THINKING IT.
TRANSLAT

TITLES OF RELATED INTEREST

Thinking Translation: A Course in Translation Method: French to English
Sándor Hervey and Ian Higgins

Thinking German Translation
Sándor Hervey, Ian Higgins and Michael Loughridge

Thinking Spanish Translation
Sándor Hervey, Ian Higgins and Louise M. Haywood

Routledge Encyclopedia of Translation Studies
ed. Mona Baker

In Other Words: A Coursebook on Translation
Mona Baker

Becoming a Translator: An Accelerated Course
Douglas Robinson

The Scandals of Translation
Lawrence Venuti

Translation Studies
Susan Bassnett

Modern Italian Grammar
Anna Proudfoot and Francesco Cardo

Modern Italian Grammar Workbook
Anna Proudfoot

The Italian Language Today
Anna Laura Lepschy and Giulio Lepschy

THINKING ITALIAN TRANSLATION

A Course in Translation Method:
Italian to English

Sándor Hervey
Ian Higgins
Stella Cragie
Patrizia Gambarotta

London and New York

First published 2000
by Routledge
11 New Fetter Lane, London EC4P 4EE

Simultaneously published in the USA and Canada
by Routledge
29 West 35th Street, New York, NY 10001

Routledge is an imprint of the Taylor & Francis Group

© 2000 Sándor Hervey, Ian Higgins,
Stella Cragie, Patrizia Gambarotta

Typeset in Times New Roman by
Florence Production Ltd, Stoodleigh, Devon
Printed and bound in Great Britain by Biddles Ltd, Guildford and King's Lynn

British Library Cataloging in Publication Data
A catalogue record for this book is available from the British Library

Library of Congress Cataloging in Publication Data
Thinking Italian translation : a course in translation method:
Italian to English / Sándor Hervey . . . [et al.].
p. cm.
Includes bibliographical references and index.
ISBN 0–415–20680–4 (hb) – ISBN 0–415–20681–2 (pb)
1. Italian language–Translating into English.
I. Hervey, Sándor G. J.
PC1498 .T45 2000 428′.0251-dc21
00–031059

ISBN 0–415–20680–4 (hbk)
0–415–20681–2 (pbk)

Contents

Acknowledgements

We owe a debt of gratitude to many people. First and foremost, it is no exaggeration to say that without Laura Leonardo and Stella Peyronel, *Thinking Italian Translation* would not be what it is. With their enthusiasm, culture, linguistic skill and generosity of spirit, they played truly major roles in piloting it and refining the course. We are deeply grateful to them. Many other friends and colleagues have helped us make improvements and avoid disasters: Wendy Anderson, Silvia Ballestra, Oliver Bennett, Bernard Bentley, Maureen Benwell, Silvana Biacca, Claudia and Pier Giuseppe Borgarelli, Paola Bortolotti, Carlo Caruso, Laura Conti, Ivor Coward, Ronnie Ferguson, Ian Henderson, Nigel Jamieson, Roger Keys, Esther Maugham, Eileen Anne Millar, John Minchinton, Georgina Nannetti, Claudia Nocentini, Éanna Ó Ceallacháin, Louise Patchett, Robert Wilson. The authors and publisher would like to thank the following people and institutions for permission to reproduce copyright material. Every effort has been made to trace copyright holders, but in a few cases this has not been possible. Any omissions brought to our attention will be remedied in future editions. Adelphi Edizioni for material from C. Fruttero and F. Lucentini, *La donna della domenica*; Antonella Antonelli Agenzia Letteraria S.R.L. for material from A. Tabucchi, *Piccoli equivoci senza importanza*; Bonacci Editore for material from Boccaccio, *Cinque novelle dal Decamerone* and Machiavelli, *Il principe. Sette capitoli scelti*; Bulzino Editore for material from G.M. Nicolai, *Viaggio lessicale nel paese dei soviet*; Cambridge University Press: extracts from the Authorized Version of the Bible (The King James Bible), the rights in which are vested in the Crown, are reproduced by permission of the Crown's Patentee, Cambridge University Press; Carcanet Press Limited for E. Morgan, 'Opening the Cage', from *The Second Life* (1968); Einaudi Editore for material from P. Levi, *Se questo è un uomo*; Electa Napoli for material from *Stagioni d'Italia*; *L'Espresso* for E. Djalma Vitale, 'Roast canguro' and material from A. Tabucchi, 'Dio ci salvi dai nipotini di Craxi'; the European Communities for material from *Euroabstracts*, 35/533–35/803; Marco Fazzini and *Forum for Modern Language Studies* for 'Aprire la gabbia a John Cage'; Feltrinelli Editore for material from *Il Gattopardo* di Tomasi di Lampedusa © Giangiacomo Feltrinelli Editore, Milan 1958; Fondazione Teatro Nuovo per la Danza for material from M. Chiriotti et al., *Piemonte dal vivo*; Garzanti Editore for material from T. Scialoja, *La mela di Amleto*; Alfredo Guida Editore for material from G. Alisio et al. (eds), *Progetti per Napoli*; HarperCollins Publishers Ltd and Arnoldo Mondadori for material from *The Path to the Nest of Spiders* by I. Calvino, translated by Archibald Colquhoun; The Harvill Press and Pantheon USA for material from THE LEOPARD, by Giuseppe Tomasi di Lampedusa, translated by Archibald Colquhoun. © Giangiacomo Feltrinelli Editore 1958. © in the English translation William Collins Sons and Co. Ltd. 1961. Reproduced by permission of The Harvill Press and Pantheon USA; IBM Italia for 'Come dicono le ricerche . . .'; Lamber di Affaba Francesco & C. snc for material from publicity brochure; Arnoldo Mondadori Editore for material from S. Ballestra, *Compleanno dell'iguana*, I. Calvino, *Il sentiero dei nidi di ragno* (© 1993 by Palomar srl e Arnoldo Mondadori) and C. Fruttero and F. Lucentini, *A che punto è la notte?*; *Panorama* for S. Petrignani, 'Lingua e linguacce. Perché il romanesco è diventato sinonimo di volgarità'; Penguin UK for extracts from *Macbeth* by William Shakespeare, edited by G.K. Hunter (Penguin Books), copyright © G.K. Hunter, 1967; Luisa Quartermaine for material from R. Pradella, 'Intervista . . .'; RCS Editore for L. Vaccari, 'Capello, ma tu che fai per un povero diavolo?'; Secker & Warburg for material from I. Welsh, *Trainspotting*; *La Stampa* for G.M. Flick, 'Un mondo imbottito di mazzette'; Ugo Guanda Editore for material from I. Welsh, *Trainspotting* (Italian translation); Vittorio Russo for material from *Santità!* and *Holiness!*

Introduction

This book is a practical course in translation from Italian into English. It has grown out of courses piloted in the universities of St Andrews and Glasgow. It has its origins in *Thinking Translation*, a course in French–English translation by Sándor Hervey and Ian Higgins first published in 1992. The approach is essentially the same as in that book, but a number of key concepts, notably cultural transposition, compensation and genre, have been considerably redefined and clarified in the light of a decade's experience in teaching all four versions of the course – German and Spanish as well as French and Italian.

The original initiative for courses along these lines came from Sándor Hervey. It is a matter of great regret for the other three authors of this book that Sándor, who was out of the country during the year in which it was first drafted, died suddenly without ever seeing the Italian incarnation of the original concept. Much of *Thinking Italian Translation* is his, however, and his co-authors gratefully acknowledge this by dedicating the book to his memory.

'Can translation be taught?' The question is asked surprisingly often – sometimes even by good translators, whom one would expect to know better. Certainly, as teachers of translation know, some people are naturally better at it than others. In this respect, aptitude for translation is no different from aptitude for any other activity: teaching and practice help anyone, including the most gifted, to perform at a higher level. Even Mozart had music lessons.

But most of us are not geniuses. Here again, anyone who has taught the subject knows that a structured course will help most students to become significantly better at translation – often good enough to earn their living at it. This book offers just such a course. Its progressive exposition of different sorts of translation problem is accompanied with plenty of practice in developing a rationale for solving them. It is a course not in translation theory, but in translation method, encouraging thoughtful consideration of possible solutions to practical problems. Theoretical issues do inevitably arise, but the aim of the course is to develop proficiency in the method, not to investigate its theoretical implications. The theoretical notions that we apply are borrowed eclectically from translation theory and linguistics, solely with this practical aim in mind. When technical or theoretical terms are first explained, they are set in bold type; they are also listed in the Glossary on pp. 211–19.

If this is not a course in translation theory or linguistics, it is not a language-teaching course, either. The focus is on how to translate. It is assumed that the student already has a good command of Italian, and is familiar with the proper use of dictionaries and, where appropriate, data banks. The course is therefore aimed at final-year undergraduates, and at postgraduates or others seeking an academic or professional qualification in translation. That said, the analytical attention given to a wide variety of texts means that students do learn a lot of Italian – and probably a fair bit of English, too.

This last point is important. While our main aim is to improve quality in translation, it must be remembered that this quality requires the translator to have an adequate command of English as well as of Italian. Assuming that this is the case, translator training normally focuses on translation into the mother tongue, because higher quality is achieved in that direction than in translating into a foreign language. Hence the predominance of unidirectional translation, from Italian into English, in this course. By its very nature, however, the course is also useful for Italian students seeking to improve their skills in translation into English: this is a staple part of English studies in Italy, and *Thinking Italian Translation* offers a new methodology and plenty of practical work in this area.

The course has a progressive structure. It begins with the fundamental issues, options and alternatives of which a translator must be aware: translation as process, translation as product, cultural issues in translation, and the nature and crucial importance of compensation in translation. Next, it looks at translation issues raised on six layers of textual variables, from the phonic to the intertextual. It then moves, via a series of semantic and stylistic topics (literal meaning, connotative meaning, register, sociolect and dialect), to the question of genre, or text-type. Further chapters are devoted to technical translation, legal and administrative translation, consumer-oriented translation, and translation revision and editing.

Chapter by chapter, then, the student is progressively trained to ask, and to answer, a series of questions that apply to any text given for translation. Pre-eminent among these are: 'What is the purpose of my translation, and what are the salient features of this text?' No translation is produced in a vacuum, and we stress throughout the course that the needs of the target audience and the requirements of the person commissioning the translation are primary factors in translation decisions. For this same reason, when students are asked in a practical to do a translation, we always include a translation brief in the assignment. As for the salient features of the text, these are what add up to its specificity as typical or atypical of a particular genre or genres. Once its genre-membership, and therefore its purpose, has been pinned down, the translator can decide on a strategy for meeting the translation brief. The student's attention is kept focused on this issue by the wide variety of genres found in the practicals: in addition to technical, legal and consumer-oriented texts, students are asked to work on various sorts of journalistic and literary text, song, film subtitling, financial texts, etc.

The sorts of question that need to be asked in determining the salient features of any text are listed in the schema of textual matrices on p. 5. The schema amounts to a check-list of potentially relevant kinds of textual feature. These are presented in the order in which they arise in the course, with one exception: as a reminder of the prime importance of purpose and genre, the genre matrix is placed at the top of the schema. There are two reasons for keeping discussion of genre as such until Chapter 11, even though its decisive importance is stressed throughout. The first is that the genre-membership of a text cannot be finally decided until the other salient features have been isolated. The second is that we have found that students are more confident and successful in responding to genre requirements *after* working on formal properties of texts, literal and connotative meaning and language variety than *before*. This is particularly true of texts with hybrid genre-features. Apart from genre, the schema of matrices outlines the investigation, in Chapters 3 and 5–10, of translation issues raised by textual features. (Compensation, the subject of Chapter 4, is not a textual feature, and so does not figure in the schema.) The student would be well-advised to refer to the schema before tackling a practical: it is a progressive reminder of what questions to ask of the text set for translation.

While the course systematically builds up a methodical approach, we are not trying to 'mechanize' translation by offering some inflexible rule or recipe. Very much the opposite: translation is a creative activity, and the translator's personal responsibility is paramount. We therefore emphasize the need to recognize options and alternatives, the need for rational discussion, and the need for decision-making. Each chapter is intended for class discussion at the start of the corresponding seminar, and a lot of the practicals are best done by students working in small groups. This is to help students keep in mind that, whatever approach the translator adopts, it should be self-aware and methodical.

The course is divided into a series of units intended to fit into an academic timetable. Each of the first eleven units comprises a chapter outlining a coherent set of notions and problems, and a practical or practicals in which students are set concrete translation tasks relevant to the chapter. These units are designed to be studied in numerical order, and are the essential foundation for the rest of the course. Chapters 12–14 give practice in various genres which commonly provide the bread and butter of professional translators.

Ideally, all of these should be worked through, but local conditions may oblige the tutor to leave one out. Chapter 15 focuses on revision and editing. Chapters 16–19 are different from the others. They can be studied at whatever points in the course seem most opportune. These chapters are devoted to four areas of 'contrastive linguistics' in which Italian–English translation problems commonly occur.

Each unit needs between 90 minutes and 2 hours of seminar time. It is vital that each student should have the necessary reference books in class: a *c.*2000-page monolingual Italian dictionary, a similar-sized Italian–English/ English–Italian dictionary, an English dictionary and an English thesaurus. Some of the practical work will be done at home – sometimes individually, sometimes in groups – and handed in for assessment by the tutor. How often this is done will be decided by tutors and students between them. Full suggestions for teaching and assessment can be found in S. Hervey, I. Higgins, S. Cragie and P. Gambarotta, *Thinking Italian Translation: Tutor's Handbook* (Routledge, 2000), which can be obtained from the address given on the opening page of this book.

Note that Practical 11 involves work on oral texts, which are easily obtainable commercially. Details are given on pp. 126–7. Some of the practicals involve work on texts that are not contained in the present volume, but are intended for distribution in class. These texts are found in the *Tutor's Handbook*.

Students doing the course often inquire about the possibility of translation as a career. The Postscript (pp. 208–10) outlines the nature, attractions and drawbacks of translation work, and contains information about professional bodies which can give detailed help and advice.

SCHEMA OF TEXTUAL MATRICES		
Question to ask about the text	Matrix of features	Examples of typical features
	GENRE MATRIX (Chapter 11)	

What genre(s) does this text belong to:	Genre types: literary
	            religious
	            philosophical
	            empirical
	            persuasive
	            hybrid
	Oral vs written:
		short story, etc.
		biblical text, etc.
		essay on good and evil, etc.
		scientific paper, balance sheet, etc.
		law, advertisement, etc.
		sermon, parody, job contract, etc.
		dialogue, song, subtitles, etc.

	CULTURAL MATRIX (Chapter 3)	
Are there significant features presenting a choice between:	Exoticism Calque Cultural borrowing Communicative translation Cultural transplantation	wholesale foreignness idiom translated literally, etc. name of historical movement, etc. public notices, proverbs, etc. Rome recast as Edinburgh, etc.
	FORMAL MATRIX (Chapters 5–7)	
Are there significant features on the:	Phonic/graphic level Prosodic level Grammatical level: lexis syntax Sentential level Discourse level Intertextual level	alliteration, layout, etc. vocal pitch, rhythm, etc. archaism, overtones, etc. simple vs complex syntax, etc. sequential focus, intonation, etc. cohesion markers, etc. pastiche, allusion to Dante, etc.
	SEMANTIC MATRIX (Chapters 8–9)	
Are there significant instances of:	Literal meaning Attitudinal meaning Associative meaning Allusive meaning Reflected meaning Collocative meaning Affective meaning	synonymy, etc. hostile attitude to referent, etc. gender stereotyping of referent, etc. echo of proverb, etc. play on words, etc. collocative clash, etc. offensive attitude to addressee, etc.
	VARIETAL MATRIX (Chapter 10)	
Are there significant instances of:	Tonal register Social register Sociolect Dialect	ingratiating tone, etc. left-wing student dropout, etc. Milan urban working class, etc. Sicilianisms, etc.

1

Preliminaries to translation as a process

This chapter examines translation as a process – what it is the translator actually does. But first, we must note a few basic terms that will be used throughout the course:

Text   Any given stretch of speech or writing assumed to make a coherent whole. A minimal text may consist of a single word – for example 'Stupendo!' – preceded and followed by a silence (however short). A maximal text may run into thousands of pages.

Source text (ST)   The text requiring translation.

Target text (TT)   The text which is a translation of the ST.

Source language (SL)   The language in which the ST is spoken or written.

Target language (TL)   The language into which the ST is to be translated.

Strategy   The translator's overall 'game-plan', consisting of a set of strategic decisions taken after an initial reading of the ST, but before starting detailed translation of it.

Strategic decisions   The first set of reasoned decisions taken by the translator. These are taken before starting the translation in detail, in response to the following questions: 'What is the message content of this particular ST? What are its salient linguistic features? What are its principal effects? What genre does it belong to and what audience is it aimed at? What are the functions and intended audience of my translation? What are the implications of these factors? If a choice has to be made among them, which ones should be given priority?'

Decisions of detail   Reasoned decisions concerning the specific problems of syntax, vocabulary and so on, encountered in translating particular expressions in their particular context. Decisions of detail are made in the light of the strategy. However, problems of detail may well arise during translating which raise unforeseen strategic issues and oblige the translator to refine the original strategy somewhat.

With these terms in mind, the translation process can be broken down into two types of activity: understanding an ST and formulating a TT. These do not occur successively, but simultaneously; indeed, it is often only when coming up against a problem in formulating the TT that translators realize they have not fully understood something in the ST. When this happens, the ST may need to be reinterpreted in the light of the translator's new understanding of it. This reinterpretation sometimes entails revising the original strategy, the revision in turn necessitating changes to some of the decisions of detail already taken. Nevertheless, it is useful to discuss ST interpretation and TT formulation as different, separable processes.

The processes of translation are not different from familiar things that everyone does every day. Comprehension and interpretation are processes that we all perform whenever we listen to or read a piece of linguistically imparted information. Understanding even the simplest message potentially involves all our experiential baggage – the knowledge, beliefs, suppositions, inferences and expectations that are the stuff of personal, social and cultural life. Understanding everyday messages is therefore not all that different from what a translator does when first confronting an ST – and it is certainly no less complicated.

In everyday communication, evidence that a message has been understood may come from appropriate practical response – for example, if your mother asks you for a spoon, and you give her a spoon and not a fork. Or it may come from appropriate *linguistic* response – such things as returning a greeting correctly, answering a question satisfactorily, or filling in a form. None of these are translation-like processes, but they do show that the comprehension and interpretation stage of translation involves an ordinary, everyday activity that simply requires an average command of the language used.

However, one everyday activity that does resemble translation proper is what Roman Jakobson actually calls **inter-semiotic translation** (Jakobson 1971: 260–6), that is, translation between two semiotic systems (systems for communication). 'The green light means go' is an act of inter-semiotic translation, as is 'The big hand's pointing to twelve and the little hand's pointing to four, so it's four o'clock'. In each case, there is translation from a non-linguistic communication system to a linguistic one. To this extent, everyone is a translator of a sort.

Still more common are various sorts of linguistic response to linguistic stimuli which are also very like translation proper, even though they actually take place within a single language. These sorts of process are what Jakobson (ibid.) calls **intralingual translation**. A brief look at the two extremes of intralingual translation will show what its major implications

are. Take the following scenario. Jill is driving Jack through the narrow
streets of a small town. A policeman steps out and stops them. As he leans
in to speak to Jill, she can see over his shoulder that, further on, a lorry
has jackknifed and blocked the street. At one extreme of intralingual translation lies the kind of response typified in this exchange:

POLICEMAN   There's been an accident ahead, Madam – I'm afraid you'll
              have to turn left down St Mary's Lane here, the road's blocked.
JILL   Oh, OK. Thanks.
JACK   What did he say?
JILL   We've got to turn left.

The policeman's essential message is 'Turn left'. But he does not want to
sound brusque. So he mollifies the driver with a partial explanation, 'There's
been an accident', and then modalizes his instruction with 'I'm afraid you'll
have to'. 'Down St Mary's Lane' gives a hint of local colour and fellow-
citizenship; but he does add 'here', just in case the driver is a stranger.
Finally, he completes his explanation.

When Jack asks what he said, however, Jill *separates the gist* of the
policeman's message from the circumstantial details and tonal subtleties,
and *reports it in her own words*. This type of intralingual translation we
shall call **gist translation**. The example also shows two other features which
intralingual translation shares with translation proper. First, Jill's is not the
only gist translation possible. For instance, she might have said 'We've got
to go down here'. Among other things, this implies that at least one of them
does not know the town: the street name has no significance. A third possibility is 'We've got to go down St Mary's Lane': if Jack and Jill do know
the town, the policeman's gist is accurately conveyed.

The other feature shared by intralingual translation and translation proper
is that the situation in which a message is expressed and received affects
how it is expressed and *how* it is received. By 'situation' here we mean a
combination of three elements: linguistic context (for example, the policeman's words and Jack's question), the non-linguistic circumstances in which
speaker and addressee find themselves (such as being stopped in a car and
having to take a diversion), and all the experiential baggage they carry with
them, all the time (knowing or not knowing the town; familiarity or unfamiliarity with conventions for giving and receiving instructions; liking or
disliking the police, etc.). There are always so many variables in the message
situation that it is impossible to predict what the gist translation will be or
how the addressee will take it. For example, Jill might simply have said
'Turn left', a highly economical way of reporting the gist – no bad thing
when she has to concentrate on driving. However, depending on how she
says it and how Jack receives it, it could give the impression that the
policeman was brusque.

Another reason why 'Turn left' could sound brusque is that, grammatically, it looks like direct speech, an imperative, whereas all the other gist translations we have given are clearly *in*direct speech (or 'reported speech'). Now *all* translation may be said to be indirect speech, inasmuch as it does not repeat the ST, but reformulates it. Yet most TTs, like 'Turn left', mask the fact that they are indirect speech by omitting such markers as 'The author says that . . .', or modulation of point of view (as in substituting 'we' for 'you', or 'he' for 'I'). As a result, it is easy for reformulation consciously or unconsciously to become distortion, either because the translator misrepresents the ST or because the reader misreads the TT, or both.

In other words, gist translation, like any translation, is a process of *interpretation*. This is seen still more clearly if we take an example at the other extreme of intralingual translation. Jill might just as easily have interpreted the policeman's words by expanding them. For example, she could build on an initial gist translation as follows:

We've got to go down St Mary's Lane – some fool's jackknifed and blocked the High Street.

This puts two sorts of gloss on the policeman's message: she adds details that he did not give (the jackknifing, the name of the street ahead) and her own judgement of the lorry driver. We shall use the term **exegetic translation** to denote a translation that explains and elaborates on the ST in this way. The inevitable part played by the translator's experiential baggage becomes obvious in exegetic translation, for any exegesis by definition involves explicitly invoking considerations from outside the text in one's reading of it – here, the jackknifed lorry, Jill's knowledge of the town, and her attitude towards other road-users.

An exegetic translation can be shorter than the ST, as in this example, but exegesis is usually longer, and can easily shade into general observations triggered by the ST but not really explaining it. Knowing the town as she does, Jill might easily have gone on like this:

That's the second time in a month. The street's just too *narrow* for a thing that size.

The explanation added in the second sentence may still just about be admissible as exegetic translation, but it does go much further than the policeman's. If she got a bit more carried away, however, her comment might still count as exegesis, but surely not as translation:

That was *another* Tory bright idea, letting juggernauts loose on British roads.

As the above examples suggest, it is sometimes hard to keep gist translation and exegetic translation apart, or to see where translation shades into comment pure and simple. It certainly seems very hard to achieve an ideal **rephrasing**, a halfway point between gist and exegesis that would use terms radically different from those of the ST, but add nothing to, and omit nothing from, its message content. Nevertheless, with its constant movement between gist and exegesis, intralingual translation happens all the time in speech. It is also common in written texts. Students regularly encounter it in annotated editions. A good example is G.K. Hunter's edition of *Macbeth*, in which the text of the play is followed by about fifty pages of notes. Here are the opening lines of the Captain's report on how the battle stood when he left it, followed by Hunter's notes and rephrasings and, in square brackets, our comments on them:

> Doubtful it stood,
> As two spent swimmers that do cling together
> And choke their art. The merciless Macdonwald –
> Worthy to be a rebel, for to that
> The multiplying villainies of nature
> Do swarm upon him – from the Western Isles
> Of kerns and galloglasses is supplied [. . .].

choke their art   make impossible the art of swimming. [An exegetic rephrasing, in so far as it makes explicit what is only implicit in the metaphor: neither army holds the advantage. At the same time, it only conveys the gist, losing the crucial implications of the image of 'choking'.]

to that   as if to that end. [Exegetic rephrasing, explaining Shakespeare's elliptical formulation.]

multiplying villainies of nature / Do swarm upon him   hosts of rebels join him like noxious insects swarming. [Exegetic rephrasing which simplifies, but distorts, Shakespeare's image, turning the metaphor into an explanatory simile: in the ST, the rebels are not *like insects*, they *are* villainous manifestations of nature.]

Western Isles   Hebrides. [Synonymous rephrasing, for readers unfamiliar with Scottish geography: a good example of how any rewording involves presuppositions regarding the target audience's experiential baggage.]

kerns and galloglasses   light and heavy-armed Celtic levies. [Virtually synonymous rephrasing, this time for readers unfamiliar with medieval Irish and Scottish armies. However, 'levies' may not be accurate in respect of galloglasses, who were mercenaries – even the simplest rephrasing may be misleading, intentionally or not.]

(Shakespeare 1967: 54, 140)

In all the examples we have been discussing, the dividing-lines between gist, exegesis, translation and comment are blurred. Things could not be otherwise. If one thing has become clear in this chapter, it is the difficulty of controlling (and even of seeing) how far an intralingual TT omits from, adds to or faithfully reproduces the ST message content. And, as we shall see in the next chapter and throughout the course, what applies to intralingual translation applies a fortiori to translation proper: the ST *message content* can never be precisely reproduced in the TT, because of the very fact that the two *forms of expression* are different.

It has also become clear that there are other important respects in which the three types of intralingual translation are on an equal footing with translation proper. They all require knowledge of the subject matter of the source text, familiarity with the source language and source culture in general, and interpretative effort. But they also require knowledge of the nature and needs of the target public, familiarity with the target culture in general – and, above all, mastery of the target language. Synopsis-writing, reported speech, intralingual rephrasing and exegesis are therefore excellent exercises for our purposes, because they develop the ability to find and choose between alternative means of expressing a given message content. This is why the first exercise in this course is a piece of intralingual translation in English.

PRACTICAL 1

1.1   Intralingual translation

Assignment
 (i)   Identify the salient features of content and expression in the following ST, and say what its purpose is.
 (ii) Recast the ST in different words, adapting it for a specific purpose and a specific public (i.e. a specific readership or audience). Define clearly what the purpose and the public are. Treat the ST as if you were recasting the whole book of Genesis, of which it is a part. (As a rule, *whenever* you do a translation as part of this course, you should proceed as if you were translating the whole text from which the ST is taken.)
 (iii) Explain the main decisions of detail you took in making the textual changes. (Insert into your TT a superscript note-number after each expression you intend to discuss, and then, starting on a fresh sheet of paper, discuss the points in numerical order. This is the system you should use whenever you annotate your own TTs.)

Contextual information

The text is from the Authorized Version of the Bible, published in 1611. The best way of making sense of it is to read the rest of Genesis 3, from which it is taken. Adam and Eve have tasted the forbidden fruit of the tree of the knowledge of good and evil. Realizing then that they were naked, and afraid to be seen by God, they have hidden among the trees. Adam has just admitted this to God, who now replies.

ST

And he said, Who told thee that thou wast naked? Hast thou eaten of the tree, whereof I commanded thee that thou shouldest not eat?

And the man said, The woman whom thou gavest to be with me, she gave me of the tree, and I did eat.

5   And the LORD God said unto the woman, What is this that thou hast done? And the woman said, The serpent beguiled me, and I did eat.

And the LORD God said unto the serpent, Because thou hast done this, thou art cursed above all cattle, and above every beast of the field; upon thy belly shalt thou go, and dust shalt thou eat all the days of thy life:

10   And I will put enmity between thee and the woman, and between thy seed and her seed; it shall bruise thy head, and thou shalt bruise his heel.

Unto the woman he said, I will greatly multiply thy sorrow and thy conception; in sorrow thou shalt bring forth children; and thy desire shall be to thy husband, and he shall rule over thee.

15   And unto Adam he said, Because thou hast hearkened unto the voice of thy wife, and hast eaten of the tree, of which I commanded thee, saying, Thou shalt not eat of it: cursed is the ground for thy sake; in sorrow shalt thou eat of it all the days of thy life;

Thorns also and thistles shall it bring forth to thee; and thou shalt eat
20 the herb of the field;

In the sweat of thy face shalt thou eat bread, till thou return unto the ground; for out of it wast thou taken: for dust thou art, and unto dust shalt thou return.

(Genesis 3, v. 11–19)

1.2 Intralingual translation

Assignment

Below are two short extracts from Italian classics, together with intralingual translations produced by Italians for foreign students. Taking each in turn,

(i) Identify the salient features of content and expression in the ST.
(ii) Identify the principal differences between ST and TT, paying special attention to cases where the TT adds to the ST, omits something from it, or rephrases it more or less faithfully.

Extract 1.
(*Contextual information*. The extract is from Machiavelli's *Il Principe* (1513), a treatise on the aims and methods of good government, and is the concluding paragraph of a chapter in which Machiavelli discusses the relative merits of mercifulness and cruelty, and whether it is better for the ruler to be loved or to be feared.)

ST
Concludo adunque, tornando allo essere temuto e amato, che, amando li uomini a posta loro e temendo a posta del principe, debbe uno principe savio fondarsi in su quello che è suo, non in su quello che è d'altri; debbe solamente ingegnarsi di fuggire l'odio, come è detto.

TT
Concludo, dunque, tornando al problema di essere temuti o amati: poiché gli uomini amano secondo ciò che fa loro comodo e temono in base alla volontà del principe, il principe saggio deve basarsi sulla sua capacità di farsi temere, non sull'amore; deve soltanto fare in modo di evitare l'odio, come si è detto.

(Machiavelli 1995: 34–5)

Extract 2.
(*Contextual information*. The extract is from 'Frate Cipolla', one of the stories in Boccaccio's *Decameron* (*c*.1353). Frate Cipolla is a Friar of St Anthony. On his annual visit to the town of Certaldo, he is celebrating Mass. He pauses from the ceremony to make the following announcement.)

Turn to p. 14

ST

'Signori e donne, come voi sapete, vostra usanza è di mandare ogni anno
a' poveri del barone messer santo Antonio del vostro grano e delle vostre
biade, chi poco e chi assai, secondo il podere e la divozion sua, acciò che
il beato santo Antonio vi sia guardia de' buoi e degli asini e de' porci e
5   delle pecore vostre; e oltre a ciò solete pagare, e spezialmente quegli che
alla nostra compagnia scritti sono, quel poco debito che ogni anno si paga
una volta. Alle quali cose ricogliere io sono dal mio maggiore, cioè da
messer l'abate, stato mandato; e per ciò con la benedizion di Dio, dopo
nona, quando udirete sonare le campanelle, verrete qui di fuori della chiesa
10   là dove io al modo usato vi farò la predicazione, e bascerete la croce; e
oltre a ciò, per ciò che divotissimi tutti vi conosco del barone messer santo
Antonio, di spezial grazia vi mostrerò una santissima e bella reliquia, la
quale io medesimo già recai dalle sante terre d'oltremare: e questa è una
delle penne dell'agnol Gabriello, la quale nella camera della Vergine Maria
15   rimase quando egli la venne a annunziare in Nazarette.' E questo detto si
tacque e ritornossi alla messa.

TT

'Signori e signore, come sapete, è vostra abitudine mandare ogni anno ai
poveri del barone messer Sant'Antonio un po' del vostro grano e della vostra
biada, chi poco e chi molto, secondo la possibilità e la devozione, affinché
il beato Sant'Antonio protegga i buoi, gli asini, i maiali e le pecore che
5   avete; di solito poi quelli che sono iscritti alla nostra confraternita pagano
una piccola quota, una volta all'anno. Io sono stato mandato dal mio superiore, cioè dal messer Abate, a raccogliere queste offerte; quindi con la
benedizione di Dio, dopo le tre del pomeriggio, quando sentirete suonare
le campanelle vi invito a venire qui fuori della chiesa, dove come sempre
10   io vi farò la predica e voi bacerete la croce. Poi, siccome so che siete tutti
molto devoti al barone messer Sant'Antonio, per una grazia speciale vi farò
vedere una reliquia bella e santissima, che io stesso tempo fa ho portato
dalla Terrasanta; è una delle penne dell'angelo Gabriele, rimasta nella camera
della Vergine Maria quando le portò l'annuncio a Nazareth.' Detto questo,
15   tacque e continuò a celebrare la messa.

(Boccaccio 1995: 40–3)

1.3   Gist translation

Assignment

You will be asked to produce a gist translation of an extract from a newspaper article (Tabucchi 1995). The text will be given to you in class by your
tutor. The tutor will tell you how long you should take over the translation.

2

Preliminaries to translation as a product

Chapter 1 viewed translation as a process. However, the evidence we had for the process was a *product* – a gist translation and an exegetic translation. It is as a product that translation is viewed in the present chapter. Here, too, it is useful to examine two diametric opposites: in this case, two opposed degrees of freedom of translation, showing extreme SL bias on the one hand and extreme TL bias on the other.

At the extreme of SL bias is **interlinear translation**, where the TT does not necessarily respect TL grammar, but has grammatical units corresponding as closely as possible to every grammatical unit of the ST. Here is an interlinear translation of an Italian proverb:

Chi non risica non rosica.   Who not risks not nibbles.

Normally only used in descriptive linguistics or language teaching, interlinear translation is of no practical use for this course. It is actually an extreme form of the much more common **literal translation**, where the literal meaning of words is taken as if straight from the dictionary (that is, out of context), but TL grammar is respected. Since TL grammar is respected, literal translation very often unavoidably involves **grammatical transposition** – the replacement or reinforcement of given parts of speech in the ST by other parts of speech in the TT. A simple example is translating 'Ho fame' as 'I am hungry': the TT has a subject pronoun where there is none in the ST, and the ST noun is rendered with a TL adjective. A literal translation of the proverb would be: 'Who does not risk does not nibble.' We shall take literal translation as the practical extreme of SL bias.

At the opposite extreme, TL bias, is **free translation**, where there is only a global correspondence between the textual units of the ST and those of the TT. A free translation of the Italian proverb might be: 'Nothing ventured, nothing gained.' Here, the implied message of the ST is made explicit, but the grammar is completely different and the image of nibbling is lost. This particular TT is a gist translation. It is also an example of what we shall call communicative translation. A **communicative translation** is produced when, in a given situation, the ST uses an SL expression standard for that situation, and the TT uses a TL expression standard for an equivalent target culture situation. 'Nothing ventured, nothing gained' is a standard modern cultural counterpart to 'Chi non risica non rosica', and in most situations would be a virtually mandatory translation. This is true of very many conventional formulae that do not invite literal translation. Public notices, proverbs and conversational clichés illustrate this particularly clearly, as in:

Senso vietato.	No entry.
Buon appetito.	Enjoy your meal.
Prego.	You're welcome/Don't mention it.
È nato con la camicia.	He was born with a silver spoon in his mouth.

Clearly, communicative translation apart, this degree of freedom is no more useful as *standard practice* than interlinear translation, because potentially important details of message content are bound to be lost.

Between the two extremes of literal and free translation, the degrees of freedom are infinitely variable. However, in assessing translation freedom, it is useful to situate the TT on a scale between extreme SL bias and extreme TL bias, with notional intermediate points schematized as in the following diagram, adapted from Newmark (1981: 39):

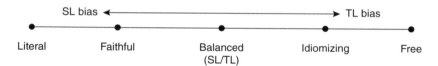

The five points on the scale can be illustrated from the simple example of someone's reaction to an anthology of fiction she has been reading: 'Le piace molto la novella del Boccaccio.'

[INTERLINEAR	To her pleases much the story of the Boccaccio.]
LITERAL	The story of Boccaccio pleases her greatly.
FAITHFUL	She likes the story by Boccaccio very much.
BALANCED	She really likes the Boccaccio story.
IDIOMIZING	She says the Boccaccio's just her cup of tea.
FREE	Boccaccio floats her boat.

By an 'idiomizing' translation, we mean one that respects the ST message content, but prioritizes TL 'naturalness' over faithfulness to ST detail; it will typically use TL idioms or phonic and rhythmic patterns to give an easy read, even if this means sacrificing nuances of meaning or tone.

Note that although the last TT is very free and colloquially plausible, it is not a communicative translation, because it is not the *standard* expression in the given situation. (For this particular situation, there *is* no standard expression.) Its freedom is therefore gratuitous and might well be considered excessive: it might be out of character for the speaker to use 'floats my boat' in this sense, and the TT is in any case avoidably different in message content and tone from the ST.

EQUIVALENCE AND TRANSLATION LOSS

In defining communicative translation, we used the term 'equivalent target culture situation'. As a matter of fact, most writers on translation use the terms 'equivalence' and 'equivalent', but in so many different ways that equivalence can be a confusing concept even for teachers of translation, let alone their students. Before going further, then, we need to say what we mean, and what we do not mean, by 'equivalence' and 'equivalent'. We shall not go in detail into the philosophical implications of the term 'equivalence': this is not a course on translation theory. Holmes (1988), Koller (1995), Nida (1964) and Snell-Hornby (1988) between them provide a useful introduction to the question.

The many different definitions of equivalence in translation fall broadly into one of two categories: they are either descriptive or prescriptive. Descriptively, 'equivalence' denotes the relationship between ST features and TT features that are seen as directly corresponding to one another, regardless of the quality of the TT. Thus, descriptively, the following pairs of utterances are equivalents:

Sempre per l'alimentazione carburante produciamo oggi carcasse per pompe di diverso tipo.	Always for the fuel's feeding we are now manufacturing frames for pumps of various type.
Windows knows every part of your PC, inside and out, so it can send your work to the right place. It also knows all the rules for storing and retrieving files, so you can find your work without a lot of hassle.	Windows conosce ogni elemento del vostro PC a menadito, così può inviare il lavoro al posto giusto. Inoltre, poiché conosce tutte le regole per archiviare e recuperare i file, potete trovare il vostro lavoro senza troppe difficoltà.

Prescriptively, 'equivalence' denotes the relationship between an SL expression and *the* canonic TL rendering of it as required, for example, by a teacher. (By 'canonic', we mean 'generally accepted as standard'.) So, prescriptively, the following pairs of utterances are equivalents:

Ho fame.	I am hungry.
Si direbbe che siamo in Italia.	You would think we were in Italy.
Non credo.	I do not think so.

An influential variant of prescriptive equivalence is the 'dynamic equivalence' of the eminent Bible translator Eugene Nida. This is based on the 'principle of equivalent effect', the principle that 'the relationship between receptor and message should be substantially the same as that which existed between the original receptors and the message' (Nida 1964: 159). Nida's view has real attractions. As we shall suggest throughout the course, there are all sorts of good reasons why a translator might not want to translate a given expression literally. A case in point is communicative translation, which may be said to be an example of 'dynamic equivalence' (cf. Nida 1964: 166: 'That is just the way we would say it'). However, there is a danger that students might see 'dynamic equivalence' as giving *carte blanche* for excessive freedom – that is, freedom to write more or less anything as long as it sounds good and does reflect, however tenuously, something of the ST message content. This danger is a very real one, as any teacher of translation will confirm. It is in fact a symptom of theoretical problems contained in the very notion of 'equivalent effect', most notably the normative ones.

To begin with, who is to *know* what the relationship between ST message and source-culture receptors is? For that matter, is it plausible to speak of *the* relationship, as if there were only one: are there not as many relationships as there are receptors? And who is to know what such relationships can have been in the past? *L'inferno*, *Il piccolo mondo di Don Camillo*: each is, and has been, different things to different people in different places – and indeed, different to the same person at different times. In any case, few texts have a *single* effect even in one reading by one person; the more literary the text, the less likely this is. And these problems apply as much to the TT as to the ST: who is to foresee the relationships between the TT and its receptors?

All this suggests that, the more normative the use of 'equivalence', the more the term risks being taken to imply 'sameness'. Indeed, it is used in this way in logic, sign-theory and mathematics. In mathematics, an equivalent relationship is one that is objective, incontrovertible and, crucially, reversible. In translation, however, such unanimity and reversibility are unthinkable for any but the very simplest of texts – and even then, only in terms of literal meaning. For example, if 'Mi piace questo vino' translates as 'I like this wine', will **back-translation** (that is, translating a TT into the SL) automatically give 'Mi piace questo vino', or will it give 'Questo vino mi piace'? The answer depends on *context* – both the context of the ST utterance and that of the TT utterance. The fact is that the simplest of contexts is usually enough to inhibit the reversibility that is crucial to equivalence in the mathematical sense.

In so far as the principle of equivalent effect implies 'sameness' or is used normatively, it seems to be more of a hindrance than a help, both theoretically and pedagogically. Consequently, when we spoke of an 'equivalent target culture situation', we were not using 'equivalent' in a sense specific to any particular translation theory; we were using it in its everyday sense of 'counterpart' – something different, but with points of resemblance in relevant aspects. This is how the term will be used in this book.

We have found it more useful, both in translating and in teaching translation, to avoid an absolutist ambition to *maximize sameness* between ST and TT, in favour of a relativist ambition to *minimize difference*: to look, not for what is to be put into the TT, but for what one might save from the ST. There is a vital difference between the two ambitions. The aim of maximizing sameness encourages the belief that, floating somewhere out in the ether, there is the 'right' translation, the TT that is 'equi-valent' to the ST, at some ideal halfway point between SL bias and TL bias. But it is more realistic, and more productive, to start by admitting that, because SL and TL are fundamentally different, the transfer from ST to TT *inevitably* entails difference – that is, loss.

It is helpful here to draw an analogy with 'energy loss' in engineering. The transfer of energy in any machine necessarily involves energy loss. Engineers do not see this as a theoretical anomaly, but simply as a practical problem which they confront by striving to design more efficient machines, in which energy loss is reduced. We shall give the term **translation loss** to the incomplete replication of the ST in the TT – that is, the inevitable loss of textually and culturally relevant features. This term is intended to suggest that translators should not agonize over the loss, but should concentrate on reducing it.

Admittedly, the analogy with energy loss is imperfect: whereas energy loss is a loss (or rather, a diversion) of energy, translation loss is not a loss *of* translation, but a loss *in* the translation process. It is a loss *of* textual effects. Further, since these effects cannot be quantified, neither can the loss. So, when trying to reduce it, the translator never knows how far there is still to go. Despite the limitations of the analogy, however, we have found it practical for translating and teaching. Once the concept of inevitable translation loss is accepted, a TT that is not, even in all important respects, a replica of the ST is not a theoretical anomaly, and the translator can concentrate on the realistic aim of reducing translation loss, rather than the unrealistic one of seeking the ultimate TT.

A few very simple examples, at the level of the sounds and literal meanings of individual words, will be enough to show some of the forms translation loss can take and what its implications are for the translator.

There is translation loss even at the most elementary level. For instance, true SL–TL homonymy rarely occurs, and rhythm and intonation are usually different as well. So, in most contexts, 'cavallo' and 'horse' will be synonyms, and there will be no loss in literal meaning in translating one with the other. But 'cavallo' and 'horse' sound completely different: there is total phonic and prosodic translation loss. Of course, in a veterinary textbook, this loss does not matter. But if the ST word is part of an alliterative pattern in a literary text or, worse, if it rhymes, the loss could be crucial; it depends on the purpose of the translation.

Even if the ST word has entered the TL as a loan-word (e.g. 'allegretto', 'chiaroscuro'), using it in the TT entails translation loss in at least two ways. English-speakers pronounce 'allegretto' differently from Italians; so using it in an English TT involves loss on the phonic level. And in any case, 'allegretto' still sounds somewhat foreign in English, despite its long use as a musical term, so that using it in an English TT introduces a touch of foreignness which is not present in an Italian ST, and thereby loses the cultural neutrality of the ST expression. These losses will virtually never matter, of course. Indeed, in a spoken TT, pronouncing 'allegretto' in an authentic Italian fashion could actually increase the translation loss, not reduce it: on top of the lexical foreignness (absent in the ST), it might increase the phonic foreignness (also absent in the ST) and introduce a comic pretentiousness which, again, is completely absent in the ST. In many contexts, this translation loss could well matter rather a lot.

In the opposite sort of case, where the ST contains a TL expression (e.g. 'hostess', 'jogging', 'scout', 'computer' in an Italian ST), there is just as much loss. For example, if Italian 'hostess' is translated as 'air-hostess', there is palpable phonic and prosodic loss, because the ST expression and the TT expression sound so different. There is also grammatical translation loss, because the TT is less economical than the ST; and there is lexical translation loss, because TT 'air hostess' loses the foreignness that 'hostess' has in Italian. In the case of TT 'jogging', the lexical loss consists not only in the loss of ST foreignness, but also in the addition of a transparent link with the verb 'to jog' that is absent in the ST.

As these examples suggest, it is important to recognize that, even where the TT is more explicit, precise, economical or vivid than the ST, this difference is still a case of translation loss. Some authorities refer to such differences as 'translation gains'. It is certainly true that the following TTs, for example, can be said to be more grammatically economical, sometimes even more elegant and easier to say, than their STs. But these so-called 'gains' are by the same token grammatical, phonic or prosodic failures to replicate the ST structures, and are therefore by definition instances of translation loss:

ST	TT
Portamonete	Purse
Imposta sul valore aggiunto	Value added tax
Exchange equalization fund	Fondo rettificativo
Multiple re-entry visa	Visto multiplo
Blind in one eye	Guercio

Conversely, if we reverse these columns, we have a set of TTs that are perhaps clearer, more precise or more vivid than their STs: these TTs, too, all show translation loss, because the ST structures have been violated:

ST	TT
Purse	Portamonete
Value added tax	Imposta sul valore aggiunto
Fondo rettificativo	Exchange equalization fund
Visto multiplo	Multiple re-entry visa
Guercio	Blind in one eye

If translation loss is inevitable even in translating single words, it is obviously going to feature at more complex levels as well – in respect of connotations, for example, or of sentence-structure, discourse, language variety, and so on. There is no need to give examples just now: many will arise in Practical 2, and plenty more later on, chapter by chapter, as we deal with these and other topics. For the moment, all we need do is point out that, if translation loss is inevitable, the challenge to the translator is not to eliminate it, but to control and channel it by deciding which features, in a given ST, it is most important to respect, and which can most legitimately be sacrificed in respecting them. The translator has always to be asking, and answering, such questions as: does it *matter* if 'I like this wine' does not reflect the nuance between 'Mi piace questo vino' and 'Questo vino mi piace'? Does it *matter* if an intralingual TT of the extract from *Macbeth* on p. 10 loses the richness of Shakespeare's metaphor? Does it matter if 'hostess' is exotic in Italian and not in English, and sounds different in each? If 'È nato con la camicia' is phonically, rhythmically, grammatically, lexically and metaphorically completely different from 'He was born with a silver spoon in his mouth'? There is no once-and-for-all answer to questions like these. Everything depends on the purpose of the translation and on what the role of the textual feature is in its context. Sometimes a given translation loss will matter a lot, sometimes little. Whether the final decision is simple or complicated, it does have to be made, every time, and the translator is the only one who can make it.

PRACTICAL 2

2.1 Translation loss

Assignment
(i) You have been commissioned to translate for publication in the United Kingdom the book from which the following ST is taken, adapting it to take into account the impact of Soviet and Russian terms in the West as a whole, not just in Italy. Discuss the strategic decisions that you have to take before starting detailed translation of this ST, and outline and justify the strategy you adopt.
(ii) Translate the text into English, *omitting ll. 5–7* (from 'Benché' to '1193').
(iii) Paying special attention to cases where you managed to reduce significant translation loss, discuss the main decisions of detail you took, explaining what the loss was and how you reduced it. (Number these points in the TT and in (iii), as you did in Practical 1.1.)

Contextual information
The text is taken from a glossary of Soviet and Russian terms that have become part of the Italian language. The glossary is over 200 pages long, and is as much an introduction to recent history as it is an essay in lexicography. This extract is followed by examples of the use of 'Černóbil' in Italian as a noun meaning 'sudden disastrous event'. (NB Misprints in the original have been corrected here.)

ST
ČERNÓBIL. Italianizzazione di *Černóbyl'*, nome di una località nell'*óblast* (grande unità amministrativa e territoriale) di Kíev, situata al confine con la Bielorussia, in cui il 26 aprile del 1986 esplose – con conseguenze devastanti – un reattore della centrale nucleare, la quale era in funzione dal 1978.
5   Benché la città sia stata costituita solo nel 1941, il luogo in cui sorge viene identificato con quello del villaggio di *Černóbyl'* menzionato nelle Cronache fin dal 1193. [. . .]
   Le dimensioni bibliche della tragedia di *Černóbyl'* indussero alcuni ad associarla alle allucinanti visioni allegoriche contenute nell'*Apocalisse*
10 attribuita a S. Giovanni, laddove, nell'ottavo capitolo, vengono descritti i flagelli – annunziati dal suono delle 'sette trombe' – che colpiranno l'umanità, chiari segni dell'ineluttabile giustizia divina. In particolare venne ricordato il passo in cui si parla del funesto suono di tromba del terzo angelo

quando 'dal cielo cadde una grande stella ardente come una fiaccola', chia-
15 mata Assenzio, la quale investì la terza parte delle acque dei fiumi e delle
sorgenti trasformandole in assenzio e 'molti uomini morirono perché queste
si erano fatte amare'.

Apocalittico, l'evento, lo fu davvero. L'equilibrio ecologico ne risultò
sconvolto. Né la scienza è in grado di indicare i limiti temporali dei suoi
20 effetti, lenti e devastanti sull'uomo e sul mondo animale e vegetale. Dal
fungo atomico alto circa un chilometro e mezzo levatosi nel cielo al momento
dello scoppio del reattore, si formarono nubi cariche di radioattività, che a
causa dei venti si propagarono rapidamente portando la contaminazione
anche in zone distanti migliaia di chilometri dal luogo del disastro (malgrado
25 ciò abbiamo visto moltiplicarsi in Italia il numero dei comuni alle cui porte
campeggiavano cartelli con su scritto 'Comune denuclearizzato': ingenuo
tentativo di esorcizzare il 'diavolo atomico', che non conosce frontiere).

(Nicolai 1994: 45–6)

2.2 Degrees of freedom; translation loss

Assignment
For each of the following STs,

(i)   Give five TTs, one corresponding to each of the five points from
'Literal' to 'Free' in the scale given on p. 16.

(ii) For each TT, show how far it is a gist translation or an exegetic
translation.

(iii) For each TT, write notes on the major elements of translation loss
incurred, and suggest circumstances in which these might matter.

ST (a)

(*Contextual information.* The text is a proverb.)

Ad ogni uccello suo nido è bello.

ST (b)

(*Contextual information.* The text is from Primo Levi's *Se questo è un uomo*,
an account of his imprisonment in Auschwitz. A trainload of deportees has
just got out onto the platform. The 'decina di SS' are waiting for them.)

Una decina di SS stavano in disparte, l'aria indifferente, piantati a gambe
larghe.

3

Cultural transposition

In this chapter, we complete the introduction to translation loss by looking at some implications of the crucial fact that translating involves not just two languages, but a transfer *from one whole culture to another.* General cultural differences are sometimes bigger obstacles to successful translation than linguistic differences. The chapter is based on comparison of certain features of the following ST and TT. (*Contextual information.* Printed together on a label, the texts were attached to a pair of Italian-made ladies' shoes bought in the United Kingdom.)

ST	TT
Complimenti! Lei ha scelto le calzature Blackpool realizzate con materiale di qualità superiore.	Compliments! You choosed the Blackpool shoes realised with materials of highly quality.
La pelle, accuratamente selezionata nei macelli specializzati, dopo una serie di processi di lavorazione viene resa più morbida e flessibile.	The leather, carefully selected in the specialised slaughter-houses, after different proceeding of manufacture, becomes softlier and supplier.
Come tutti i prodotti naturali la tonalità di colore sulla calzatura può variare a seconda delle venature caratteristiche della vera pelle.	As all the natural products, the colour tonality on the shoe can change following the grains, characteristic of the true leather.
Le Blackpool, calzature di fine lavorazione, vengono eseguite con la stessa particolare cura dei vecchi ciabattini.	The Blackpool, shoes of fine manufacturing are executed with the same particular care of the old cobbler.

The TT is rich in translation loss! This loss is mostly lexical and grammatical. We will just look at four cases which are good examples of loss arising from differences in cultural expectations between ST public and TT public.

First, 'Blackpool shoes'. An informal survey of British reactions suggests that the term 'Blackpool shoes' strikes most people as comic. Doubtless the name was chosen to give the shoe a touch of foreign chic. It is easy to imagine a British maker calling a style the 'Sorrento' or the 'Manhattan'. From the translation point of view, keeping 'Blackpool' in the TT loses the consumerist cachet of the exotic. If this loss matters to the manufacturer, two alternatives suggest themselves. A different name could be adopted for the British market ('Sorrento'? 'Capri'?), or the translator could drop all reference to a name and try to win respect for the shoes by some other means.

Dealing with names in translation is not usually a major issue, but, as the 'Blackpool' example shows, it can sometimes require attention. If we pause for a moment to look at this question, it will prove a useful introduction to the cultural dimension of translation.

There are two main alternatives in dealing with names. The name can be taken over unchanged into the TT, or it can be adapted to conform to the phonic/graphic conventions of the TL. Assuming that the name is an SL name, the first alternative introduces a foreign element into the TT. This loss will not usually matter. More serious is the sort of case where using the ST name introduces into the TT different associations from those in the ST. Brand names are a typical danger area. The 'Blackpool' shoe is an example. So is San Pellegrino's 'Dribly' lemonade: Italian sales may be enhanced by the footballing connotations, but the English connotations are completely inappropriate. Translating an Italian ST in which someone washed down a pot of Mukk yoghurt with a glass of Dribly, one would have to drop the brand names altogether, or perhaps invent English ones with more product-enhancing associations.

Simply using the ST name unchanged in the TT may in any case sometimes prove impracticable, if it actually creates problems of pronounceability, spelling or memorization. This is unlikely with 'Michelangelo', but can easily happen with, say, Polish or Russian names. The second alternative in dealing with names, **transliteration**, to some extent solves these problems by using TL conventions for the phonic/graphic representation of an ST name. This is the standard way of coping with Russian and Chinese names in English texts. There is a good example in the text in Practical 2.2, where the first thing requiring a decision was what transliteration to use for the Russian name: Černóbyl', Cernóbil, Chernobyl', or the accepted British version, Chernobyl? When the disaster happened, of course, few in the West had heard of Chernobyl, and the first Western correspondents had to devise their own transcriptions. However, once a TL consensus had emerged, there was little choice: in translating from Russian, Italian or any other language, translators will generally have felt constrained to use the established TL convention. This is normal practice; the translator simply has to be aware that standard transliteration varies from language to language and is common in the translation of place names: compare Venezia/Venice/Venise/Venedig, Salzburg/Salisburgo/Salzbourg, etc.

Some names do not need transliteration at all, but have standard TL equivalents. Compare Italian 'S. Giovanni', French 'Saint Jean' and German 'St. [= Sankt] Johannes'; or Flemish 'Luik', French 'Liège', German 'Lüttich' and Italian 'Liegi': in these cases there is little choice but to use 'St John' and 'Liège', unless the translator wants deliberately to draw attention to the foreign origin of the text. The same applies to initials and acronyms: compare Italian 'ONU' and English 'UNO' (or 'the UN'), Italian 'OMS' and English 'WHO', Italian 'IVA' and English 'VAT', etc. Keeping the Italian form here would normally introduce needless obscurity and undermine confidence in the translator.

To return to the 'Blackpool' text. The second example we want to look at is the reference to slaughterhouses. Although leather shoes are all made from animals that have been killed, people in the United Kingdom do not on the whole like to be reminded of this, just as they are often reluctant to eat small birds, or little animals (like rabbits) that have not been dismembered to stop them *looking* like little animals. A symptom of this is the fact that 'abattoir' is often used instead of 'slaughterhouse': to an English-speaker, 'slaughterhouse' refers much more explicitly than 'abattoir' to the bloody act of killing an animal. Italians are by and large less squeamish about such things. 'Macelli' will probably provoke less revulsion in an Italian lady buying Blackpool shoes than 'slaughterhouse' will in her British counterpart. Even in the ST, of course, it is odd to refer to 'macelli'; but, in this particular instance, there is such a big cultural difference between Italy and the United Kingdom that the translator is better advised to abandon all reference to slaughterhouses than to look for some subtle way of conveying the unusualness of 'macelli' in this ST. In other words, the lexical translation loss is a lesser evil here than serious consumer resistance would be.

The other two examples of loss arise from another sort of cultural difference. Whereas 'Blackpool' and 'slaughterhouses' trigger *extralingual* associations (associations in the world outside the TL, such as candyfloss and saucy postcards, or blood and death), 'execute' and 'the old cobbler' trigger *intralingual* associations. Coming so soon after 'slaughterhouses', 'execute' sounds like a bad pun. 'The old cobbler' irresistibly evokes 'a load of old cobblers'. Even if 'old cobbler' were acceptable in terms of literal meaning, the connotation would be enough to make it unusable in an advertising puff, which would self-destruct at the last moment.

We shall return to all these examples from the 'Blackpool' text when discussing compensation in Chapter 4.

CULTURAL TRANSPOSITION

As the discussion so far has shown, there may be ST expressions that, for cultural reasons, must be taken over unchanged into the TT, or need to be 'naturalized' in some way, or must be dropped altogether. We shall use the general term **cultural transposition** for the main types and degrees of departure from literal translation that may be resorted to in the process of transferring the contents of an ST from one culture into another. Any degree of cultural transposition involves the choice of features indigenous to the TL and the target culture in preference to features with their roots in the source culture. The result is to reduce foreign features in the TT, thereby to some extent naturalizing it into the TL and its cultural setting.

The various degrees of cultural transposition can be visualized as points along a scale between the extremes of exoticism and cultural transplantation:

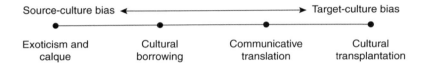

Source-culture bias			Target-culture bias
Exoticism and calque	Cultural borrowing	Communicative translation	Cultural transplantation

Exoticism and calque

The extreme options in signalling cultural foreignness in a TT fall into the category of **exoticism**. A TT marked by exoticism is one which constantly uses grammatical and cultural features imported from the ST with minimal adaptation, thereby constantly signalling the exotic source culture and its cultural strangeness. This may be one of the TT's chief attractions, as with some translations of Icelandic sagas or Persian poetry that deliberately trade on exoticism. A TT like this, however, has an impact on the TL public quite unlike any that the ST could have had on an SL public, for whom the text has fewer features of a different culture.

Even where the TT as a whole is not marked by exoticism, a momentary foreignness is sometimes introduced in the form of calque. A **calque** is an expression that consists of TL words and respects TL syntax, but is unidiomatic in the TL because it is modelled on the structure of an SL expression. This lack of idiomaticity may be purely lexical and relatively innocuous, or it may be more generally grammatical. The following calques illustrate decreasing degrees of idiomaticity:

Chi dorme non piglia pesci.	He who sleeps catches no fish.
In casa sua ciascuno è re.	In his house each is king.

Le Blackpool vengono eseguite con la stessa particolare cura dei vecchi ciabattini.	The Blackpool are executed with the same particular care of the old cobblers.

For most translation purposes, it can be said that a bad calque imitates ST features to the point of being ungrammatical in the TL, while a good one compromises between imitating ST features and offending against TL grammar. It is easy, through haste or ignorance, to mar the TT with bad calques. However, it is conceivable that in some TTs the momentary foreignness of calque may be desirable or necessary, even if its effects need to be palliated by some form of compensation. We shall return to this point in a moment, when looking at communicative translation.

Sometimes, what was originally a calqued expression actually becomes a standard TL cultural equivalent of its SL original. An English example is 'world-view', calqued on 'Weltanschauung'. Italian examples are 'peso mosca', calqued on 'flyweight'; 'la Casa Bianca', calqued on 'the White House'; and 'giardino d'infanzia', calqued on 'Kindergarten'.

Cultural transplantation

At the other end of the scale from exoticism is **cultural transplantation**, whose extreme forms are hardly translations at all, but more like adaptations – the wholesale transplanting of the entire setting of the ST, resulting in the entire text being completely rewritten in a target-culture setting. Hollywood remakes of European films are familiar cases of this. An example of a transplantation of an Italian film into America is Arau's *A Walk in the Clouds*, adapted from Blasetti's *Quattro passi fra le nuvole*. Cultural transplantation on this scale is not normal translation practice, but it can be a serious option, especially in respect of points of detail – as long as they do not have knock-on effects that make the TT as a whole incongruous. Some of Robert Garioch's Scots translations of Giuseppe Belli's *Sonetti* are examples of successful cultural transplantation from nineteenth-century Rome to twentieth-century Edinburgh (e.g. Garioch 1983: 266, 272).

By and large, normal translation practice avoids the two extremes of exoticism and cultural transplantation. In avoiding the two extremes, the translator will consider the alternatives lying between them on the scale given on p. 27.

Cultural borrowing

The first alternative is to transfer an ST expression verbatim into the TT. This is termed **cultural borrowing**. It introduces a foreign element into the TT. Of course, something foreign is by definition exotic; this is why, when the occasion demands, it can be useful to talk about *exotic elements* introduced by various translation practices. But cultural borrowing is different from exoticism as defined above: unlike exoticism, cultural borrowing does not involve adaptation of the SL expression into TL forms. So, in the 'Blackpool' TT, 'the same particular care of the old cobblers' contributes to the exoticism that marks that text, but keeping an SL expression in the TT would introduce an element of cultural borrowing into the exoticism: 'the same particular care of the old *ciabattini*'. Translators often turn to cultural borrowing when it is impossible to find a suitable indigenous TL expression. As with calque, such borrowings sometimes become standard TL terms – think of all the Italian musical terms that entered English in the eighteenth and nineteenth centuries. Cultural borrowing is also frequent in texts on history or social or political matters, where an institution or concept specific to the source culture – such as 'Signoria', 'Risorgimento' or 'mafia' – is defined in the TT the first time it occurs, and thereafter simply used as a loan-word.

Cultural borrowing only presents the translator with a true choice in cases where previous translation practice has not already firmly established the ST expression in the TL. So unless there are special contextual reasons for not doing so, it is virtually mandatory to render loan-expressions like 'andante sostenuto', 'pizza', 'dolce far niente', 'terza rima', 'breccia' or 'intaglio' verbatim into an English TT, because they have become the standard conventional equivalents of the Italian expressions.

However, caution needs to be exercised in translating SL words that have become TL loan-words, because they often have more meanings in the SL than in the TL, and sometimes even have a different meaning in the TL from their SL one. In Italian, for example, 'breccia' may denote crushed stone for road-mending *or* the geological type of stone (as well as 'breach'). Italian 'ballerina' denotes any kind of female dancer – ballerina, ballroom dancer, variety dancer, etc. Conversely, in Italian, 'un drink' can only be an alcoholic drink, generally a fashionable imported spirit. And in contemporary Italian journalism, 'baby' is commonly used to denote not a baby, but someone who is surprisingly young for whatever they are doing: so a 'baby killer' is an unexpectedly young murderer, and a 'baby pensionato' is someone who has retired unusually early. Similarly, prime ministers' or presidents' wives are sometimes given the title 'Lady', regardless of rank: 'Lady Blair' is a recent example.

Communicative translation

As we saw on p. 16, communicative translation is usually adopted for all those clichés, idioms, proverbs, etc. which have readily identifiable communicative equivalents in the TL. Only special contextual reasons could justify not choosing communicative translation in such cases as the following:

– In bocca al lupo! – Crepi!	'Good luck!' 'Thanks!'
Piove a catinelle.	It's raining cats and dogs/bucketing it down.
Ha trent'anni suonati.	He won't see thirty again/He's the wrong side of thirty.
Non si può tenere il piede in due staffe.	You can't run with the hare and hunt with the hounds/You can't have your cake and eat it.
Magro come un chiodo.	As thin as a rake.

Literal translation of expressions like these would introduce a potentially comic or distracting foreignness not present in the ST. Sometimes, however, the obvious communicative equivalent will not be appropriate in the context. For instance, in a TT clearly set in Italy and involving only Italian characters, it would be comic to translate 'In casa sua ciascuno è re' as 'An Englishman's home is his castle'. If this comic effect were not wanted, the translator would have either to substitute something like 'My home is my castle', or to invent a generalization with a proverbial ring to it ('Every man's home is his castle', 'Every man is master in his own house', etc.), or to substitute a related proverb ('Every dog is a lion at home', etc.). Each of these has its own connotations; which – if any – is appropriate will depend on what nuance is required in the context.

This example lies halfway between cases where communicative translation is virtually inescapable (as for 'Magro come un chiodo'), and cases where – as commonly happens – a set phrase in the ST does not have a standard communicative equivalent in the TL. In cases like these, the translator has a genuine choice between literal translation and some degree of communicative translation. Take the following scenario. It is nearly midday, and hot and stuffy in the classroom. Gianluca is gazing vacantly out of the window. The teacher rebukes him and, wagging a finger, sententiously quotes the proverb: 'Chi dorme non piglia pesci.' The temptation is to render proverb with proverb and to translate: 'The early bird catches the worm.' This translation is indeed the one given in a number of dictionaries. But in this case it does not work. For one thing, it is practically noon, so that earliness does not come into it. In any case, the message of the Italian proverb is that you won't get results if you don't concentrate on the matter in hand (the image is of the angler watching intently so as to hook the fish as soon as the float moves). The teacher is telling Gianluca to pay attention, not to leap out of bed and tackle a job that is waiting to be done. It is conceivable, of course, that in certain situations the TL proverb would overlap with the Italian one and be usable in the context – say, if a parent is getting a sleepyhead out of bed. But this would be a lucky chance, and in most cases

'The early bird catches the worm' is not a communicative translation of 'Chi dorme non piglia pesci.'

Given that there is no standard communicative equivalent here, what are the translator's options? Literal translation is one possibility: 'Who sleeps catches no fish.' However, this calque both introduces an exotic element and makes the teacher into some kind of whimsical wordsmith or parodist instead of someone simply quoting a well-worn saying. Whether these effects were acceptable would depend on the context.

A less stylistically marked option is communicative paraphrase, a cross between gist translation and exegetic translation – something like 'Gazing into space won't get your verbs learnt/sums done.' In most cases, this would be the least risky solution, but it does lose the stylistic flavour of 'speaking in proverbs'. This loss could be significant if, in the ST, it is a notable part of the teacher's character that she regularly uses proverbs or maxims. If that were the case, one might keep the literal translation, but add a clause to make it clear that the teacher is quoting an existing proverb and not making one up: 'You know the saying: "He who sleeps catches no fish/Watch your float or you'll catch no fish"', or some such.

Translators themselves clearly need to 'watch the float', and not ruin the message with ill-judged attempts at communicative translation. It is easy to be misled by semantic resemblances between SL and TL expressions, especially in respect of proverbs. For example, 'To run with the hare and hunt with the hounds' is not the communicative equivalent of 'Una volta corre il cane e un'altra la lepre.' Depending on context, this Italian proverb might be rendered with something like 'He who laughs last laughs longest' (but cf. 'Ride bene chi ride ultimo'), 'Every dog has his day', 'The biter bit', or 'My/your/their turn will come', etc. Each of these has its own nuances, and each is susceptible to the same sorts of translation loss as the various renderings of 'In casa sua ciascuno è re' and 'Chi dorme non piglia pesci'.

PRACTICAL 3

3.1 Cultural transposition

Assignment
(i) You have been commissioned by a broadsheet to translate the following ST for inclusion in a series entitled 'How the Continentals See Us'. Discuss the strategic decisions that you have to take before starting detailed translation of this ST, and outline and justify the strategy you adopt.
(ii) Translate the text into English.
(iii) Paying special attention to the options for cultural transposition that you rejected and adopted, discuss the main decisions of detail you took.

Contextual information
The text is a short article published in *L'Espresso* in November 1996.

ST

ROAST CANGURO

Il roast beef è obsoleto (e lo era già prima ancora che le angliche bocche fossero turbate dal disdicevole evento della vacca pazza). Anche il tacchino è démodé, anzi declassato al rango di vivanda plebea. Per gentlemen e ladies di Sua Maestà britannica è già tempo di rivolgere un pensierino ai menù
5   natalizi. Che trionfino le carni e i pesci. In omaggio alla nobile tradizione zoofila, la gentebene di Britannia dimostra, ancora una volta, di amare gli animali. Anche a tavola, e ben cotti.

Da alcuni anni, gli inglesi sono tra i più solleciti importatori di carni esotiche: di coccodrillo dello Zimbabwe (ne parlammo il 10/1/88), di iguana
10 (24/4/88), struzzo (7/1/94), emù e nandù (15/10/95). Per il prossimo Natale (mala tempora currunt anche per i marsupiali), arriverà nel Regno Unito (ma non ancora in Italia) perfino la carne surgelata di canguro (kangaroo, in inglese).

Questo timido, buffo, simpatico animale erbivoro, che finora aveva saltato
15 (e sono salti di nove metri di lunghezza per tre di altezza!) libero e felice nelle zone verdi dell'Australia e della Tasmania, è ora malinconicamente allevato in grandi recinti. Finirà, ancora cucciolo, nelle spietate fauci di Homo sapiens (et insatiabilis).

I promotori commerciali assicurano che si tratta di carne 'magra, saporita
20 e a basso contenuto di colesterolo': stesso ritornello ascoltato per alligatore, iguana, struzzo, emù, nandù. Un gourmet giramondo mi segnala, però, che non ha gradito il sentore 'di selvatico'. Caro, mite canguro, ti confesso di non essere vegetariano. Eppure mi disturba sapere che anche tu puoi finire nello stomaco degli umani e nelle scatole per gatti.

(Djalma Vitali 1996: 185)

4

Compensation

In Chapter 3, we spoke of the need to palliate certain TT effects by the use of compensation. To see what is meant by this, we can return to Gianluca and the teacher (pp. 30–1). One way of translating the proverb was 'You know the saying: "He who sleeps catches no fish".' 'You know the saying' is added to show that the aphorism is an established proverb and not a flight of poetic creativeness on the part of the teacher. Without the addition, the quaint unfamiliarity of the calque would have an exotic quality that is completely absent from the ST, and it would also imply something about the teacher's personality that the ST does not imply at all. Depending on the purpose of the TT, these two effects could be instances of serious translation loss, a significant betrayal of the ST effects. Adding 'You know the saying' does not make 'He who sleeps catches no fish' any less unfamiliar *in itself*, but it does make it less likely to have these misleading effects. This procedure is a good example of **compensation**: that is, where any conventional translation (whether literal or otherwise) would entail an unacceptable translation loss, this loss is reduced by the freely chosen introduction of a less unacceptable one, such that important ST effects are rendered approximately in the TT by means other than those used in the ST. Thus, in this example, adding 'You know the saying' incurs great translation loss in terms of *economy* and *cultural presupposition*, but this is accepted because it significantly reduces an even greater loss in terms of *message content*.

Translators make this sort of compromise all the time, balancing loss against loss in order to do most justice to what, in a given ST, they think is most important. Our aim in this book is to encourage student translators to make these compromises as the result of deliberate decisions taken in the light of strategic factors such as the nature and purpose of the ST, the purpose of the TT, the nature and needs of the target public, and so on. In taking these decisions, it is vital to remember that compensation is not a matter of putting any old fine-sounding phrase into a TT in case any weaknesses have crept in, but of countering a specific, clearly defined, serious loss with a specific, clearly defined, less serious one. Compensation illustrates better than anything else the *imaginative rigour* that translation demands. The following examples will show some of the forms it can take.

In discussing the 'Blackpool' text in Chapter 3, we suggested that a translator might try to get round the TL drawbacks of the name 'Blackpool' by dropping the name and trying to win respect for the shoes by some other means. If the manufacturer were reluctant to substitute an Italian name for 'Blackpool', one might compensate for losing the consumerist cachet of the foreign element in the ST like this:

Complimenti! Lei ha scelto le calzature Blackpool realizzate con materiale di qualità superiore.	Congratulations! You have chosen a pair of shoes crafted from the finest of materials.

In this TT, there are two features that highlight the uniqueness of the new shoes: 'a pair' and 'finest of materials'. Saying 'a pair' points to the shoes as something apart. Superiority is also suggested in the relatively formal tone of 'the finest of materials' as compared with, say, 'the finest materials' or 'top-quality materials'. From the point of view of literal meaning, these expressions are unnecessary departures from the TL structures indicated by the ST grammar: 'you have chosen shoes' and 'top-quality materials' would have been perfectly acceptable. These translation losses have been deliberately incurred in order to compensate for the loss of ST 'Blackpool' by conferring superiority on the shoes by other means than the exotic.

This compensation has also been calculated to fit in with the implications of another one. In the ST, 'realizzate' (as distinct from 'prodotte' or 'fabbricate') has connotations of vision and fulfilment (cf. 'realizzare uno scopo/un'aspirazione/un progetto', etc.). The English verb 'realize' can have the same connotations, but it can hardly be used here, because it sounds very odd with 'shoes' as its object: there would be unacceptable translation loss in terms of idiomaticity. The obvious alternative, 'made', would incur almost as big a loss, because it does not have the connotations of 'realizzate'. This loss is compensated for with the connotations of 'crafted' – skill, care and exclusiveness. These connotations are different from those of 'realizzate', but they have the same communicative function – to convince the purchaser that she has made a good choice. And, because they do not clash with the connotations of 'a pair' and 'the finest of materials', they fit into the context.

Note that none of these departures from literal translation has been forced on the translator by the constraints of TL grammar. The changes – that is, the losses – have been deliberately chosen in order to compensate for losing the exotic element in 'Blackpool' and the connotations of 'realizzate'. Whereas 'Blackpool' and 'realized' would have betrayed the manufacturer's purpose, the three TT expressions between them convey a similar message to that of the ST: that this, truly, is a superior shoe. This question of choice versus constraint is vital to the understanding of compensation, as we shall see.

The second paragraph of the 'Blackpool' text offers another good example of the need for compensation. The lexical translation loss entailed in not translating 'nei macelli specializzati' is a lesser evil than the consumer resistance that would be provoked by the connotations of 'slaughterhouses'. But is it worth spending time working out how to compensate for this loss? As always, before deciding whether to compensate for a loss, the translator has to ask what the *function* of the ST feature is in the context. In this ST, one of the functions of 'nei macelli specializzati' is to draw attention to the care exercised at every stage: the skins are singled out; even the slaughterhouses are specialized, as if exceptional know-how is needed for these select animals. And the stress on the provenance of the skins perhaps reinforces the impression of authenticity (cf. 'vera pelle' in the third paragraph): one can almost smell the animal the leather comes from. Whatever the translator thinks of this hype, it is there in the ST, and it has a commercial purpose. So, if reference to slaughterhouses is taboo, the loss of the implication of 'nei macelli specializzati' must be compensated for. Here is one possibility:

La pelle, accuratamente selezionata nei macelli specializzati, dopo una serie di processi di lavorazione viene resa più morbida e flessibile.	The leather is taken from specially selected hides, and then goes through a series of careful procedures which make it softer and more supple.

'Hides' denotes skins taken from large animals. It therefore retains an allusion to where the leather has come from, and implies the realities of slaughter and flaying without naming them. Literal meaning ('macelli') has been replaced with connotation, a common form of compensation. Further, as a technical term, 'hide' may be less upsetting than 'skins', and certainly than 'slaughterhouses'. Since the notion of 'specialization' is typically product-vaunting, it is retained in the TT; but it has had to be transferred from the now unmentioned slaughterhouses to the selection of the hides. The adjectival past participle 'specializzati' is rendered with the adverb 'specially'. This change of place, and the grammatical change, are also very common in compensation. And, again typically, one change of place entails another, the notion of 'care' now being applied to the processes, not the selection: 'carefully specially selected' or 'specially carefully selected' would have been clumsy and near-tautologous. Here too, a grammatical change, from the adverb 'accuratamente' to the adjective 'careful', accompanies a change in place.

Like any structural change, all these changes are by definition instances of translation loss. But, as with the previous example, the point is that they are not forced on the translator by the constraints of TL grammar: they are consciously and carefully chosen in order to avoid a greater translation loss, namely the communicative ineffectiveness which would have resulted from using 'slaughterhouses'. It is this deliberateness and precision that makes them into compensation rather than simply examples of standard structural differences between SL and TL.

In the last paragraph of the 'Blackpool' ST, 'vecchi ciabattini' cannot be translated as 'old cobblers', because of the unwanted connotations. Yet the reference to traditional craftsmen is vital in the ST. Omitting it would mean serious translation loss. Luckily, literal meaning in the ST is again subservient to the commercial blarney, which makes it easier to compensate for this loss:

Le Blackpool, calzature di fine lavorazione, vengono eseguite con la stessa particolare cura dei vecchi ciabattini.	Your new shoes are proof positive that the old traditions of skilled craftsmanship still flourish in Italy.

This TT is a good example of how compensation can be relatively complex in even the simplest-looking TTs. To begin with, the adjective 'new' is introduced, for two reasons. First, while 'Blackpool' had to be dropped, both publicity and normal usage require an adjective before 'shoes' – 'your shoes' sounds oddly as if it refers to the ones you are wearing, not the new ones. Second, contrasting 'new' with 'old' (in 'old traditions') helps to compensate for some of the major translation loss incurred in not translating the sentence literally. This loss primarily concerns the ST implications of traditional skill and perfectionism, as we shall see. In the case of 'new', its specific compensatory role is to counter the loss of the connotations of 'eseguite'. 'Executed' or 'performed' is impossible in this context. Yet 'eseguite' is an unusual term to apply to making shoes (contrast 'fatte', 'fabbricate' or 'prodotte'), and is presumably chosen for its connotations of performance, of artistic creation or re-creation. By contrasting 'new' with 'old' in the context of this sentence, the TT suggests that these shoes are a new manifestation of traditional Italian shoemaking genius. The image is different from the ST implications of a new *performance* of a masterpiece. But, like the ST, the TT is dealing not in rational argument, but in emotive connotations. What the two sets of connotations have in common is the continuing vigour of a creative tradition.

'Old' renders 'vecchi', but it qualifies something different in the TT, 'traditions'. This word has been added to strengthen the emphasis on skill and craftsmanship, in an attempt to compensate for the loss of specific reference to shoemakers and the replacement of 'ciabattini' with 'craftsmanship', which is abstract and more general. While 'craftsmanship', in this TT, corresponds to 'ciabattini', it also overlaps with 'lavorazione' in the sense of 'workmanship'. It is therefore made to carry too big a semantic load, so that 'lavorazione' is somewhat weakened in the TT; to compensate for this loss, 'skilled' has been added to 'craftsmanship'. 'Skilled' is chosen to correspond to ST 'fine', but collocates better with 'craftsmanship' than 'subtle', 'detailed' or even TL 'fine'. It does, however, introduce a different viewpoint from the ST expression: 'skilled' denotes a quality displayed by the shoemakers as they work, whereas ST 'fine' denotes a quality of the finished object. Despite the change, the global message is the same: great care has gone into making these shoes. This sort of switch in viewpoint is common in compensation (as indeed in translation in general); there is another example in 'proof positive', as we shall see in a moment.

Compensation is also required on the level of sentence structure in this final paragraph. In the ST, the insertion of 'calzature di fine lavorazione' after the subject has a rhetorical effect, creating a certain suspense before the climactic predicate finally comes. Ideally, the translator will want to ensure a similar effect in the TT. But calquing the parenthetical ST structure (e.g. 'Your new shoes, skilfully crafted, are made . . .') would perhaps be unidiomatic, certainly less convincing than following the subject directly with the main verb ('Your new shoes are . . .'). Hence the use of 'are proof positive' instead of, say, 'show' or 'prove' or even 'are proof': inserting the longer expression holds the climax back, and therefore highlights it. In this way, the rhetorical impact of the TT is similar to that of the ST, but it is achieved by different means.

Another reason for choosing 'proof positive' is that it connotes careful scrutiny of evidence – in this case, the details of the finished shoe. This helps to compensate for the loss of significant connotations in 'la stessa particolare cura'. If this phrase is translated literally, the result is a comic calque. Before translating the phrase, the translator has to pin down its function. 'Stessa' and 'vecchi' together stress the continuity of a traditional craft. 'Particolare' denotes 'special', 'exceptional', but has a strong connotation of 'going into particulars', 'attention to detail'. In other words, what makes the 'cura' special is that it is so painstaking. In so far as 'proof positive' connotes careful scrutiny, some of this stress on detail may be saved, by compensation. As we have said, this piece of compensation, like the use of 'skilled', involves a change in viewpoint: in the TT it is implied that the purchaser scrutinizes the finished shoe, whereas in the ST the implied scrutiny is the shoemaker's, as he concentrates on creating the shoe. As in the case of 'skilled', this change in viewpoint is saved from illogicality or nonsense by the fact that the global message is the same in the TT as in the ST: what is scrutinized in the TT is the triumphant result of the shoemaker's own scrutiny, the superb shoe.

However, the connotation of scrutiny is in itself too slight to convey all the force of 'la stessa particolare cura'. This is why we have used the phrase 'still flourish': 'still' compensates for the loss of 'same' or 'very' ('stessa'), while 'flourish' introduces the notions of *vigour and success* to compensate for the loss of the ST stress on *painstaking attention to detail*. All that the two ideas have in common is an implication of 'superlative merit', but that is all that is needed for the purposes of this publicity puff.

Finally, 'in Italy' was added to compensate for the loss of the exotic dimension contained in ST 'Blackpool': the purchaser is reminded that her shoes are Italian-made, and therefore excellent. Purely from the compensation point of view, of course, there would be less need for 'in Italy' if the manufacturer called the shoes something like 'Sorrento' for the English-speaking market. Stylistically, however, there is another reason for adding these words: they supply a complement for 'flourish', so that the sentence does not end with unidiomatic abruptness.

CATEGORIES OF COMPENSATION

In discussing TTs, it is sometimes helpful to distinguish between different categories of compensation. We shall suggest three. Remember, however, that most cases of compensation belong in more than one category. The most important thing is not to agonize over what label to give an instance of compensation, but to be clear *what loss* it compensates for and *how* it does so. Remember, too, that the question of how to compensate can never be considered in and for itself, in isolation from other crucial factors: context, style, genre, the purpose of the ST and of the TT.

Compensation is needed whenever consideration of these factors confronts the translator with inevitable, but unwelcome, compromise. Simply put, it is a less unwelcome compromise. It usually entails a difference in mode between the ST textual effect and the TT textual effect. This **compensation in mode** can take very many forms. For instance, it may involve making explicit what is implicit in the ST, or implicit what is explicit. Literal meaning may have to replace connotative meaning, or vice versa. Compensation may involve substituting concrete for abstract, or abstract for concrete. It nearly always involves using different parts of speech and syntactic structures from those indicated by literal translation. There are examples of all these devices in our 'Blackpool' TT. In other texts, the same approach may result in replacing, say, a snatch of Dante with an analogous snatch of Milton. An ST pun may have to be replaced with a different form of word play. All these sorts of substitution may be confined to single words, but they more usually extend to whole phrases, sentences, or even paragraphs. Sometimes, a whole text is affected. For instance, quite apart from lexical and grammatical considerations, if a poem is heavily marked by rhyme and assonance, and the translator decides that for some reason rhyme and assonance would lead to unacceptable translation loss, compensation might consist of heavily marking the TT with rhythm and alliteration instead.

Compensation also usually entails a change in place, the TT textual effect occurring at a different place, relative to the other features in the TT context, from the corresponding textual effect in the ST context. We shall call this **compensation in place**. A simple example in the 'Blackpool' text is the use of 'old' to qualify 'traditions' instead of 'craftsmanship'.

Compensation also often involves a change in 'economy', ST features having to be spread over a relatively longer length of TT. We shall call this **compensation by splitting**. The following sentence, from an unpublished essay by the composer Luca Francesconi, provides an excellent example of the need for compensation by splitting:

Anzi, la sensazione brutale è che si voglia eliminare tutto ciò che non è evasione e naturalmente anche la ricerca musicale, che è prima di tutto ricerca instancabile di identità e di valori fondanti, linguistici ed umani. Ricerca che porta con sé nel bene e nel male il retaggio del grande, antichissimo pensiero occidentale.

The term 'ricerca' is central to the author's thinking throughout this essay. Now in many contexts, it clearly means *either* 'research', *or* 'search', *or* 'quest', *or* 'investigation', *or* 'study'. In such cases, the translator simply has to choose the right term. But in many other contexts, including this one, it means several of these things at once. There is no single English word that can carry these same combinations of meanings. This is where compensation by splitting comes in. In the following TT, we have tried to divide up the semantic load of 'ricerca' and spread it over several TL expressions:

On the contrary, the brutal impression is that there is a wish to do away with anything that is not escapism, including of course research in and through music – that is, above all, a search, an indefatigable quest for founding values, linguistic and human. A quest that brings with it, for better or for worse, the great and ancient heritage of Western thought.

In this TT, the use of 'in and through music' instead of 'musical' triggers two of the four sorts of 'ricerca' that are implied in the ST: *research into* music, and the *use of* music as a tool for acquiring knowledge. The other two are conveyed as nouns in apposition to 'research': 'search' and 'quest'. The complexity of 'ricerca' is therefore split up into its components and spread over three nouns and two prepositions. Note that, as happens more often than not, this compensation by splitting also entails grammatical transposition – that is, there is also an element of compensation in mode. There are three instances of this. First, part of the *noun* 'ricerca' is expressed by *prepositions*. Second, these prepositions need a noun after them, so the *noun* 'music' corresponds to the *adjective* 'musicale'. Third, introducing the noun 'music' means that 'che' cannot be translated with a relative pronoun, because 'research in and through music, which is . . .' is ambiguous: hence the change in syntax, the *relative pronoun* being replaced with a dash and the *conjunction* 'that is'.

This complex example raises very clearly the issue of the parameters of compensation. What we have done is deliberately introduce loss in economy and grammar in order to avoid more serious loss in message content. Now, since it is after all the translator's job to convey the message content, it could be reasonably argued that splitting 'ricerca' as we have done is not strictly speaking compensation, but simply a constraint. That is, to do full justice to the ST's semantic complexity, the translator does not have a choice, because this expansion is the only adequate solution – using fewer or other possible meanings of 'ricerca' would simply have given a mistranslation.

It is of course true that if, in this context, 'ricerca' is seen as having four meanings, a TT that does not in some way convey them all should be considered defective. In deciding whether the changes introduced amount to compensation, the crucial factor is the role of context. If an ST expression has a standard TL counterpart that, regardless of context, spreads it over a relatively longer stretch of TT, then this is a constraint, an instance of canonic expansion, not of compensation. So, for example, 'fondo rettificativo' will always be translated as 'exchange equalization fund', whatever the context – in every case, the translation is predictable; that is, the differences between ST expression and TT expression only reflect lexical and syntactic differences between Italian and English. The 'ricerca' example is not like this, however. It does reflect lexical differences between Italian and English, but our expansion is not canonic or predictable; in fact it is virtually unrepeatable. To the extent that it is a specific reaction to specific occurrences of 'ricerca' in a specific context, it is a case of compensation.

Distinguishing the three sorts of compensation is a rough-and-ready categorization. Each could be refined and subdivided. In any case, most cases of compensation involve more than one category. However, our purpose here is not to elaborate a taxonomy, but simply to alert students to the possibilities and mechanisms of compensation. In fact, in the case of compensation in mode and compensation in place, it is not usually even necessary to label them as such, because virtually all compensation entails difference in mode and place. The most important lesson to be learned from this chapter is that compensation is a matter of *choice and decision*. It is the reduction of an unacceptable translation loss through the calculated introduction of a less unacceptable one. Or, to put it differently, a deliberately introduced loss is a small price to pay if it is used to avoid the more serious loss that would be entailed by conventional translation of the expression concerned. So where there is no real choice open to the translator, the element of active compensation is minimal. The easiest way of illustrating this is to look at communicative translation. Communicative translation does certainly involve compensation, in that it reduces translation loss by deploying resources like those mentioned in the previous paragraph. But the element of compensation is, in a sense, 'automatic': the original compensation was created long ago, by the first person who decided that, say, 'Chi non risica non rosica' was best rendered with a TL equivalent like 'Nothing ventured, nothing gained'. Certainly, ever since then, translators confronted with this proverb have had to be alert enough to recognize the need for communicative translation – to that extent, producing the TL equivalent does, like all translation, involve choice and decision. But in cases like this one, the translator is not required to devise the TT expression from scratch. Therefore, in discussing TTs, such cases are generally more usefully noted as communicative translation than analysed as instances of compensation.

The same is true of the myriad cases where the canonic literal translation involves grammatical transposition. Take a simple exchange like 'Ho fame. – Anch'io': there is little option but to translate as "'I'm hungry." "So am I"', although, in a colloquial context, 'Anch'io' could be translated as 'Me too'. In most contexts, the unidiomatic exoticism of "'I have hunger." "Also I"' would constitute grievous translation loss. So preserving TL idiomaticity does in a way compensate for the loss of the ST grammatical structures. But this compensation is even more automatic than that involved in communicative translation. In so far as the canonic literal translation is unavoidable, little choice is involved, and there is no point in discussing such cases as examples of compensation.

In both these sorts of mandatory translation, then, the only element of choice is in the decision *not* to depart from the standard rendering. Similar remarks apply to differences in 'economy' between ST and TT, as we saw in the 'ricerca' example. Occasionally, however, there may be a case for departing from the norm to some extent. This more often happens with communicative translation than with canonic literal translation. For a good example, see the discussion of 'quando i buoi sono scappati' in Chapter 9 (pp. 96–7).

Compensation, then, is a matter of conscious choice, and is unlikely to be successful if inspiration is not allied with analytical rigour. So, before deciding on how to compensate for a translation loss, it is best to assess as precisely as possible what the loss is and why it matters both in its immediate context and in the ST as a whole. This reduces the likelihood of inadvertently introducing, somewhere in the TT, more serious translation losses than the one that is being compensated for.

PRACTICAL 4

4.1   Compensation

Assignment
Comparing the ST and TT printed on pp. 44 and 45–6,

(i)   Take any three suitable examples and explain why you think they are
      more a matter of balanced (SL/TL) translation (cf. p. 16) than of
      compensation.
(ii) Analyse the principal cases where the translator seems to have used
      compensation to alleviate translation loss. Say why you think the
      compensation is successful or unsuccessful; if you think it could be
      improved, give your own translation, and explain why you think it is
      better.
(iii) Analyse any cases where you think that significant translation loss is
      incurred without the translator apparently having tried to alleviate it
      with compensation. Give your own translation of these cases, and
      explain why you think it is better.

Contextual information
The ST is taken from early in Italo Calvino's novel, *Il sentiero dei nidi di
ragno* (set in wartime Italy, and first published in 1947). Pin, a young
apprentice, lives in the rough part of a small town on the Ligurian coast.
He associates with the drinkers in a local bar, who like getting him to sing
lurid or earthy adult songs. He acts tough by smoking and drinking, but
still has not learned to enjoy either. His sister is a prostitute; his 'bedroom'
is a cubby hole next to her room, and he often watches what she is up to
through a crack in the partition. When this episode occurs, Pin is exchanging
banter with the men sitting drinking at tables in the bar. He promises good
news to anyone who'll buy him a drink, and someone asks: 'Has your sister
cut her prices?' The translation was first published in 1956.

Turn to p. 44

ST

Gli altri ridono a gola spiegata e lo scappellottano e gli versano un bicchiere. Il vino non piace a Pin: è aspro contro la gola e arriccia la pelle e mette addosso una smania di ridere, gridare ed essere cattivi. Pure lo beve, tracanna bicchieri tutto d'un fiato come inghiotte fumo, come alla notte spia con 5 schifo la sorella sul letto insieme a uomini nudi, e il vederla è come una carezza ruvida, sotto la pelle, un gusto aspro, come tutte le cose degli uomini; fumo, vino, donne.

– Canta, Pin, – gli dicono. Pin canta bene, serio, impettito, con quella voce di bambino rauco. Canta *Le quattro stagioni*.

10
Ma quando penso all'avvenir
della mia libertà perduta
vorrei baciarla e poi morir
mentre lei dorme... all'insaputa...

Gli uomini ascoltano in silenzio, a occhi bassi come fosse un inno di 15 chiesa. Tutti sono stati in prigione: chi non è stato mai in prigione non è un uomo. E la vecchia canzone dei galeotti è piena di quello sconforto che viene nelle ossa alla sera, in prigione, quando i secondini passano a battere le grate con una spranga di ferro, e a poco a poco tutti i litigi, le impre-cazioni si quetano, e rimane solo una voce che canta quella canzone, come 20 ora Pin, e nessuno gli grida di smettere.

Amo la notte ascoltar
il grido della sentinella.
Amo la luna al suo passar
quando illumina la mia cella.

25 Pin proprio in prigione non è mai stato: quella volta che volevano portarlo ai *discoli*, è scappato. Ogni tanto lo acchiappano le guardie municipali, per qualche scorribanda per le tettoie del mercato della verdura, ma lui fa impazzire tutto il corpo di guardia dagli strilli e dai pianti finché non lo liberano. Ma nella guardina dei vigili un po' c'è stato rinchiuso, e sa cosa 30 vuol dire, e perciò canta bene, con sentimento.

Pin sa tutte quelle vecchie canzoni che gli uomini dell'osteria gli hanno insegnato, canzoni che raccontano fatti di sangue; quella che fa: *Torna Caserio...* e quella di Peppino che uccide il tenente. Poi, a un tratto, quando tutti sono tristi e guardano nel viola dei bicchieri e scatarrano, Pin fa una 35 piroetta in mezzo al fumo dell'osteria, e intona a squarciagola:

– E le toccai i capelli – e lei disse non son quelli – vai più giù che son più belli, – amor se mi vuoi bene – più giù devi toccar.

Allora gli uomini dànno pugni sullo zinco e la serva mette in salvo i bicchieri, e gridano 'hiuù' e battono il tempo con le mani. E le donne che 40 sono nell'osteria, vecchie ubriacone, con la faccia rossa, come la Bersagliera, ballonzolano accennando un passo di danza.

(Calvino 1993: 6–7)

TT

The others roar with laughter and clap him on the back and pour him out a glass. Pin does not like wine; it feels harsh against his throat and wrinkles his skin up and makes him long to laugh and shout and stir up trouble. Yet he drinks it, swallowing down each glassful in one gulp, as he swallows cigarette
5   smoke, or as at night he watches with shivers of disgust his sister lying with some man on her bed, a sight like the feel of a rough hand moving over his skin, harsh like all sensations men enjoy; smoke, wine, women.

'Sing, Pin,' they say. And Pin begins singing, seriously, tensely, in that hoarse childish voice of his. He sings a song called 'The four seasons':

10   *When I think of the future*
And the liberty I've lost
I'd like to kiss her and then die
While she sleeps . . . and never knows.

The men sit listening in silence, with their eyes lowered, as if to a hymn.
15   All of them have been to prison; no one is a real man to them unless he has. And the old jail-birds' song is full of melancholy which seeps into the bones in prison, at night, when the warders pass hitting the grills with a crowbar, and gradually the quarrels and curses die down, and all that can still be heard is a voice singing this song which Pin is singing now, and
20   which no one shouts for him to stop.

At night I love to hear
The sentry's call,
I love to watch the passing moon
Light up my cell.

25   Pin has never been in a real prison yet; once when they tried to take him off to a reformatory he escaped. Every now and again he is picked up by the municipal guards for some escapade among the stalls in the fruit-market, but he always sends the guards nearly crazy with his screams and sobs, until finally they let him go. He has been shut up in their guardroom once
30   or twice, though, and knows what prison feels like; that's why he is singing this song so well, with real emotion.

Pin knows a lot of old songs which have been taught him by the men of the tavern, songs about violence and bloodshed such as 'Torna Caserio' or the one about a soldier called Peppino who killed his lieutenant. Then,
35   when they are all feeling sad and gazing into the purple depths of their glasses, Pin suddenly twirls round the smoky room and begins singing at the top of his voice:

And I touched her hair –
And she said not there . . .

40 Then the men begin pounding on the tables and shouting 'hiuú', and clap-
ping time, while the servant-girl tries to save the glasses. And the women
in the tavern, old drunks with red faces like the one called the Bersagliera,
sway to and fro as if to the rhythm of a dance.

(Calvino 1976: 4–5)

The formal properties of texts: Introduction

We have suggested that translation is most usefully taken as a challenge to reduce translation loss. The threat of loss is most obvious when the translator confronts general issues of cultural transfer like those discussed in Chapter 3. However, a threat of greater translation loss is actually posed by the formal properties of the ST.

In assessing the formal properties of texts, it is helpful to borrow some fundamental notions from linguistics. Linguistics offers a hierarchically ordered series of discrete levels on which formal properties can be discussed in a systematic way. Of course, although it is essential to *distinguish* between these levels when analysing texts, they do not actually function *separately* from one another: textual features on a given level always have their effect in terms of features on all the other levels.

In any text, there are many points at which it could have been different. Where there is one sound, there might have been another (compare 'road tolls' and 'toad rolls'). Or where there is a question mark there might have been an exclamation mark (compare 'What rubbish?' and 'What rubbish!'). Or where there is an allusion to the Bible there might have been one to Shakespeare. All these points of detail where a text could have been different – that is, where it could have been *another* text – are what we shall call **textual variables**. These textual variables are what the series of levels defined in linguistics make it possible to identify.

Taking the levels one at a time has two main advantages. First, looking at textual variables on a series of isolated levels makes it easier to see which are important in the ST and which are less important. As we have seen, all ST features inevitably fall prey to translation loss in some respect or other. For example, even if the TT conveys literal meaning exactly, there will at the very least be phonic loss, and very likely also loss in terms of connotations, register, and so on. It is therefore excellent translation strategy to decide in broad terms which category or categories of textual variables are indispensable in a given ST, and which can be ignored.

The other advantage in scanning the text level by level is that a proposed TT can be assessed by isolating and comparing the formal variables of ST and TT. The translator or reviser is thus able to see precisely what textual variables of the ST are absent from the TT, and vice versa. This makes the assessment of translation loss less impressionistic, which in turn permits a more self-aware and methodical way of reducing it.

We suggest six levels of textual variables, hierarchically arranged, in the sense that each level is built on top of the preceding one. Using the term 'hierarchy' is not meant to imply that features on a 'higher' level are by definition more important than those on a 'lower' level: the variables only have their effect in terms of one another, and their relative importance varies from text to text or even utterance to utterance. Other categories and hier-archies could have been adopted, but arguing about alternative frameworks belongs to linguistics, not to translation method. We shall progress 'bottom up', from phonic details to intertextual matters. We find that students are more comfortable with this than with a 'top down' approach. In Chapters 5–7, we shall work our way up through the levels, showing what kinds of textual variable can be found on each, and how they may function in a text. Together, the six levels constitute part of a checklist of questions which the translator can ask of an ST, in order to determine what levels and proper-ties are important in it and most need to be respected in the TT. This method does not imply a plodding or piecemeal approach to translation: applying the checklist quickly becomes automatic and very effective. (For the whole checklist, see above, p. 5.)

5

The formal properties of texts: Phonic/graphic and prosodic issues in translation

Although they are the 'lowest' in the hierarchy, the phonic/graphic and prosodic levels of textual variables are as potentially significant as any other.

THE PHONIC/GRAPHIC LEVEL

Taking a text on the **phonic/graphic level** means looking at it as a sequence of sound-segments (or *phonemes*), or as a sequence of letters (or *graphemes*), or as both. Oral texts are normally only looked at in phonic terms. Written texts are always first encountered on the graphic level, but they may need to be looked at in phonic terms as well – in fact, from a translation point of view, they are more often considered phonically than graphically. Although phonemes and graphemes are different things, they are on the same level of textual variables. To help keep this in mind, we shall normally refer to the 'phonic/graphic level', whether the text in question is oral or written.

The occasional coincidence apart, no text in a given language can reproduce exactly the same sequence of sound-segments/letters as any text in another language. This automatically constitutes a source of translation loss. The real question for the translator is whether this loss matters at all. The answer, as usual, is that it all depends.

Generally, we take little notice of the sounds or shapes of what we hear and read, paying attention primarily to the message of the utterance. We do tend to notice sounds that are accidentally repeated, but even then we attach little importance to them in most texts. Often, however, repetition of sounds is a significant factor, so it is useful to have precise terms in which to analyse it.

Repetition of sounds in words can generally be classified either as alliteration or as assonance. We define **alliteration** as the recurrence of the same sound or sound-cluster at the beginning of words occurring next to or near one another, as in '*t*wo *t*ired *t*oads', '*cl*ever *kl*eptomaniacs' or '*a*ll *a*wful *or*nithologists'. We define **assonance** as the recurrence, within words occurring next to or near one another, of the same sound or sound-cluster, as in 'a gr*ea*t d*ay*'s p*ai*nting' or 'a sw*ift* sn*ift*er *aft*erwards'. The two often occur together, of course, as in '*Fren*ch *infl*uence *al*so *expl*ains *Fred*erick *II*'s *spl*endid *ca*stles *in* the *S*outh of *I*taly and *S*icily'. Terminal sounds that are the same, but are not strictly speaking rhyme, are best defined as assonance; so the five [z] sounds in the following are most simply described as assonance: 'ja*zz*y photo*s* of animal*s* in *z*oos'. A vital point to remember is that it is the sound, not the spelling, that counts in discussing alliteration and assonance.

In general, the more technical or purely informative the text, the less account is taken of repetitions or other sound patterns, because they hardly ever seem to have any thematic or expressive function. That is true of the sentence about Frederick II's castles (taken from an article on Italian architecture), and it is true of the following sentence from a text on coalmining: 'Testwork has been carried out on screenbowl centrifuges dewatering frothfloated coal.' The alliteration and assonance in these two examples are incidental to the message.

However, many texts are marked by the expressive use of phonic patterns, including rhyme. We shall say that two words **rhyme** where the last stressed vowel, and all the sounds that follow it, are identical and come in the same order, as in 'br*eam* / s*eem*', '*W*arw*ick* / euph*oric*', 'incid*entally* / m*entally*', 's*ol* / su*ol*', 'fel*ice* / Beatr*ice*', 'voluttu*osa* / p*osa*'. The less the text is purely factual, the more alliteration, assonance and rhyme tend to be exploited. The most obvious example is poetry. However, on the phonic/graphic level, the only difference between poetry and many other genres is one of degree: alliteration, assonance and even rhyme are often exploited in fiction, drama, journalism, polemic, etc.

What are the implications of these observations for translators? As always, the translator must be guided by the purpose of the text, the needs of the target public and the function of the phonic feature in its context. In general, the sorts of feature we have been looking at will not have expressive function in a scientific, technical or other purely informative text, so the translator can happily ignore them: even considerable loss on the phonic/graphic level will simply not matter. In literary STs, on the other hand, marked phonic features very often do have thematic and expressive functions – that is, the message would be less complex and have less impact without them. Whether these effects are triggered or not is very much a matter of what the text is for and what the public is expecting.

Sometimes, even if the ST contains no marked phonic features, a draft TT will inadvertently contain a grotesque concentration of sounds. This might introduce an unwanted comic note, or even make the TT difficult to read. So, even in written texts, the translator will generally want to avoid *introducing* tongue-twisters or other phonic effects that impair the TT's communicative function.

The use of phonic echoes and affinities for thematic and expressive purposes is sometimes called sound-symbolism. It takes two main forms. In the context, the sounds of given words may evoke other words that are not present in the text. Or the sound of a given word occurs in one or more others, and sets up a link between the words, conferring on each of them connotations of the other(s). The first two lines of Keats's 'To Autumn' offer simple examples of both:

> Season of mists and mellow fruitfulness,
> Close bosom-friend of the maturing sun; [. . .]
> (Keats 1958: 273)

The context is crucial. Given the title of the poem and the reference to fruitfulness, 'mellow' is almost sure to evoke 'yellow', a colour of fruit and autumn leaves. In its turn, the 'sun' is likely to be a rich yellow, glowing like a ripe fruit through the autumn haze. These two effects ensure that the 'mists' are received positively by the reader/listener, and not as cold, damp and grey. The alliteration in 'mists . . . mellow . . . maturing' reinforces the effect, and also gives 'maturing' an intransitive sense as well as its transitive one: the sun itself is growing mature as the year advances. And if the sun is maturing (whether in the year or in the day), it may well be low in the sky; if so, it looks larger when seen through mist, like a swelling fruit. The [m] in 'bosom' links this word, too, with the other three; so the mellow fruits are perhaps reminiscent of milk-filled breasts, as if the season, sun and earth affectionately unite in maternal bountifulness. This suggestion is itself reinforced by the alliteration and assonance in 'fruitfulness . . . friend', and by the alliteration and assonance on [s] throughout the two lines, which associates all these key words still more closely with one another.

Not many translators earn their living translating poetry. But in respect of sound-symbolism – as of many other things – poetry offers very clear examples of two vital factors which all translators do need to bear in mind. The Keats example is useful for this very reason. Practically none of the images and associations we saw in those two lines derive from literal meaning alone – that is why perceiving and reacting to sound-symbolism is bound to be subjective. All of them are reinforced or even created by phonic features. Yet those phonic features are objectively present in the text. This points to the first factor that needs to be remembered: unlike many other sorts of symbol, those in sound-symbolism do not have a single, unchanging meaning. In fact, none of the phonic features in the lines from Keats has any *intrinsic* meaning or expressive power at all. Such expressiveness as they have derives from the context – and that is the second vital factor. In a different context, the same features would almost certainly have a different effect. The *sounds* of the words have their effect in terms of the literal and connotative *meanings* of the words. So, without the title, 'mellow' might very well not evoke 'yellow'. Neither is there anything intrinsically mellow, maternal or mature about the sound [m]: the smell in a pig-yard might be described as 'the mingling miasmata from the slime and muck'. And, in [fr], there is as much potential for frightful frumpishness as for fruitfulness and friendship.

In other words, a translator confronted with sound-symbolism has to decide what its function is before starting to translate. The aim will be to convey as much of the ST message as possible. Even if it is essential to this message that the TT include sound-symbolism, it is almost certain that the TL sounds involved will be *different* from the ST ones: trying to reproduce phonic patterns in the TT usually entails too much loss in respect of literal and connotative meaning. The translator's question therefore has to be: is what matters the *specific sounds* in the ST's alliteration, assonance, etc., or is it rather *the fact that there is* alliteration, assonance, etc.? Fortunately, the latter is generally the case, and it is usually possible to compensate for the loss of given ST phonic details by replacing them with TL ones that are different but have a comparable effect.

These points are perhaps obvious, but it does no harm to be reminded of them, because student translators often get themselves into difficulties by assuming that they have to *replicate* ST sounds in the TT. In reality, the translator is only likely to want to try replicating ST sounds when they are onomatopoeic. Onomatopoeia must not be confused with alliteration and assonance. An **onomatopoeia** is a word whose phonic form imitates a sound – 'splosh', 'bang', 'cuckoo', etc. In translating onomatopoeia, there will virtually always be some phonic translation loss. This is usually inconsequential, for instance in translating 'Pam!' as 'Bang!'. It could be less inconsequential, of course, if 'Pam!' were part of an alliterative pattern with specific expressive function. In such a case, some form of compensation might have to be used.

Similar remarks apply to rhyme. There can be no hard and fast rule regarding rhyme in translation. Each TT requires its own strategic decision. Often, producing a rhyming TT means an unacceptable sacrifice of literal and connotative meaning. With some sorts of ST (especially comic or sarcastic ones), where the precise nuances of meaning are less important than the phonic mockery, it is often easier, and even desirable, to stock the TT with rhymes and echoes that are different from those of the ST, but have a similar effect.

So far, our examples of textual variables on the phonic/graphic level have concerned the *sounds* of words, because the *shapes* are less commonly a source of textual effects on this level. However, written texts often do depend to some extent on their visual layout. Advertisements and publicity material make frequent use of visual effects on the phonic/graphic level. But the most extreme examples are perhaps in literary texts. Concrete poetry, for example, depends to a great extent on layout for its effect. Sometimes a poem is laid out pictorially, to look like something mentioned in it – a bird, a telegraph-pole, falling rain, etc. Here is a different sort of case, a text by Edwin Morgan together with a translation by the eminent poet and translator Marco Fazzini. (*Contextual information.* John Cage was an American composer who often incorporated an element of the random into his music.)

OPENING THE CAGE

14 variations on 14 words
I have nothing to say and I am saying it and that is poetry
John Cage

I have to say poetry and is that nothing and am I saying it
I am and I have poetry to say and is that nothing saying it
I am nothing and I have poetry to say and that is saying it
I that am saying poetry have nothing and it is I and to say
5   And I say that I am to have poetry and saying it is nothing
I am poetry and nothing and saying it is to say that I have
To have nothing is poetry and I am saying that and I say it
Poetry is saying I have nothing and I am to say that and it
Saying nothing I am poetry and I have to say that and it is
10   It is and I am and I have poetry saying say that to nothing
It is saying poetry to nothing and I say I have and am that
Poetry is saying I have it and I am nothing and to say that
And that nothing is poetry I am saying and I have to say it
Saying poetry is nothing and to that I say I am and have it
(Morgan 1968: 51)

APRIRE LA GABBIA A JOHN CAGE

13 variazioni su 13 parole
io non ho nulla da dire e lo dico e questo è poesia
John Cage

poesia è dire e io non ho nulla da questo e lo dico
da questo dire nulla è e non ho e io lo dico poesia
dico nulla non da dire e io ho questo e poesia lo è
io lo dico e ho poesia da dire e non è questo nulla

5   nulla e poesia e non da questo io dico è dire lo ho
     dire non è poesia e io ho questo e da nulla lo dico
     io ho e dico poesia è questo e non lo dire da nulla
     io non ho nulla e questo è poesia e lo dico da dire
     non è e da questo nulla io ho e lo dico dire poesia
10   io ho poesia e questo dire da nulla è e non lo dico
     da questo dire nulla io ho e lo dico poesia e non è
     io lo dico e è da non dire nulla e ho questo poesia
     io nulla poesia questo ho da dire e non lo dico e è
                                      (Morgan 1997: 32–3)

The ST is a set of permutations of the words in the epigraph. By obeying his very constricting self-imposed rule, Morgan has in fact given his text a random quality (just as Cage does in his music) – there is a limit to what you can say with these fourteen words, but, in exploring those limits, you find yourself saying things you would never have dreamt of saying! The rectangular layout imitates a cage or cell. Each permutation exemplifies the feisty affirmation expressed in the epigraph, while all the permutations taken together exultantly confirm that even the severest physical constraints, far from preventing expression, actually inspire and permit it. The translator has clearly decided that the layout in permutations is paramount: as in the ST, any phonic effects are subsidiary, deriving accidentally from the repetitions of words. Once graphic considerations are prioritized, literal translation of each line becomes impossible: the vital thing is to have as many permutations as there are words in the epigraph, while not losing the overall thematic exuberance of the ST.

We have quoted the Morgan and Fazzini texts because they offer extreme examples of basic truths of translation. First, they show very clearly how reducing one sort of loss – here, graphic loss – entails increasing other sorts of loss, deemed less important – here, lexical and grammatical. And second, they are especially good illustrations of the importance of prosodic factors.

THE PROSODIC LEVEL

On the **prosodic level**, utterances count as 'metrically' structured stretches. 'Metric' here covers three sorts of thing. First, in a given utterance, some syllables will conventionally always be accented more than others; on top of this standard accentuation, voice stress and emphasis will be used for greater clarity and expressiveness. Second, clarity and expressiveness also depend on variations in vowel pitch and voice modulation. And third, the speed of vocal delivery also varies, for similar reasons. On the prosodic level, therefore, groups of syllables may form *contrastive* patterns (for example, short, fast, staccato sections alternating with long, slow, smooth ones), or *recurrent* ones, or both. Morgan's 'Opening the Cage' shows very clearly the crucial role of prosodic features. Because they are grammatically so unusual, many of the lines mean very little when scanned silently on the printed page, as one normally reads. For all the grammatical vagaries, however, they do make sense if they are read out loud, with appropriate pauses and variations in speed, intonation and stress. The same is true of the Italian TT. Indeed, it is true of any text. Go back to the start of this paragraph, and try reading it in a monotone and without any variations in stress: this is very difficult to do, because it is so unnatural; and if you do succeed, the text becomes virtually incomprehensible.

For the translator, there are four factors to be borne in mind when considering the prosodic level. The first is that English and Italian are as different from one another on the prosodic level as on the phonic/graphic level. This is vividly illustrated by listening to an Italian speaking on the radio, with the tuning not quite on the station, so that it is not quite possible to distinguish the words. This brings the prosodic features to the foreground. It only takes a few seconds to realize that the tempi, rhythms and melodic undulations sound very different from those of English. It is virtually impossible to produce a TT that both sounds natural and reproduces the prosodic characteristics of the ST. Just occasionally, it is worth aiming for similar rhythms in the TT to those of the ST. For instance, if part of the ST's expressive effect stems from imitative rhythms – galloping horses, breaking waves, dripping water, etc. – there would be significant translation loss on the prosodic level if the TT failed to use similar rhythms to similar effect.

However, prosodic translation loss far more commonly arises from a failure to heed one or more of the other three factors. For example, it is vital to recognize the nature and function of ST intonation and stress. This is relatively straightforward in the case of oral texts. Even in written texts, either the grammatical structure or the context will usually show what the intonation is and what its communicative purpose is. Take the following two sentences:

Anch'io sono pittore. (Correggio)

Io sono anche pittore.

It is impossible to confuse these two sentences. In each, the grammatical structure engenders a specific prosodic profile – intonation and stress pattern – and a specific meaning.

Following from this factor is the third: the need to select an intonation and a stress pattern which ensure that the TT sentence has the same communicative purpose as its ST counterpart. So the Correggio quotation and its variant might be translated thus:

I'm a painter, too (*or*: I, too, am a painter) [e.g. as well as you].

I'm a *painter*, too [e.g. as well as a writer].

The fourth factor arises from the third, and is perhaps the one that needs closest attention. Even where the TL expression does not seem grammatically or prosodically problematic, the translator must be sure not to introduce prosodic features that are inappropriate to the message content. Perhaps the commonest cases of significant translation loss on the prosodic level arise when a grammatical choice in the TT implies a stress pattern and an intonation that lead the reader/listener to expect a different sort of message from the one that actually materializes. This often happens when the translator chooses an inappropriate conjunction or conjunctive phrase. Here is a typical example. (*Contextual information.* Micòl is in bed. The narrator climbs onto the bed and tries to kiss her, but she turns her head away.)

'Perché fai così' disse Micòl.   'Why d'you behave like that?' asked
'Tanto, è inutile.'   Micòl. 'In any case, it's no use.'
       (Bassani 1991: 176)   (Bassani 1989: 218)

The English expression 'in any case' sounds odd after a question. It typically accompanies a second affirmation in support of a quite different one that has just been made, as in 'I can't afford a satellite dish. In any case, I'm too busy with the farm' (or: 'I'm too busy with the farm, in any case'). The tone in the second sentence is emphatic and authoritative, strengthening the previous assertion into a positive refusal to buy the dish. In the Bassani TT, the translator may have been influenced by the absence of a question mark in the ST; but the fact remains that 'in any case' does not work after the TT question, because it implies intonations for the two sentences which clash with the message-content of Micòl's words. The only way of making the TT convincing would be to speak the question as a sneering exclamation, as if Micòl were contemptuously saying '*That's* not the way to do it!' – but that is not the sense of the ST question at all. The weakness of the TT is primarily a matter of literal meaning, not of prosodic features, but scanning the TT on the prosodic level is the best way of confirming, or even discerning, the fault in literal meaning. A better TT might be: 'What are you doing that for? You *know* there's no point.'

Here, for discussion in class, is a similar example from the same novel; the expression at issue is 'As far as I was concerned'. (*Contextual information.* The characters in question are all Jews, friends of the narrator. One had died of illness in 1942. The others were arrested by Mussolini's fascists in September 1943.)

Dopo una breve permanenza nelle carceri di via Piangipane, nel novembre successivo furono avviati al campo di concentramento di Fòssoli, presso Carpi, e di qui, in seguito, in Germania. Per ciò che riguarda me, tuttavia, debbo dire che durante i quattro anni intercorsi fra l'estate del '39 e l'autunno del '43 di loro non avevo visto più nessuno.

(Bassani 1991: 240)

After a short stay in the prison at via Piangipane, they were sent to the concentration camp at Fòssoli, near Carpi, the following November, and thence to Germany. As far as I was concerned, though, during the four years between the summer of '39 and the autumn of '43 I never saw any of them.

(Bassani 1989: 291)

Rudiments of Italian and English versification

A special set of features on the prosodic level are those found in verse, which present specific translation challenges. Our aim in the following short introduction to the rudiments of Italian and English versification is to give students a foundation for discerning and interpreting the conventional patterns in Italian verse, and for making an informed choice between English metres if the strategic decision is to produce a verse TT. We shall look only at the metrical side of versification. But do not forget that tempo and melodic pitch are also vital prosodic textual variables requiring as much attention in verse translation as in prose. We shall not consider other aspects of verse, such as types of stanza or the phonic question of rhyme. For fuller information on these and on metrical questions, see Menichetti 1993, Bausi and Martelli 1993, and Hollander 1981.

Italian
A line of verse in Italian is defined in terms of the number of syllables it contains. There are four specifically metrical devices that affect how the syllables in a line are counted. In the following examples, the divisions between metrical syllables are shown as oblique lines.

1. The fundamental principle is that, when a word ending with a vowel is followed by one beginning with a vowel, the vowels are generally considered as one syllable. This is known as *sinalefe*. For example:

   Pa/ne/ di/ ca/s*a e*/ lat/t*e a*p/pe/na/ mun/to/.

In performance, *sinalefe* usually entails partial elision of the two vowels, so that they sound like a diphthong. An exception is when the speaker makes a pause for effect, or if a punctuation mark after the first vowel suggests it.

2. Sometimes, however, the vowels at the end and beginning of the two words are counted separately. This is known as *dialefe*. It is normal when the first vowel or both vowels are accented. For example:

El/la/ giun/se e/ le/vò/ *a*m/be/ le/ pal/me/.

3. Two consecutive vowels within a word are often counted as one syllable, even where they do not normally form a diphthong. This is known as *sineresi*. In performance, the effect is similar to that of *sinalefe*, the two vowels sounding like a diphthong. For example:

Dis/se/: B*ea*/tri/ce/, lo/da/ di/ D*io*/ ve/ra/.

4. Sometimes, two consecutive vowels within a word which do normally form a diphthong are pronounced separately. This is usually shown by a diaeresis over the first vowel, and is known as *dieresi*. For example:

For/se/ per/ché/ del/la/ fa/tal/ qu*ï*/*e*/te/.

There is another factor that affects how the syllables are counted: the stress pattern of the final word in the line. When the main stress of the final word is on the last syllable but two, the line may have an extra syllable. Here is a hendecasyllable (a notionally eleven-syllable line) ending with such a word:

a/ pa/ro/le/ for/mar/ dis/con/ve/ne/*vole*.

If, however, the main stress is on the very last syllable, the line will have one syllable fewer than expected. Here is a hendecasyllable ending with such a word:

Pren/di/ sol/ un/ non/ti/scor/dar/di/mé/.

If the poem as a whole consists of hendecasyllables, variants like the last two examples also count as such, metrically speaking. The same principle holds for other standard line lengths as well.

Every line has its own stress pattern: a hendecasyllable must have a main accent on the tenth syllable, a decasyllable (ten-syllable line) on the ninth, and so on. The distribution of other stresses within the line can vary slightly, depending how many syllables it contains, although generally lines with an even number of syllables follow a constant rhythm.

In reading Italian verse, then, there is no need to look for some rigid pattern of feet that has to be imposed on the text. The pattern of stresses in the line virtually always coincides with the 'natural' stresses the words have in prose. The reader should therefore read the verse as the sense dictates, while taking due account of the rules given above. Observing these rules will automatically have certain rhythmic consequences and mean highlighting certain words: that is, the versification will have specific thematic and expressive functions. These functions are special effects on the prosodic level, and the translator simply has to be as aware of them as of every other feature of the ST. If the verse is in rhyme, the phonic/graphic functions of the rhymes will also be affected by these prosodic features.

The foregoing applies to texts in traditional, regular, verse. The very fact that a text is in regular verse is usually significant, marking the text as belonging to a particular genre. This in itself is a factor that will weigh in deciding a strategy.

If a text is in *free* verse, this fact is similarly strategically important. Apart from that, all the student translator needs to remember is to read the text as the sense demands, while taking due account of the phonic/graphic and prosodic effects of the line-ends.

English
English metre is syllable-and-stress metre. That is, the line is defined in terms of feet. A line of traditional verse consists of a fixed number of particular feet. For example:

The ***cur***/few ***tolls***/ the ***knell***/ of ***par***/ting ***day***/

This line has five feet; that is, it is a pentameter. In this particular case, the feet have one unstressed followed by one stressed syllable. This is known as an *iamb*, or iambic foot. A line consisting of five iambs is an iambic pentameter. It is the most common English line, found in the work of the great playwrights and poets. The commonest other feet are:

trochee (adj. *trochaic*):	***When*** the/ ***pie*** was/ ***o***pened/
dactyl (adj. *dactylic*):	***M***errily/ ***chat***ting and/ ***clat***tering/
anapest (adj. *anapestic*):	And made ***ci***/der in***side***/ her in***side***/

Most poems do not have a regular beat throughout. This would be intolerably dreary. Even limericks are very rarely exclusively anapestic or dactylic. The opening lines of Keats's 'To Autumn', quoted on p. 51, are examples of typical variations on the basic iambic pentameter. These lines still count as iambic pentameters, because they do have five feet, they are predominantly iambic, and the rest of the poem has these qualities.

One other sort of English metre is worth mentioning, strong-stress metre. This is different from syllable-and-stress metre, in that only the stresses count in describing the line, the number of weak syllables being variable. Much modern verse uses this metre, often in combination with syllable-and-stress metre. The important thing to remember, then, is that the translator of a verse text has to ask what the *function* of the verse is. Is it decorative? Does it have thematic and/or expressive effect? What is the effect of its regularity or irregularity? Would there be significant translation loss in writing a prose TT? (And, of course, similar questions have to be asked on the phonic/graphic level.) Only when these questions have been answered can a reasoned decision be taken either to translate into prose or to couch the TT in an appropriate verse-form. The introduction to versification given above will help in deciding what, if any, this 'appropriate' TL verse-form is to be.

PRACTICAL 5

5.1   Phonic/graphic and prosodic issues

Assignment
Taking the following text and the translations,
  (i)   Determine the salient features of the ST on the phonic/graphic and prosodic levels, and say what, if any, their function is in the text.
 (ii)   Discuss each of the TTs in turn, concentrating on significant translation loss that you think has been incurred on the phonic/graphic and prosodic levels, and explaining any successful instances of compensation that you find.
(iii)   Drawing conclusions from (i) and (ii), discuss briefly what you think your main strategic decisions would be if you had to translate this ST into English.

Contextual information
The text is one of a series of playful short poems about animals written in the late 1970s by Toti Scialoja. These poems are marked by vivid, quirky and sometimes disturbing imagery, which almost seems at times to have been generated by the words themselves rather than by thematic intention.

ST

> La lepre ha il più crudele dei musi quando morde
> i leggeri lillà sulla radura brulla,
> strappa i fiori d'aprile, li ricaccia nel nulla,
> col labbro che strafà profumato di verde.
>
> (Scialoja 1984: 95)

TT (a)
The hare has the most cruel of mouths when it bites the light lilacs on the bare clearing, rips out the flowers of April and drives them back into the void, with an exaggerating lip perfumed with green.

TT (b)

> The hare has the meanest of mouths when he bites
> the lightsome lilacs on the barren branch,
> and, lip scented with his leafy lunch,
> returns devoured spring flowers to blackest night.

5.2 Phonic/graphic and prosodic issues

Assignment
(i)   The following advertisement having proved successful in Italy, you
      are to translate it for a British campaign. Concentrating mainly on
      phonic/graphic features and their implications, discuss the strategic
      decisions that you have to take before starting detailed translation of
      this ST, and outline and justify the strategy you adopt.
(ii) Translate the text into English.
(iii) Discuss the main decisions of detail you took, paying special atten-
      tion to phonic/graphic issues.

Contextual information
The text is printed opposite a picture of a smartly dressed man looking into
a mirror at six reflections of himself.

ST

COME dicono le ricerche di mercato, i profitti generati da un
unico cliente affezionato sono pari al costo necessario per acquisirne
sei nuovi. Poiché la ragione principale per cui si perdono clienti è un servizio
inadeguato, vorremmo farti una semplice ma vantaggiosa proposta. Un modo
5 rapido per migliorare la qualità della relazione e **OTTENERE** ottimi
risultati è installare un Call Center basato su soluzioni IBM. Il tempo impie-
gato **DAI** tuoi operatori per gestire gli ordini diminuirà, dal momento che
tutti i dati relativi ai **TUOI CLIENTI** appariranno automatica-
mente sullo schermo non appena telefoneranno. Potrai così sapere qual è
10 l'ordine fatto, la situazione dei pagamenti e valutare, sulla base delle loro
abitudini di acquisto, se è il caso di offrire loro qualcos'altro. E se ci chiedi
il progetto per un sito Internet, i tuoi prodotti saranno disponibili non soltanto
cinque o **SEI** giorni alla settimana, ma tutte le **VOLTE** che sarà
necessario. Pensaci: non hai bisogno di spendere molto per dare ai tuoi
15 clienti un servizio migliore. E quindi per avere da loro **TANTO** di più.
(IBM Italia 1996: 87)

6

The formal properties of texts: Grammatical and sentential issues in translation

We saw in Chapter 5 that the alliteration and assonance of 'Season of mists and mellow fruitfulness' trigger effects over and above the literal meaning of this phrase. We were considering the alliteration and assonance as features on the phonic/graphic level. But, like all utterances, this one can also be considered on the other five levels of textual variables. The extra meanings, for instance, are features on the *grammatical* level, while part of the effect of Keats's phrase derives from features on the *sentential* level. It is these two levels that we shall look at in the present chapter.

THE GRAMMATICAL LEVEL

On the **grammatical level** are considered two things: (1) words, and their formation by affixation, inflection, derivation and compounding; (2) syntax, the arrangement of words into phrases and sentences. It is on the grammatical level that translation loss is generally most immediately obvious, whenever grammatical transposition occurs. Because loss on this level is so common, we shall only give a few examples here. As ever, the question is not whether there is translation loss, but what it consists of and whether it matters. The question does have to be asked, because an essential part of interpreting any text lies in construing the literal meaning conveyed by its grammatical structure.

Words

We are all familiar with dictionaries. They list the practical totality of the words in a given language. This totality is known as the **lexis** of a language (adj. **lexical**). But it is vital to remember that meanings are not found exclusively in the words individually listed in the dictionary. Any text shows that the combination of words creates meanings that they do not have in isolation, and even meanings that are not wholly predictable from the literal senses of the words combined.

In translation, lexical loss is very common, but it is just one kind of translation loss among many. It can occur for all sorts of reasons. It very often arises from the fact that exact synonymy between SL words and TL words is relatively rare. 'Ricerca' (p. 39) is a good example. We shall return to this issue in Chapter 8. Another common source of lexical translation loss is the fact that, in any text, words acquire associative overtones on top of their literal meaning. The lines from Keats are a good example. It is difficult, and usually impossible, to find TL words that will convey an appropriate literal meaning *and* produce appropriate overtones. We shall return to these questions in Chapter 9.

Grammatical arrangement

Lexical issues are a particular category of grammatical issue, so it is not surprising that some of them are most conveniently examined under the heading of grammatical arrangement. Under this heading, we subsume two types of grammatical structure: (1) patterns affecting individual words – affixation/inflection, compounding and derivation; (2) **syntax** (adj. **syntactic**), the patterns whereby words are linked to form more or less complex phrases and sentences. In both, what concerns the translator is the fact that the structural patterns differ from language to language. For instance, English more readily adds *-ly* to words to form adverbs than Italian does *-mente*, particularly if two or more adverbs occur together. Compare the following:

I lavori procedono con confortante rapidità.	The work is progressing reassuring*ly* quick*ly*.

Sometimes, an ST adverb can be rendered either with a TT adverb or with affixation. For example:

Sono stati oltremodo gentili.	They were ***extremely*** kind.
Sei oltremodo prudente.	You're ***excessively*** cautious, *or* You're ***over***cautious.

Compounding, too, differs from language to language. German is capable of long compounds, English less so. Italian, like French, is a more analytical language, in that the relations between the elements in a compound expression tend to be marked explicitly, through either syntax (generally prepositions) or inflection, or both. Here is a simple example:

Flüssigkristallanzeige = liquid crystal display = visualizzatore *a* cristall*i* liquid*i* = affichage *à* crista*ux* liquide*s*.

English compounds in particular are potentially ambiguous. For instance, a bodyguard guards the body, but a mudguard guards *against* the mud. In the example above, only knowledge of the topic makes it possible to say whether the reference is to a display of liquid crystals, a liquid display of crystals, or a display that is liquid and crystal. The Italian expression, however, is less ambiguous, thanks to the preposition and the plural inflexions.

The fact that Italian is more analytical than English gives rise to frequent and typical grammatical differences between the two. We can use the Keats example again here. Keats could have written: 'Season of mists and of mellow fruitfulness', or 'Season of mists, of mellow fruitfulness'. In both, repeating 'of' means that the mists and the fruitfulness are identified as two distinct things, whereas Keats's actual phrase melds them into a single, complex sensation. A literal translation of his phrase into Italian could incur significant translation loss on the grammatical level, since Italian syntax offers no choice but to repeat 'di', as in 'Stagione di foschie e di fecondità matura'. Some form of compensation would be needed to convey the 'single-ness' of the sensation expressed in the ST.

Things often work the other way round, of course, English grammar not having a nuance that Italian enjoys. An obvious example of this is the fact that the subject pronoun tends to be omitted in Italian, unless it is needed to avoid ambiguity, or for contrast or emphasis. So 'Ho aperto la porta' clearly means 'I opened the door'. In the following sentence, on the other hand, the 'io' is inserted to mark the contrast between two actions : 'Ha chiuso la finestra e così io ho aperto la porta.' In such a sentence, the subject of 'Ha chiuso' will normally be clear from the context; but if it is not, it will be inserted – 'Lei', 'lei', 'lui', etc. In all these cases, however, English *must* use a pronoun. In many cases, losing the Italian nuance is of no consequence. But where emphasis is involved, the translator may have to find some form of compensation, as we shall see in discussing the sentential level.

Grammatical differences are especially clear in differences in verb systems between languages, which can require special care in translating. To illustrate this, we can start with a simple example from Chapter 2, where we saw that the canonic translation of 'Si direbbe che siamo in Italia' is 'You would think we were in Italy.' In some contexts, however, a better translation might be: 'One/you would say we are in Italy.' Conversely, depending on context, 'You would say we were in Italy' could be rendered in various different ways:

Diresti/direste/direbbe/direbbero che siamo/eravamo in Italia.

Dicevi/dicevate/diceva/dicevano che eravamo in Italia.

In all these cases – not to mention 'Sembra di stare in Italia' – SL and TL grammatical structures are so different that there is obvious translation loss on the grammatical level. This will not usually matter, as long as the sense is accurate and as clear as in the ST. The many differences in systems of tense and aspect between Italian and English do, however, mean that the translator has always to be careful to avoid unwanted ambiguities or outright mistranslation. The Italian conditional and imperfect offer simple examples. Depending on context, each of the following Italian sentences could be translated in two or three ways:

Pensavo che sarebbe venuto.	*Either* I thought he would have come *or* I thought he would come.
Poteva partire subito.	*Either* He could [= was able to] leave immediately *or* He could have left immediately *or* He might have left immediately.

These few examples are simple, but they are the tip of a big iceberg. The translation loss caused by differences in grammatical structure between SL and TL is often not serious, but it is all too easy, through inattention, to let a degree of calque make the TT unidiomatic. We have already seen plenty of examples of this, especially in Chapter 3, and we shall see plenty more. In fact, translation issues on the grammatical level are so significant that certain problem areas will be illustrated in detail in Chapters 16–19.

Generally, as the discussion so far has suggested, translators give priority to the *mot juste* and to constructing idiomatic TL sentences, even where this entails translation loss in terms of grammatical structure or economy. Exceptions may be made where, for whatever reason, exoticism is required in the TT. More often, the ST may have salient textual properties resulting from the manipulation of grammatical structure. The marked manipulation of grammatical structure is a common feature in literary or critical texts. The translator has always to decide how distinctive the grammatical structures are, what their function is, and what the aim of the ST is. Only then can a decision be taken about how distinctive the TT's grammar should be. A typical issue is that of syntactic streamlining versus syntactic complexity. The following two texts should be compared in class from this point of view. The first is from an article on art history, the second from Andrea De Carlo's *Treno di panna*:

Con una tecnica compositiva di facile applicazione, che gli consentiva, come nelle composizioni presepiali contemporanee e con effetti teatrali e situazioni da 'commedia dell'arte' quasi simili, di combinare elementi reali e fantastici del paesaggio napoletano lucidamente percepito e oggettivamente riprodotto come nelle vedute urbane di Antonio Joli (ma almeno inizialmente anche con esiti di brillantezza decorativa cui non dovette essere estranea la conoscenza di esempi recenti di Carlo Bonavia) con episodi di vita quotidiana ripresi con cordiale e divertita partecipazione nei sobborghi e nei quartieri popolari sul lungomare napoletano, Pietro Fabris del resto non solo sembrava offrire soluzioni adeguate e tempestive alle recenti esigenze di una colta committenza internazionale interessata alla documentazione di usi, costumi e tradizioni della gente di Napoli, secondo moderne istanze culturali e rinnovati interessi antropologici di matrice illuminista, ma soprattutto forniva l'occasione e i contenuti per una pittura d'immediata presa visiva, piacevole, di facile collocazione e quindi di sicuro successo commerciale.

(Spinosa 1990: 17)

Jill mi ha fatto un cenno con la mano. Ha detto 'Okay, vado'. Poi si è sporta verso di me e ha chiesto se ero libero sabato. Le ho detto di sì. Lei ha detto 'Magari facciamo qualcosa'. Ho detto 'Bene. Ciao'. Ho chiuso la portiera. Lei è andata via veloce verso la freeway.

(De Carlo 1981: 75)

THE SENTENTIAL LEVEL

We can use the lines from 'To Autumn' to show how different grammatical arrangements create different assumptions in the listener or reader as regards the communicative purpose of an utterance. Keats's own lines –

Season of mists and mellow fruitfulness,
Close bosom-friend of the maturing sun; [. . .] –

are partly an address to Autumn and partly an exclamation about it: the very structure of the utterances leads the listener/reader to expect an expression of wonderment and enthusiasm. A different grammatical arrangement, however, would most likely announce a different communicative purpose. For instance:

Autumn is a season of mists and mellow fruitfulness.
It is a close bosom-friend of the maturing sun.

This structure announces a more purely informative text – even though, in the event, phonic and lexical features do give the utterances something more than simply informative value. In each version, the grammatical arrangement marks the utterances as having a particular communicative purpose, whatever overtones may turn out to be involved. When, as here, one looks at the *communicative purpose* of a given grammatical arrangement, rather than at the grammatical arrangement in its own right, one is looking at the utterance on the **sentential level**. On this level are considered sentences. A **sentence** is defined as a complete, self-contained and ready-made vehicle for communication: nothing needs to be added before it can be uttered and understood in concrete situations. The starter's command 'Go!' is a sentence. So is 'No way!' as an expression of refusal or disbelief. (Note that, in this definition, a sentence does not necessarily contain a verb.)

Any text counts on the sentential level as a succession of sentences, each with a built-in communicative purpose. This purpose is usually conveyed by one or more of three features: (1) prosodic features, such as intonation or stress (for example the rising pitch that signals a question in Italian and English); (2) grammatical features, such as sequential focus (for example, 'On this level are considered sentences', which puts emphasis on 'sentences'); (3) **illocutionary particles** (for example, the question-forming particle 'non è vero', or the particle 'ma andiamo', which qualifies an utterance as an expression of scoffing disbelief; illocutionary particles do not fit into syntax proper – their function is to tell the listener/reader what affective force the utterance is intended to have).

Thus, in spoken texts, a number of different sentences, marked for different purposes, can be created purely through intonation and stress – even though they comprise exactly the same words, in exactly the same order. Here are some examples, adapted from Pittàno (1993: 76, 273):

Lui non va a pesca [with falling intonation: *statement*].

Lui non va a pesca [with rising intonation: *question, focusing on whether he is going*].

Lui non va a pesca [with fall-rise intonation and stress on 'pesca': *amazed question, focusing on the activity*].

Lui non va a pesca [with low, level intonation: *menacing prohibition*].

The same five words could be spoken in yet other ways, to express joy, encouragement, despair, and so on.

As these examples suggest, the sentential level of spoken language is extremely rich, fine shades of intonation and stress distinguishing sentences with subtly different nuances. These refinements largely disappear in written texts, mostly because the only ways of conveying intonation and stress in writing are punctuation (usually question mark and exclamation mark) and typography (usually italics, sometimes capitals). These offer far fewer alternatives than the rich nuances of speech. Try saying 'Lui non va a pesca' in the four ways described above, and compare the result with the following attempts at achieving the same result in written mode:

Lui non va a pesca.

Lui non va a pesca?

Lui non va a *pesca*?!

LUI NON VA A PESCA!!

All these written versions can in fact be spoken in a number of ways, each with its own emphases and affective force. Consequently, if punctuation and typography cannot clearly convey the desired nuance, the writer or translator has to fall back on adding explicit information about how the sentences are spoken, as in 'she exclaimed in surprise', 'she said angrily', and so on.

In translating both oral and written texts, then, the sentential level requires as much care as any other. Sequential focus and illocutionary particles are easier to represent in written texts than prosodic features are; but how to translate them still cannot be taken for granted. Both are generally accompanied by appropriate prosodic features, notably intonation and stress; the translator has to be sure not to introduce *inappropriate* prosodic features in the TT (as happens in the Bassani examples on pp. 56–7).

As regards sequential focus, something else needs to be remembered: Italian and English differ in how and when they vary word-order. We saw a simple example in comparing 'Anch'io sono pittore' and 'Io sono anche pittore' (p. 55). Sometimes, then, what is expressed by Italian sequential focus may best be expressed in English simply with intonation and stress. But on other occasions, English may need to use an illocutionary particle as well as intonation, stress and – possibly – grammatical arrangement, especially if typography and punctuation are not enough to convey the full force of the ST. This can be seen in translating three more versions of the sentence about not going fishing, which all use sequential focusing for sentence-marking purposes:

Non va a pesca, lui [emphasis on 'lui'].

Lui, a pesca, non va [hints at hostility to fishing].

A pesca, lui non va [emphatic hostility to fishing].

Neither is it self-evident how to render the illocutionary particles in such sentences as 'Ma andiamo! Non ci crederà!'; or 'Tacete un po'!'; or the indignant 'Avrebbe potuto telefonarci, però!'.

One final point to remember is that whereas a *speaker* can easily use intonation, stress, gesture and facial expression to mark a sentence for a specific communicative purpose, the absence of these features in a *written* TT means that compensation often has to be resorted to if significant translation loss is not to be incurred on the sentential level.

PRACTICAL 6

6.1 Grammatical and sentential issues

Assignment
(i) You are translating for publication in a literary journal the short story from which the following ST is taken. Concentrating mainly on grammatical and sentential issues, discuss the strategic decisions that you have to take before starting detailed translation of this ST, and outline and justify the strategy you adopt.
(ii) Translate the text into English.
(iii) Discuss the main decisions of detail you took; pay special attention to grammatical and sentential issues, but do not overlook other major decisions.

Contextual information
The text comprises two extracts from Antonio Tabucchi's 'Rebus' (1985). In this story, 'fact' and 'fantasy' are impenetrably interlocked – as the narrator will say, life is not only an 'ingranaggio', but also a 'rebus'. Lines 1–11 are the opening paragraph of the story; lines 11–20 (from 'Io ero sudato') are from near the end, after a near-collision in a car rally from Paris to San Sebastián in northern Spain. The mysterious Miriam had hired the narrator to drive her car in the rally, with her as passenger. There was an overnight stop in Biarritz, in south-western France.

ST
Stanotte ho sognato Miriam. Indossava una lunga veste bianca che da lontano sembrava una camicia da notte; avanzava lungo la spiaggia, le onde erano paurosamente alte e si frangevano in silenzio, doveva essere la spiaggia di Biarritz, ma era completamente deserta, io stavo seduto su una poltrona a
5 sdraio, la prima di un'interminabile fila di poltrone deserte, ma forse era un'altra spiaggia, perché a Biarritz non mi ricordo poltrone come quelle, era solo l'idea di una spiaggia, e le ho fatto cenno col braccio invitandola a sedersi, ma lei ha continuato a camminare come se non si fosse accorta

di me, guardando fisso in avanti, e quando mi è passata vicino mi ha investito
10 una folata di aria gelida, come un alone che si portava dietro: e allora, con
lo stupore senza sorpresa dei sogni, ho capito che era morta. [. . .] Io ero
sudato da capo a piedi, di un sudore freddo. Miriam mi stringeva un braccio.
Non ti fermare, ti prego, non ti fermare. Proseguii la corsa, San Sebastiano
era proprio sotto di noi, credo che alla scena non avesse assistito nessuno.
15 Dopo avere tagliato il traguardo entrai nel box allestito all'aperto, ma non
scesi. È stato intenzionale, dissi, lo hanno fatto apposta. Miriam era pallidis-
sima, non diceva niente, pareva pietrificata. Io vado alla polizia, dissi, voglio
denunciare l'accaduto. Ti prego, mormorò lei. Ma non capisci che lo
hanno fatto apposta, gridai, volevano ammazzarci. Lei mi guardò, aveva
20 un' espressione stravolta e allo stesso tempo implorante.

(Tabucchi 1988: 29, 42–3)

6.2 Grammatical and sentential issues

Assignment
Comparing the ST and TT printed on pp. 72–3,

(i)   Determine the salient features of the ST on the grammatical and
      sentential levels, and say what, if any, their function is in the text.
      (Note that, because you are *comparing* an Italian text with an English
      one, there are likely to be features in the ST that will strike you as
      salient even though, if you were looking only at the ST, they would
      be unremarkable in Italian.)
(ii) Discuss the TT, concentrating on cases of translation loss on the gram-
      matical and sentential levels and saying how important you think they
      are. Where you can improve on the TT, give your own edited TT,
      explaining why it is better.

Contextual information
Both ST and TT are reproduced, by kind permission, from a publicity brochure
(*c.*1996) for Lamber, a manufacturer of industrial washing equipment.

Turn to p. 72

ST

La storia

Era il 1948 quando il Cav. Raimondo Affaba, attuale presidente della Lamber, cominciava la sua prima attività nel settore del lavaggio lattiero caseario. Nel 1958 egli dava inizio ad una nuova attività di produzione di
5   macchine lavastoviglie industriali per il settore alberghiero.

Già in quegli anni dimostrava la sua forte vocazione all'innovazione: allora si trattava di essere tra i primi a produrre lavastoviglie e sistemi di lavaggio a traino ed a nastro, oggi di sviluppare le più sofisticate tecnologie informatiche per la progettazione e la produzione di modelli d'avanguardia.
10 Sempre con l'apporto creativo e attento dell'uomo.

L'azienda

Flessibilità ed informatizzazione spinta dal processo costruttivo per adattare la produzione alle esigenze ed ai desideri di ciascun cliente, sistemi di produzione e consegna just in time: grazie all'innovazione costante e ad
15 una sapiente organizzazione, la Lamber ha saputo diventare in questi anni un'importante realtà di riferimento del settore. L'iniziale strategia volta ad estendere la propria presenza sui mercati internazionali permette oggi alla Lamber di destinare al mercato estero l'80% della propria produzione.

La qualità come riferimento costante

20 CE, VDE, DVGW, UL, UL Sanitation e CSA: dotata al proprio interno di un laboratorio di progettazione e ricerca, la Lamber ha saputo ottenere le più alte certificazioni internazionali del settore. Per la Lamber vocazione ai mercati esteri significa costruire nel rispetto delle norme più restrittive per essere in grado di rispondere produttivamente alla domanda espressa dai
25 mercati soprattutto i più evoluti. Un'esperienza che si traduce in una progettazione che utilizza le più sofisticate tecnologie CAD, ed in uno studio che incontra ed anticipa le richieste del mercato in continuo sviluppo.

TT
The history
It was in 1948 that Raimondo Affaba, Managing Director of Lamber, established his first business in the sector of dairy equipment washing. A decade later, he also started up a new company, which manufactured industrial
5 washing machines for the hotel sector.

Even at that time, Affaba showed his strong vocation for innovation, a property that led his firm to a position of leadership among the producers of unit and system washing machines. Today the accent still lies very much on innovation, which now exploits cutting-edge information technology in
10 the areas of design and manufacture – while keeping a close contact with the creative and careful input of man.

The firm
Flexibility and IT prompted by the manufacturing process to adapt production techniques to each customer's requirements, production systems and
15 just-in-time delivery. Consistent innovation and operational excellence are the cornerstones to Lamber's success. The initial strategy, which was aimed at development at an international level, has brought Lamber to the current level of exports: 80% of total output.

Quality as the constant reference
20 CE, VDE, DVGW, UL, UL Sanitation and CSA. With its in-house design and research facilities, Lamber has shown it has what it takes to obtain the top international certifications. A strong vocation towards exports means manufacturing to the most stringent standards and being able to productively respond to the markets' demand – especially the most developed ones.
25 This broad-based experience translates into design functions that use the most sophisticated CAD technologies, as well as into marketing studies that meet – and indeed anticipate – the continuously changing market demands.

7

The formal properties of texts: Discourse and intertextual issues in translation

In the last chapter, we briefly discussed a grammatical rearrangement of the two lines from 'To Autumn':

> Autumn is a season of mists and mellow fruitfulness.
> It is a close bosom-friend of the maturing sun.

We saw that, on the sentential level, this arrangement marks the text as informative, rather than as an expression of excitement. Now, part of this sentential effect derives from the pronoun 'It', which explicitly links the second sentence to the first as conveying additional information about Autumn. Such linking of one sentence to another is the most significant feature found on the discourse level.

THE DISCOURSE LEVEL

The textual variables considered on the **discourse level** are those that distinguish a cohesive and coherent textual flow from a random sequence of unrelated utterances. Strictly speaking, this level is concerned with inter-sentential relations (relations between sentences) and with relations between larger units, such as paragraphs, chapters, stanzas, and so on. For our purposes, however, it is sometimes useful also to consider relations between *parts of* sentences on the discourse level, as if the parts were sentences in their own right. We shall see examples of this below, but for the most part we shall be concentrating on intersentential issues, because these are what most clearly illustrate translation issues on the discourse level.

It is useful to distinguish between two aspects of discourse: cohesion and coherence. Following Halliday and Hasan (1976), we define **cohesion** (adj. **cohesive**) as the transparent linking of sentences (and larger sections of text) by explicit discourse connectives like 'then', 'so', 'however', and so on. These act as signposts pointing out the thread of discourse running through the text. **Coherence** (adj. **coherent**) is a more difficult matter than cohesion, because, by definition, it is not explicitly marked in a text: it is a tacit, but discernible, thematic or emotional development running through the text. We can illustrate the difference with a simple example:

I was getting hungry. I went downstairs. I knew the kitchen was on the ground floor. I was pretty sure the kitchen must be on the ground floor. I didn't expect to find the kitchen so easily. I made myself a sandwich.

I was getting hungry. *So* I went downstairs. *Well* . . . I knew the kitchen was on the ground floor. *I mean*, I was pretty sure *it* must be *there*. *Still*, I didn't expect to find *it* so easily. *Anyway*, I made myself a sandwich.

The first text has no intersentential connectives. But it is coherent, thanks to the underlying chronological narrative structure. In the second text, a train of thought is restored by inserting connectives (printed in italics). These act as cohesion markers, setting up a transparent intersentential structure. Some of the cohesion markers link the sentences by explaining or commenting on the speaker's actions: 'So', 'I mean', 'Still', 'Anyway'. Others are instances of **grammatical anaphora** – that is, the replacement of previously used words and phrases by expressions referring back to them; here, the anaphoric elements are 'it' (replacing 'the kitchen') and 'there' (replacing 'on the ground floor').

The sentential and discourse levels are by definition closely related. In this example, many of the intersentential connectives also function on the sentential level; rather like illocutionary particles, they give each utterance a particular tone and tell the listener how to take it – 'So', 'Well', 'I mean', 'Still', 'Anyway'. For example, the two versions of the second sentence will almost certainly be spoken differently, because, on the sentential level, they have different functions: the first announces a new fact out of the blue, while in the second, 'So' marks the sentence as expressing a response to a situation. 'So' therefore has both a sentential and a discourse function here. Punctuation can have a similar double function, as in Practical 6.2 – for instance the full stop in line 9, the colon in line 14, the full stop in line 25. It is instructive to see how these have been rendered in the TT, and with what results.

Furthermore, many connectives can be used to join short sentences together to make longer ones. Conjunctions such as 'so', 'and' or 'but' are

simple examples. This is another way in which intersentential and sentential functions are often close in practice, even though they are distinguishable
in analysis. For instance, 'I was getting hungry, so I went downstairs' will
probably have a different communicative impact from 'I was getting hungry.
So I went downstairs'. Similarly, **rhetorical anaphora** – that is, the repetition of a word or words at the start of successive or closely associated
clauses or phrases – can have a discourse function even where it occurs
within a single sentence. Take these lines from Carducci's 'Pianto antico':

> Sei ne la terra fredda,
> Sei ne la terra negra;
> Né il sol più ti rallegra
> Né ti risveglia amor.
> (Carducci 1994: 104)

Each of these lines could just as easily be a sentence on its own. Either
way, the anaphora has a discourse function, connecting the separate
clauses/sentences with one another. It is therefore advisable, when examining texts on the discourse level, to pay as much attention to features *within*
sentences as to *intersentential* features.

To show the importance of these considerations for translation, we can
subject a short Italian text to a bit of intersentential and sentential restructuring and see what difference this makes. If an intralingual restructuring
makes a significant difference, it is likely that an interlingual one will also
do so. Take the De Carlo text from p. 66 (Jill and the narrator are saying
goodbye in a deserted street in Los Angeles):

> Jill mi ha fatto un cenno con la mano. Ha detto 'Okay, vado'. Poi si è
> sporta verso di me e ha chiesto se ero libero sabato. Le ho detto di sì.
> Lei ha detto 'Magari facciamo qualcosa'. Ho detto 'Bene. Ciao'. Ho
> chiuso la portiera. Lei è andata via veloce verso la freeway.
> (De Carlo 1981: 75)

This terse, staccato writing might suggest the dispassionate eye of a camera.
In fact, however, there are connective elements which deny it any such
'objectivity'. First, the adverb 'Poi' is a cohesion marker, denoting a chronological succession of events. The conjunction 'e' does the same. Both imply
a degree of narratorial control (which the camera can never have), and, in
the situation narrated, they imply some degree of intention, cause and effect.
Second, '*Le* ho detto *di* sì' denotes a reply to a previous question; this link
is more explicit than it would be in the more simple 'Ho detto "Sì"'. Finally,
the subject pronoun 'Lei', which occurs twice, is not absolutely necessary
for clarity, because Jill and the narrator are the only two people involved.
Its presence explicitly marks the characters' utterances as linked with one

another: they are a coherent exchange, not a random accumulation of disconnected sentences.

Let us see what happens if the text is stripped of its connective elements:

Jill mi ha fatto un cenno con la mano. Ha detto 'Okay, vado'. Si è sporta verso di me. Ha chiesto se ero libero sabato. Ho detto 'Sì'. Ha detto 'Magari facciamo qualcosa'. Ho detto 'Bene. Ciao'. Ho chiuso la portiera. È andata via veloce verso la freeway.

Interestingly, the text remains coherent, because of the chronological narrative structure and the reader's knowledge of the context.

However, additional coherence, with different implications, can be created if connective elements are introduced both on the sentential level and on the intersentential level:

Facendomi un cenno con la mano Jill ha detto che sarebbe andata e, sporgendosi verso di me, ha chiesto se fossi libero il sabato seguente. Alla mia risposta affermativa ha detto che avremmo potuto fare qualcosa, al che ho acconsentito e l'ho salutata. Poi, dopo che ho chiuso la portiera, lei è andata via veloce verso la freeway.

'Facendomi' creates a temporal link between Jill's wave and her words, and welds them into a single complex action. The same is true of her leaning out ('sporgendosi') and asking if he will be free. The 'e' then links these two complex actions so closely with one another that they in turn become one, an even more complex action. In this restructuring, there are also three instances of indirect speech: 'ha detto che' (twice) and 'ha chiesto se'. These integrate her words seamlessly into the narrative, which loses the discontinuities of the original. Likewise, 'Alla mia risposta' explicitly links her next words with his reply to her question, binding all three into a smoothly unfolding single event; 'al che' has a similar function. Finally, 'Poi, dopo che' introduces an explicit chronological connection.

The effect of these devices is to introduce a greater degree of explicit coherence than there is in the original. Taken together, they imply that, before embarking on the narrative, the narrator has thought about these events and sorted them out into a significant pattern. This smooth, controlled narrative flow has a very different effect from De Carlo's original, where the narrator does not seem to have stood back and got events into perspective. In the original, the relative lack of connective elements implies a narrator who either cannot or will not make much sense of events; a whole text written in this style might even suggest that the world itself is absurd. In our restructuring, on the other hand, the connective elements perhaps imply that the world can be understood, and that the narrator has the self-confidence and intellectual ability to understand it.

Other connectives than these could have been used, of course – for instance 'Quando le ho detto di sì' instead of 'Alla mia risposta affermativa', or 'allora ho detto "Bene"' instead of 'al che ho acconsentito'. These would result in a less formal register, certainly less elegant, and perhaps giving less of an impression of narrative control.

An important conclusion from these analyses is that translators should be aware of the affective and thematic consequences of wholesale interference with the sentential and intersentential functions of cohesion markers and other connectives. For instance, if the first paragraph of the Tabucchi text in Practical 6.1 were translated into a set of shorter sentences, the effect would be significantly different from that of the ST, even without cohesion markers. Adding them would give yet another effect.

It must be remembered that languages have different expectations in respect of cohesion and coherence. For example, it is more common in Italian than in English for texts to be explictly structured by the use of connectives ('dunque', 'magari', 'pure', 'appunto', etc.) that signpost the logical relationship between sentences. Consequently, an English TT that used explicit connectives to reproduce all those found in an Italian ST would most likely seem stilted, pedantic or patronizing. This piece of dialogue is a simple example:

– Giulio sarebbe la persona giusta.
– Sì, è proprio a lui che pensavo.

This 'proprio' is a good example of how a sentential feature (the high-lighting of 'lui') can double as a discourse feature (the link between the two sentences). In an oral TT, it would probably be rendered not with a cohesion marker, but with prosodic features:

'Giulio would be the (right) man.'
'Yes, I was *thinking* of him.'

In this spoken version, there would be voice stress on 'thinking' and a fall-rise intonation on '-ing of him', highlighting 'him'. In a written TT, on the other hand, 'proprio' might well be rendered with a cohesion marker: 'I was indeed thinking of him'; or it might be rendered with intonation and sequential focus: 'It was him I was thinking of.' Like the ST, each of these three versions contains a sentential feature that also has a discourse function.

This example is typical. In translating, the intersentential link could be marked either prosodically, or with a cohesion marker, or with sequential focus. The decision will be heavily influenced by genre and context. In a play or a novel, italics (indicating voice stress and intonation) would be a likely option. But in an academic text, or if the character in the play or the novel were a pompous type, the cohesion marker would be more likely.

Even in cases where SL and TL do both habitually use discourse connectives, this is often a weak spot in translation. This is because some cohesion markers can be *falsi amici*, or require grammatical transposition in the TT. We have already seen an example on p. 56, where translating 'Tanto' as 'In any case' made near-nonsense of the TT. Other examples are easily found. For instance:

– Non ti ho visto in ufficio ieri.	'I didn't see you in the office
– In effetti, non mi sentivo bene.	yesterday.' 'No/That's right – I wasn't feeling well.'

Here, translating 'In effetti' as 'In effect' or 'In fact' would be near-nonsensical. If the context showed that the speaker was a bit pedantic, an alternative rendering of 'In effetti' might be 'No, indeed' or 'Indeed you didn't'.

The following example shows that finding accurate and idiomatic discourse connectives often necessitates grammatical transposition:

Guadagna poco, ma in compenso il lavoro gli piace.	He doesn't earn much, but he does enjoy his work.

The intensive 'in compenso' is rendered with the verb 'do' used as an auxiliary.

Similarly, an adverb may most idiomatically be rendered with a conjunction. This is often the case with 'invece', for example. But because 'invece' has greater contrastive force than 'ma', English 'but' sometimes needs to be strengthened. For instance:

Volevo telefonargli, invece andai di persona.	I wanted to phone him, but in fact I went round to see him; *or* but I went round to see him instead.
Mario ha studiato legge, invece suo fratello ha scelto medicina.	Mario studied law, but his brother (has) opted for medicine.

In both examples, spoken English could make the contrast through prosodic features alone. But in the first, it is virtually impossible to show the necessary stress and intonation in writing: if the translator decides that 'invece' here has strong contrastive force, something like 'in fact' or 'actually' becomes virtually inevitable. In the second example, 'brother' could be italicized in a written text. However, if the translator decides that italics are inappropriate in the TT context, 'invece' might best be rendered with 'on the other hand' or 'however', or with 'but [. . .] medicine instead'.

Languages also differ in their use of punctuation as a cohesion marker. There are two typical examples in Practical 6.2 (pp. 72–3), where the translator has perhaps failed to spot the function of colons in the ST (ST ll. 14, 20; TT ll. 15, 20). Translators should always be alert to the specific discourse function of ST punctuation and select appropriate TL punctuation.

In respect of intersentential features, then, translators have to ask three simple, but very important, questions. Assuming that the ST is coherent, are the connective elements explicit (e.g. cohesion markers, or sequential focus acting as a connective) or implicit (e.g. prosodic features, or narrative chronology)? What is the thematic and expressive function of the connective elements? And what, in context, is the most accurate and idiomatic TL way of marking a given intersentential relation – should it be explicit or implicit, and does it require grammatical transposition?

As for relations between larger units on the discourse level (paragraphs, chapters, etc.), these are generally less problematic than intersentential relations. As usual, the translator must first ask what the function of such features is in the ST. If they have no marked purpose, but simply reflect SL conventions, altering them to match TL conventions is unproblematic. Commercial considerations may also come into play: for instance, a publisher may be afraid that a text full of long paragraphs would not sell.

The English translation of *Il Gattopardo* is perhaps influenced by both sorts of consideration. For example, Chapter 5 of the ST is entitled thus: 'Arrivo di padre Pirrone a S. Cono – Conversazione con gli amici e l'erbuario – I guai familiari di un Gesuita – Risoluzione dei guai – Conversazione con l''uom di onore' – Ritorno a Palermo' (Tomasi di Lampedusa, 1963a: 128). In the TT, the chapter is entitled simply 'Father Pirrone Pays a Visit' (Tomasi di Lampedusa, 1963b: 154). And it is not uncommon in the same TT to find several short paragraphs corresponding to one longer one in the ST. In both respects, the effect of the changes is to deprive the TT of some of the self-consciously 'archaic' feel of the ST. This may or may not be regrettable; but it does less damage than would wholesale interference with Tabucchi's paragraphs in Practical 6.1.

THE INTERTEXTUAL LEVEL

No text, and no part of any text, exists in total isolation from others. Even the most innovative texts and turns of phrase form part of a whole body of speaking and writing by which their originality or unoriginality is measured. We shall give the term **intertextual level** to the level of textual variables on which texts are viewed as bearing significant external relations to other texts in a given culture or cultures.

There are two main sorts of intertextual relation that particularly concern translators. The most common is that of genre membership. Genre as such is the subject of Chapter 11, but we do need to outline some of its implications here. An instruction manual, for example, will or will not be typical of a certain sort of instruction manual in the SL culture; a play will or will not be typical of a certain sort of play, and so on. Before translating an ST, then, the translator must judge how typical it is of its genre. If it is utterly typical of an established SL genre, it may be necessary to produce a similarly unoriginal TT. This will be relatively straightforward in the case of, say, scientific abstracts or thrillers. It can prove tricky where there is no TL genre corresponding to that of the ST. For instance, where are the poetic and musical counterparts in English to singers like Gino Paoli and Francesco de Gregori? And, whatever its genre, the more innovative the ST is, the more the translator may feel impelled to formulate a TT that is equally innovative in the TL. Alternatively, if accuracy of content is more important than considerations of style, it may be necessary to sacrifice the stylistic originality of the ST. This will usually be the case with scientific or technical texts.

A variation on genre membership is imitation, which may shade into parody. The translator must be alert to this, and also have a mastery of the TL style appropriate to the genre parodied. Umberto Eco's *Diario minimo*, for example, is a collection of short parodies of writers and journalists, both Italian and foreign. This poses such intricate problems as how to render into English an Italian parody of the French *nouveau roman*.

Parody brings us to the second category of intertextual relation, that of quotation or allusion. A text may directly quote from another. In such cases, the translator has to decide whether to borrow the standard TL translation of the quoted text. If it is very familiar in the TL culture, there will have to be special reasons for departing from it, as for instance with Dante's 'Lasciate ogni speranza, voi ch'entrate': the translator would seem to be making a special point if this appeared as 'Give up all hope, you who come in' and not 'Abandon all hope, ye who enter here'. But there will often be more than one TL version of the quotation. In translating the verse from Revelation in Practical 2.2, for example, the translator has either to choose an existing English translation (but which one?) – or to translate the Italian version (which may result in what looks to the TL reader like paraphrase). A relevant factor in the decision will be how standard the form of the ST quotation is.

Sometimes, an ST quotation that is full of resonances for the SL reader would be completely lost on the TL reader. In such cases, the translator may either leave it out altogether, or simply translate it literally, or, if it has an important function in the ST, use some form of compensation. It depends on what exactly the function is. Umberto Eco gives an example from the translation of his novel *Il pendolo di Foucault*, in which the characters constantly speak in literary quotations. A quotation from Leopardi's 'L'infinito' ('al di là della siepe') is rendered with 'Like Darien', an allusion to Keats: in context, it was vital to have *a* literary reference, but it did not matter if this was not to Leopardi or a hedge (Eco 1994: 20).

Translation problems can become acute where ST intertextual features are more a matter of allusion than of simple quotation. The text in Practical 5.1, for instance, appears to contain an allusion to the beginning of T.S. Eliot's 'The Wasteland': 'April is the cruellest month, breeding / Lilacs out of the dead land, mixing / Memory and desire, stirring / Dull roots with spring rain' (Eliot 1963: 63). The example bristles with problems. First, one has to spot the allusion in the first place. Second, this allusion is not to an Italian intertext, but to an English one; for those Italian readers who do spot it, therefore, it has a recherché and exotic flavour which it would not have in English. Third, Eliot's lines are themselves an allusion, to the start of Chaucer's 'General Prologue': 'Whan that Aprill with his showers soote / The droghte of March hath perced to the roote, / And bathed every veyne in swich licour / Of which vertu engendred is the flour' (Chaucer 1974: 17) – an intertext likely to be lost on all but a few Italian readers, and even on most English-speakers. Before translating this text, the translator must decide what the function of the allusions is, and how important the intertextual considerations are relative to factors on other levels.

There is a further problem with allusions. An allusion is normally something deliberate, but we often see allusions where none was intended. An accidental allusion may be more accurately called an echo. Whatever one calls it, when readers or listeners respond to intertextual features of this sort, they are real factors in the meaning and impact of the text. We know, for example, that Keats was not alluding to Donovan's 'They call me mellow yellow' in 'To Autumn'; but, for many modern readers, Donovan's line will be a major intertext in their response to 'mellow' when they first encounter Keats's poem. Conversely, when Donovan first sang his song, many listeners will immediately have recalled Keats. What we do *not* know is whether Keats was alluding to Thomson's 'roving mists', or to Wordsworth's 'mellow Autumn charged with bounteous fruit'; and we do not know whether his readers in 1820 responded to these and other echoes and allusions. But, for readers who do hear these possible echoes and allusions, they are part of the richness of Keats's lines.

Intertextual questions like these are perhaps the simplest illustration of why, in Chapter 2, we were reluctant to accept the notion of 'equivalent effect': any text will have different resonances – even different meanings – for different people and for different generations. This is truer of literary than of scientific or technical texts, but it is a crucial factor that translators cannot ignore in assessing the relevance of intertextual features. And, as ever, the translator must also be careful to avoid *introducing* inappropriate features.

PRACTICAL 7

7.1 Discourse and intertextual issues

Assignment
(i)   You are translating for publication in the United Kingdom the work
     from which the following ST is taken. Concentrating mainly on
     discourse and intertextual issues, discuss the strategic decisions that
     you have to take before starting detailed translation of this ST, and
     outline and justify the strategy you adopt. (Remember to look for
     discourse features within sentences as well as for intersentential
     features.) After finishing your translation, you would find it revealing
     to compare it with the published TT (Levi 1996: 42–3).
(ii) Translate the text into English.
(iii) Discuss the main decisions of detail you took; pay special attention
     to discourse and intertextual issues, but do not overlook other major
     decisions.

Contextual information
The text is from Primo Levi's *Se questo è un uomo*, an account of, and
reflection on, Levi's terrible experiences in Auschwitz. It is not bombastic
or melodramatic, but thought-provoking and very moving in its combination of factuality, humaneness, rationality and discreet rhetorical urgency.
Thematically, the book explores binary opposites – good and evil, justice
and injustice, freedom and imprisonment, etc. This extract is from Chapter
2, 'Sul fondo', where Levi has been inducted into the camp and reached
rock-bottom in this nightmare world. His fellow-prisoners are of various
nationalities, and include a small group of Italians.

ST
Se fossimo ragionevoli, dovremmo rassegnarci a questa evidenza, che il
nostro destino è perfettamente inconoscibile, che ogni congettura è arbi-
traria ed esattamente priva di fondamento reale. Ma ragionevoli gli uomini
sono assai raramente, quando è in gioco il loro proprio destino: essi
5 preferiscono in ogni caso le posizioni estreme; perciò, a seconda del loro
carattere, fra di noi gli uni sono convinti immediatamente che tutto è perduto,
che qui non si può vivere e che la fine è certa e prossima; gli altri, che,
per quanto dura sia la vita che ci attende, la salvezza è probabile e non
lontana, e, se avremo fede e forza, rivedremo le nostre case e i nostri cari.
10 Le due classi, dei pessimisti e degli ottimisti, non sono peraltro così ben
distinte: non già perché gli agnostici siano molti, ma perché i più, senza
memoria né coerenza, oscillano fra le due posizioni-limite, a seconda dell'interlocutore e del momento.

Eccomi dunque sul fondo. A dare un colpo di spugna al passato e al
15 futuro si impara assai presto, se il bisogno preme. Dopo quindici giorni
dall'ingresso, già ho la fame regolamentare, la fame cronica sconosciuta
agli uomini liberi, che fa sognare di notte e siede in tutte le membra dei
nostri corpi;[1] già ho imparato a non lasciarmi derubare, e se anzi trovo in
giro un cucchiaio, uno spago, un bottone di cui mi possa appropriare senza
20 pericolo di punizione, li intasco e li considero miei di pieno diritto. Già mi
sono apparse, sul dorso dei piedi, le piaghe torpide che non guariranno.
Spingo vagoni, lavoro di pala, mi fiacco alla pioggia,[2] tremo al vento; già
il mio stesso corpo non è più mio: ho il ventre gonfio e le membra stec-
chite, il viso tumido al mattino e incavato a sera; qualcuno fra noi ha la
25 pelle gialla, qualche altro grigia: quando non ci vediamo per tre o quattro
giorni, stentiamo a riconoscerci l'un l'altro.

Avevamo deciso di trovarci, noi italiani, ogni domenica sera in un angolo
del Lager; ma abbiamo subito smesso, perché era troppo triste contarci, e
trovarci ogni volta più pochi, e più deformi, e più squallidi. Ed era così
30 faticoso fare quei pochi passi: e poi, a ritrovarsi, accadeva di ricordare e di
pensare, ed era meglio non farlo.

(Levi 1976: 49–51)

---

[1]Cf. Leopardi, *Appressamento della morte*, III, ll. 41–2: 'su lor crespa fronte e su la cava / lor
mascella parea seder la fame.'
[2]Cf. Dante, *L'inferno*, VI, ll. 53–4: 'per la dannosa colpa de la gola, / come tu vedi, a la pioggia mi fiacco.'

8

Literal meaning and translation issues

Translation is concerned with meaning. However, the term 'meaning' is elastic and indeterminate, especially when applied to a whole text. This is true even of **literal** (or 'cognitive' or 'denotative') **meanings** – that is, those that are fully supported by ordinary semantic conventions, such as the convention that 'window' refers to a particular kind of aperture in a wall or roof. In the case of words, it is this literal meaning that is given in dictionary definitions. Yet even the dictionary definition of a word has its problems. This is because it imposes, by abstraction and crystallization of a core meaning, a rigidity of meaning that words do not often show in reality. In addition, once words are put into a context, their literal meanings become even more flexible. These two facts make it difficult to pin down the precise literal meanings in any text of any complexity. The more literary the text, the more this is so; but it is true even of the most soberly informative texts. In this chapter, we shall discuss three degrees of semantic equivalence – that is, how close given expressions are to having identical literal meanings.

SYNONYMY

Literal meaning is a matter of categories into which a language divides the totality of communicable experience. Thus, the literal meaning of the word 'pencil' consists in the fact that all over the world there are similar objects that are included in the category of 'pencil' – and all sorts of other objects that are excluded from it. To define a literal meaning is to specify the 'range' covered by a word or phrase in such a way that it is clear what items are included in that range or category and what items are excluded. It is helpful to visualize literal meanings as circles, because circles can be used to give a rough measure of semantic equivalence. So, for instance, the expressions 'my mother's father' and 'my maternal grandfather' may be represented as two separate circles. The two ranges of literal meaning, however, coincide perfectly: that is, in every specific instance of use, 'my mother's father' and 'my maternal grandfather' include and exclude exactly the same referents. This can be visualized as drawing two circles of exactly the same size, sliding them on top of each other and seeing that they cover one another exactly, as in the figure:

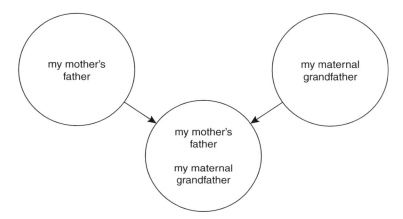

This exemplifies the strongest form of semantic equivalence, full **synonymy**: the two expressions are **synonyms** of one another, having exactly the same range of literal meaning.

Comparisons of literal meaning can also be made between expressions from different languages. For example, 'The carburettor is blocked' and 'Il carburatore è bloccato' cover exactly the same range of situations, and are therefore fully synonymous, as in the figure:

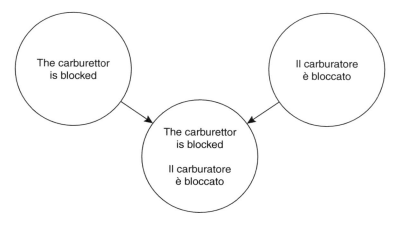

HYPERONYMY–HYPONYMY

Unfortunately, full synonymy is exceptional. Even the nearest semantic equivalent for translating the literal meaning of an ST expression usually falls short of being a full TL synonym. Compare 'The carburettor was blocked' with 'Il carburatore era bloccato'. The English phrase could be referring to an event, not a state. This would have to be expressed in Italian as 'Il carburatore fu bloccato', 'Il carburatore si è bloccato', 'Il carburatore si bloccò' or 'Il carburatore è stato bloccato'. In fact, in some contexts, Italian would even require a pluperfect – 'era stato bloccato' or 'si era bloccato'. (Strictly speaking, there are even more possibilities: 'fu stato bloccato' and 'si fu bloccato'. But these are unlikely, so we shall leave them out of the diagram.) The English phrase, then, covers a range of situations that is divided between at least seven different expressions in Italian: the English phrase is wider than any of the Italian ones. This can be shown as follows:

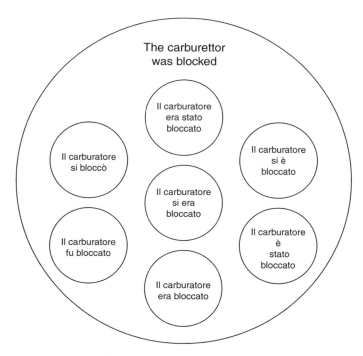

The relationship between 'The carburettor was blocked' and each of the seven Italian expressions is known as **hyperonymy–hyponymy**. An expression with a wider, less specific, range of literal meaning is a **hyperonym** (or 'superordinate') of one with a narrower and more specific literal meaning. Conversely, the narrower one is a **hyponym** of the wider one. So 'The carburettor was blocked' is a hyperonym of 'Il carburatore era bloccato',

'Il carburatore è stato bloccato', etc.; and they are all hyponyms of the English phrase.

Hyperonymy–hyponymy is so widespread that one can say that the entire fabric of linguistic reference is built up on such relationships. The same external reality can be phrased in an indefinite number of ways – compare 'I bought a Collins–Sansoni dictionary' with these increasingly general phrasings: 'I bought an Italian dictionary', 'I bought a dictionary', 'I bought a book', 'I bought something'. Each of these phrasings is a hyperonym of the ones before it.

When there is no full TL synonym for a given ST expression (e.g. 'The carburettor was blocked'), the translator has to look for an acceptable TL hyperonym or hyponym. In fact, translators do this automatically. For example, in most contexts SL 'nipote' can only be translated by a TL hyponym, *either* 'granddaughter' *or* 'grandson' *or* 'niece' *or* 'nephew'. Each of these is narrower in literal meaning than 'nipote'. Conversely, each of the English words can only be translated into Italian with a hyperonym, the wider and less specific 'nipote'.

PARTICULARIZING TRANSLATION AND GENERALIZING TRANSLATION

Translating by a hyponym results in a TT expression with a narrower and more specific literal meaning than the ST expression. TT 'niece' is more specific than ST 'nipote', adding particulars not present in the ST expression. We shall call this **particularizing translation**, or **particularization** for short.

Translating by a hyperonym results in a TT expression with a wider and less specific literal meaning than the ST expression. TT 'nipote' is more general than ST 'grandson', omitting particulars given by the ST. We shall call this **generalizing translation**, or **generalization** for short.

Particularization and generalization both entail a degree of translation loss on the grammatical level: detail is added to, or omitted from, the ST message. However, translating by a hyponym or a hyperonym is standard practice and entirely unremarkable, unless the TL hyponym or hyperonym is unnecessary, inappropriate or misleading.

Particularizing translation, for instance, is acceptable if the TL offers no suitable alternative and if the added detail does not clash with the overall context of ST or TT. Thus 'Facciamo un giro' could be translated in several ways: 'We're going for a walk/ride/drive/sail', etc. Each of these particularizations is unavoidable. Only the context will make it clear which hyponym to use. Even translating 'Facciamo' inevitably entails particularization, since it can be either declarative ('We're going for . . .') or imperative ('Let's go for . . .'): English is forced to choose one or the other.

Particularizing translation is *not* acceptable if the TL does offer a suitable alternative to the addition of detail or if the added detail does clash with the overall context of ST or TT. Take 'ballerine' and the four TTs in the following example:

Le ballerine dei night sono sexy.

(a) The nightclub ballerinas are sexy.

(b) Nightclub ballerinas are sexy.

(c) The nightclub dancers are sexy.

(d) Nightclub dancers are sexy.

In all four TTs, there is unavoidable particularization, because '*Le* ballerine' can denote either *all* dancers in general or *the particular* dancers who are the subject of discussion. Which option to choose depends on the context. As long as the option chosen is the right one, this particularization is unremarkable. (Likewise, only context will show whether 'ballerine *dei* night' is best rendered as 'nightclub dancers', 'dancers *in/from* nightclubs' or 'dancers in/from *the* nightclubs'.) However, in TTs (a) and (b), there is a truly unacceptable particularization. Italian 'ballerina' can denote a ballerina, a ballroom dancer, a go-go dancer, etc. English 'ballerinas' clashes with the context of nightclubs. 'Dancers' is a better translation, because it collocates well with 'nightclub'.

This example shows very clearly how difficult it is to avoid some degree of particularization or generalization. In fact, on its own, 'dancers' is actually a *generalization*: it omits the gender-specific detail of ST 'ballerine' (as distinct from 'ballerini'). In most contexts, this would not matter. If it were absolutely necessary to specify the gender, the translator would probably be better advised to make it clear by compensation in the TT context than to commit a stylistic horror like 'nightclub dancing girls' or 'female nightclub dancers'.

Similar considerations apply to generalizing translation as to particularizing translation. Generalization is acceptable if the TL offers no suitable alternative and if the omitted detail is either unimportant in the ST or is implied in the TT context. As long as these conditions obtain, 'nightclub dancers' is probably the best rendering of 'ballerine dei night'. Here is another example. In the sitting room, all there is to sit on is a sofa, covered with papers, and two armchairs, one of them occupied. The priest comes to call and his host says: 'Si accomodi in poltrona'. The most natural translation is 'Have a/the chair', not 'Have an/the armchair': if the only chairs in the room are armchairs, English normally makes do with the hyperonym 'chair'. In this situation, the generalization is not only acceptable, but arguably more idiomatic than 'armchair'.

Generalizing translation is *not* acceptable if the TL does offer suitable alternatives, or if the omitted details are important in the ST but not implied or compensated for in the TT context. For example, in the sitting room there are two armchairs, both occupied, and an ordinary chair with no arms. The priest is at the front door and the daughter of the house asks where she should invite him to sit. Her anticlerical father says: 'Che prenda la sedia'. In this case, the hyperonym 'chair' is no use, because there are three chairs in the room. 'He can have the chair with no arms' is accurate in literal meaning, but implausible. An idiomatic translation needs compensation – something like 'He's not having an armchair', or a particularization of 'sedia', as in 'He can have the dining/kitchen/wooden/hard chair'. Any of these particularizations would be acceptable, as long as it fitted in contextually.

For an example of compensation in handling the relation between hyperonymy and hyponymy, see the translation and discussion of 'ricerca' on pp. 39–40.

PARTIALLY OVERLAPPING TRANSLATION

There is a third degree of semantic equivalence. Take the phrase 'My niece's joke'. In the context of joking, 'La battuta di mia nipote' is as close a literal rendering as possible. But the English does not specify the kind of joke, whereas the Italian TT specifies that it is a witty remark. That is, 'battuta', as opposed to 'scherzo' (practical joke) or 'barzelletta' (funny story), is a particularization. Conversely, in the English phrase, the relationship between the speaker and the girl is specified unambiguously, whereas the Italian TT leaves it ambiguous: here, the TT generalizes, because 'mia nipote' can mean either 'my niece' or 'my granddaughter'. This TT, then, combines particularization and generalization: it *keeps* the reference to a jest on the part of a junior female relative, but it *adds* a detail not found in the ST and it *omits* a detail that is given in the ST. This can be visualized as two partially overlapping circles, as in the figure opposite. The unshaded area, where the circles overlap, represents the material the ST and TT have in common. The shaded areas represent what is omitted and what is added in the TT. This is another category of degree in the translation of literal meaning. We shall call it **partially overlapping translation**, or **partial overlap** for short.

Partial overlap is almost unavoidable in whole sentences, common in phrases, and not infrequent even in single words. Take the word 'professoressa'. If, in a given context, this is translated as 'teacher' and not 'lecturer', the TT certainly keeps the reference to someone who instructs. But it also particularizes, because it *adds* the specific detail that she works in a school and not a university; and at the same time it generalizes, because it *omits* the detail of her gender.

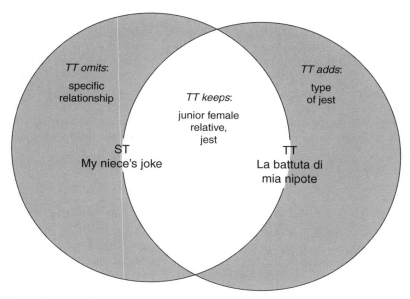

When the TL offers no suitable alternatives, partial overlap is acceptable if the *omitted* detail is unimportant or is implied in the overall TT context, and if the *added* detail does not clash with the overall ST or TT contexts. Translating 'professoressa' as 'teacher' or as 'lecturer', for example, will in most contexts be harmless and unavoidable.

Partial overlap is unacceptable if the *omitted* detail is important in the ST but is not implied in the overall context of the TT, or if the *added* detail clashes with the overall ST or TT contexts. If the TL does not offer suitable alternatives, then only compensation can counteract the omission or addition. So the teacher's gender can be made clear through anaphora ('she' or 'her'), and a reference to her workplace can if necessary be inserted into the TT.

PRACTICAL 8

8.1 Particularizing, generalizing and partially overlapping translation

Assignment
(i) Make a detailed analysis of examples of particularizing, generalizing and partially overlapping translation in the TT printed opposite the ST.
(ii) Where possible, give a revised TT that is a better translation, and explain your decision.

Contextual information

The ST is from Lampedusa's *Il Gattopardo* (1958). Sicily is full of political tension, the threat to the Bourbon king and to the established social
order growing daily. The political situation, together with the Prince's auto-
cratic presence, can make mealtimes tense and silent affairs. Today, the
Prince's mood is not improved by the departure of his beloved nephew
Tancredi to join the rebels. However, a conversation with padre Pirrone
before lunch helps him to come to terms with the situation to some extent:
he is resigned to a future where the lower orders rule the roost. Carolina
and Concetta are daughters of the Prince, Paolo a son. The TT was first
published in 1960.

ST

Quando la campanella del pranzo li richiamò giù, tutti e due erano rasser-
enati, tanto dalla comprensione delle congiunture politiche quanto dal
superamento di questa comprensione stessa. Un'atmosfera di inconsueta
distensione si sparse nella villa. Il pasto di mezzogiorno era quello princi-
5   pale della giornata, e andò, grazie a Dio, del tutto liscio. Figurarsi che a
Carolina, la figlia ventenne, accadde che uno dei boccoli che le incornici-
avano il volto, sorretto a quanto pare da una malsicura forcina, scivolasse
e andasse a finire sul piatto. L'incidente che, un altro giorno, avrebbe potuto
essere increscioso, questa volta aumentò soltanto l'allegria: quando il fratello,
10 che era seduto vicino alla ragazza, prese il ricciolo e se lo appuntò al collo,
sicché pendeva lì come uno scapolare, financo il Principe acconsentì a
sorridere. La partenza, la destinazione, gli scopi di Tancredi erano ormai
noti a tutti, e ognuno ne parlava, meno Paolo che continuava a mangiare
in silenzio. Nessuno del resto era preoccupato, tranne il Principe che però
15 nascondeva l'ansia non grave nelle profondità del suo cuore, e Concetta che
era la sola a conservare un'ombra sulla bella fronte. 'La ragazza deve avere
un sentimentuccio per quel briccone. Sarebbe una bella coppia. Ma temo
che Tancredi debba mirar più in alto, intendo dire più in basso.'

(Tomasi di Lampedusa 1963a: 33)

TT

When the bell for luncheon called them downstairs, both had regained their serenity, due to understanding the political scene and to setting that understanding aside. An atmosphere of unusual relaxation had spread over the house. The midday meal was the chief one of the day, and went, God be
5 thanked, quite smoothly. This in spite of one of the ringlets framing the face of the twenty-year-old Carolina, the eldest daughter, dropping into her soup plate because apparently of an ill-secured pin. Another day the incident might have had dreadful consequences, but now it only heightened the gaiety; and when her brother, sitting next to her, took the lock of hair and
10 pinned it on his neckerchief where it hung like a scapular, even the Prince allowed himself a smile. Tancredi's departure, destination and reasons were now known to all, and everyone talked of them, except Paolo who went on eating in silence. No one was really worrying about him, in fact, but the Prince, who showed no signs of the anxiety he still felt deep down, and
15 Concetta who was the only one with a shadow on her pretty forehead. 'The girl must have her eye on the young scamp. They'd make a fine couple. But I fear Tancredi will have to aim higher, by which of course I mean lower.'

(Tomasi di Lampedusa 1963b: 40)

9

Connotative meaning and translation issues

Literal meaning is only one aspect of verbal meaning. The meaning of a text comprises a number of different layers: referential content, emotional colouring, cultural, social and personal associations, and so on. This many-layered nature of meaning is another crucial translation issue.

Even within a single language, synonyms are usually different in their overall semantic effects – compare 'clergyman' and 'sky-pilot', 'adder' and 'viper', 'go away' and 'piss off', etc. Each of these has overtones which differentiate it from its synonym. We shall call such overtones **connotative meanings** (or **connotations**) – that is, associations which, over and above the literal meaning of an expression, form part of its overall meaning. Connotative meanings are many and varied, and it is common for a single piece of text, or even a single expression, to combine more than one kind into a single overall effect. However, it is useful at this stage to distinguish six major types of connotative meaning (some of them adapted from Leech 1974: 26). Learning to identify these sharpens awareness of the presence and significance of connotations in STs and TTs alike. Note that, by definition, we are only concerned here with socially widespread connotations, not personal ones. Translators do not normally let personal connotations influence a TT if they can help it.

ATTITUDINAL MEANING

Attitudinal meaning is that part of the overall meaning of an expression which consists of some widespread *attitude to the referent*. The expression does not merely denote the referent in a neutral way, but also hints at some attitude to it.

For instance, in appropriate contexts, 'the police', 'the filth' and 'the Old Bill' are synonyms in terms of referential content, but they have different overall meanings. These attitudes are not part of the literal meaning of the expressions, but it is impossible to ignore them in responding to the expressions. It is therefore important not to overlook them when translating. Translating 'la pula' as 'the police' accurately renders the literal meaning of the ST, but fails to render the hostile attitude connoted by 'la pula' (the filth', 'the pigs'). Translating 'la pretaglia' as 'clergy' rather than something like 'the dog-collar brigade' would miss the point. Conversely, the translator must be careful not to introduce significant connotations that are absent from the ST and clash with the TT context, as in translating 'il clero' as 'the dog-collar brigade'.

ASSOCIATIVE MEANING

Associative meaning is that part of the overall meaning of an expression which consists of expectations that are – rightly or wrongly – widely *associated with the referent* of the expression. The word 'nurse' is a good example. Most people automatically associate 'nurse' with 'woman'. This unconscious association is so widespread that the term 'male nurse' has had to be coined to counteract its effect: 'he is a nurse' sounds odd, even today.

We have seen good examples of unwanted associative meaning in the 'Blackpool' TT (p. 24), where 'Blackpool' connotes things like candy-floss and what the butler saw, and 'slaughterhouses' connotes blood, suffering and eating meat – all of which clash with the intentions of the ST (see pp. 25–6).

Any area of reference where prejudices and stereotypes, however innocuous, operate is likely to give examples of associative meaning. Even something as banal as a date can trigger an associative meaning – think of 1 April or 5 November. There is a good example of associative meaning in the last sentence of Pascoli's short poem 'Novembre'. The air is bright and spring-like, but there are no birds. The poem ends:

> Silenzio, intorno: solo, alle ventate,
> odi lontano, da giardini ed orti,
> di foglie un cader fragile. È l'estate,
> fredda, dei morti.
>
> (Pascoli 1905: 130)

Given the title and the context, the inescapable association in the last sentence is 2 November, 'il giorno dei morti' (All Souls' Day), when prayers for the dead are said. The associative meaning is that of 'graveside prayer for the dead'. A TT that omitted this connotation of liturgy and prayer might incur unacceptable translation loss. It is tempting to trigger the All Souls' Day association with a translation like 'It is the cold summer of dead souls'; but this might introduce unwanted connotations of Gogol's *Dead Souls*. Perhaps a reference to remembrance in a stylized, quasi-ritual diction would compensate: 'This is the summer, cold summer, of the remembered dead.'

ALLUSIVE MEANING

The unwanted echo of Gogol is an example of **allusive meaning**. Allusive meaning occurs when an expression evokes an associated saying or quotation in such a way that the meaning of that saying or quotation becomes part of the overall meaning of the expression. Good examples are the allusions to Leopardi and Dante in the Levi text on p. 84. The lines from Pascoli contain another. Because the poem is entitled 'Novembre', 'l'estate' evokes the expression 'estate di San Martino'. This allusive meaning joins with the associative meaning of 'graveside prayer for the dead' to give to the description of a November day an overall meaning that is more powerful than the literal meanings of the expressions used. In fact, this overall meaning is reinforced still more by another associative meaning: the St Martin's summer in Italy is often accompanied by winds, so that 'ventate' makes the listener/reader more receptive to the connotation of 'San Martino' in 'estate'. (This connotation is in turn reinforced on the phonic/graphic level, by the end-rhyme in 'ventate/estate'.)

Like all intertextual features, allusive meaning needs to be discerned in the first place. Even when the translator decides there is an allusion, it may be relevant to ask whether it is deliberate innuendo or sheer accident. When Roberto Baggio declined to take a penalty against his old club, how many fans recognized the next day's headlines, 'Il Gran Rifiuto', as an allusion to Dante? Did the reporters themselves know that this common expression is from *L'inferno*? If the translator decides that the allusion has no textual function, 'The Great Refusal' will do. If it *is* judged to be relevant, then something like 'The Great Renunciation' or 'Baggio's Betrayal' might be suitable, depending on how the translator interprets the author's reading of Dante.

Humorous allusive meanings can pose delicate translation problems. Here is one from Michele Saponaro's short story 'Il cavallo morello'. Cosimo's beloved horse Alano has disappeared from the stable. The *brigadiere* observes critically that the stable door is coming off its hinges. The following exchange ensues:

– [. . .] Ma farò mettere la porta nuova, oggi stesso.
– Già, quando i buoi sono scappati...
Rideva anche il brigadiere.
– Cavallo, signor brigadiere, era cavallo. Il mio vecchio Alano!

(Saponaro 1992: 161)

The *brigadiere* alludes to the proverbial expression: 'Chiudere la stalla dopo che i buoi sono scappati.' Cosimo is too upset to see the allusion, hence the comic inappropriateness when he corrects the *brigadiere*. The first idea will be to draw on the stock communicative translation of the Italian saying: 'To shut the stable door after the horse has bolted.' This is apt in the circumstances, but makes nonsense of Cosimo's reply. The Italian allusion could be translated literally – but then the exotic touch of 'oxen' might draw too much attention to itself. One possibility might be to compensate for the loss of reference to oxen by using a different TL saying and adapting Cosimo's reply accordingly:

'But I'll get the new door put on this very day.'
'I'd say that's putting the cart before the horse . . .'
And the sergeant laughed as he said it.
'I *can't* – he's not there, he's gone. My old Alano!'

Another possibility would be to keep the TL communicative equivalent, but use it differently from its ST counterpart:

'But I'll get the new door put on this very day.'
'Well make sure it's the door that's bolted this time, not the horse.'
And the sergeant laughed as he said it.
'But he *has* – I told you, he's gone. My old Alano!'

Here, Cosimo's failure to respond to the pun in 'bolted' compensates for the loss of his failure, in the ST, to respond to the allusion.

REFLECTED MEANING

Like 'l'estate [. . .] dei morti', 'bolted' in our second TT shows more than one sort of connotative meaning. In the Pascoli example, associative meaning and allusive meaning reinforce one another. In 'bolted', there is an allusive meaning – 'it's too late'. This is reinforced by a reflected meaning. **Reflected meaning** is the meaning given to an expression over and above its literal meaning by the fact that *its form calls to mind the completely different meaning of an expression that sounds, or is spelled, the same, or nearly the same*. In our example, 'bolted' has two completely different meanings. The idea of '*bolting* the door' is triggered in the sergeant's mind (and the reader's) by the allusion to shutting the stable door after the horse has *bolted*. Another example is the evocation of 'yellow' by 'mellow' in 'To Autumn'. We saw good Italian examples in the 'Blackpool' ST (p. 24), where 'realizzate' and 'eseguite' are applied to shoemaking. (See the discussion on pp. 34–6.)

It is easy to spoil a TT by letting an unwanted reflected meaning creep in. There is an example in the 'Blackpool' TT (p. 24), where the earlier reference to slaughterhouses triggers the connotation of 'put to death' in 'executed'. And there is a threat of unwanted reflected meaning in Practical 2.2: in the context of Chernobyl, 'oblast' could look like a sick pun in the TT, whereas in the ST 'óblast' has no reflected meaning of 'explosion' or 'Oh blast'.

Reflected meanings do not usually occur spontaneously to the listener or reader. When an expression is taken in isolation, its reflected meaning or meanings are usually merely latent. It is the context that triggers these latent reflected meanings. In the Saponaro example, the two meanings of 'bolt' that are activated are appropriate to the situation. But there are others, such as 'to eat hurriedly' or 'to sieve', that are irrelevant to this situation in this context. These are therefore very unlikely to occur to the listener/reader. Translators should remember that being receptive to connotative meaning is not the same as looking up every possible use of a word in the dictionary and assuming that they are all relevant in the particular context in question.

COLLOCATIVE MEANING

Collocative meaning is given to an expression over and above its literal meaning by *the meaning of some other expression with which it collocates to form a commonly used phrase*. Some collocative meanings are so strong that they hardly need triggering by context; for example, 'chauvinism' (literally, 'fanatical patriotism') can hardly be used today without evoking its collocative partner 'male', and has virtually become a synonym of 'male chauvinism'. Others need to be activated by the context; in 'I rode shotgun on the way to his wedding', the innuendo is based on activating the collocative echo of 'shotgun wedding'.

For the translator, collocative meanings are important, not only because they contribute to the overall meaning of the ST, but also because of the need to avoid unwanted collocative clashes in the TT. This is easily seen from comparison of a few Italian phrases with alternative English renderings:

Una serpe in seno	A snake in my breast (cf. snake in the grass; Cleopatra's asp) *vs* A viper in my bosom
Un mare di lacrime	A sea of tears (cf. [take up arms against] a sea of troubles) *vs* Floods of tears

There is an example of unintentional collocative meaning in the 'Blackpool' TT (p. 24), where 'old cobbler' irresistibly evokes 'a load of old cobblers'.

There is another good example in l. 15 of the *Gattopardo* TT on p. 93. 'Concetta was the only one with a shadow on her pretty forehead' has two unfortunate effects. Evoking the cliché '[don't you worry] your pretty little head [about that]', it turns Concetta into a bit of a bimbo, and the narrator (or the Prince) into a male chauvinist.

Collocative meaning is often inseparable from allusive meaning. To take an earlier example, 'quando i buoi sono scappati' acquires its allusive meaning from the unmissable evocation of its collocative partner, 'chiudere la stalla'.

AFFECTIVE MEANING

Affective meaning is an *emotive effect worked on the addressee* by the choice of expression, and which forms part of its overall meaning. The expression does not merely denote its referent, but also hints at some attitude of the speaker or writer to the addressee.

Features of linguistic politeness, flattery, rudeness or insult are typical examples of expressions carrying affective meanings. Compare, for instance, 'Le dispiacerebbe fare silenzio?' with 'Chiudi il becco!'. These expressions share the same core literal meaning of 'Be quiet', but the speaker's implied attitude to the listener produces a different affective impact in each case: polite in the first, rude in the second.

Translators must obviously be able to recognize affective meanings in the ST. But they must also be careful not to introduce unwanted ones into the TT. For example, a customer at the baker's asks for some rolls: 'Mi dia quattro panini.' This might sound rude if translated literally as 'Give me four rolls', although the ST does not have that affective meaning at all. A safer TT would cushion what sounds to the English-speaker's ear like the brusqueness of the Italian: '(I'd like) four rolls, please.'

As we have seen, although these six types of connotative meaning are distinguishable from each other, it often happens that two or more occur together and nourish each other. In acquiring a translation method, it is useful to learn to distinguish exactly which sorts of connotative meaning are in play. Practical 9 involves detailed analysis of connotations, because it is designed to help in the acquisition of this ability. Once the ability has been acquired, however, it becomes relatively easy to respond to the sometimes complex connotations of a given piece of text without labelling every last component in them. All that remains then is to find a way of rendering the connotative meanings without too much translation loss!

PRACTICAL 9

9.1 Connotative meaning

Assignment
Taking the expressions printed in bold type in the ST printed on p. 102:

(i)   Categorize and discuss those in which connotative meaning plays a
       part, and discuss the translation of them in the TT printed opposite.
       Where necessary, give a revised TT rendering the ST connotations
       more successfully into English, and explain why you think your TT
       is better.
(ii)   Identify and discuss expressions where unwanted connotative mean-
       ings have been introduced into the printed TT. Give a revised TT in
       each case, and explain your decisions.

Contextual information
The ST is from *Santità!* (1996), a novel by Vittorio Russo. God has appeared
to a contemporary pope, and is criticizing the record of the Church. Here,
arguing about the rights and wrongs of the Spanish Inquisition, they are
discussing the case of Elvira del Campo, who was accused of sympathizing
with Jews, tortured and put on trial for heresy. When the passage begins,
God is responding to the pope's reminder that the court did finally acknowledge her innocence. (NB The TT was produced from a pre-publication
version of the ST.)

Turn to p. 102

ST

'Sì, dopo averla umiliata e trattata come la più immonda delle bestie, dopo averla denudata e ricoperta appena di *paños de verguenza*, dopo averne fiaccato la personalità e averle strappato fino all'ultimo brandello di dignità, dopo averla seviziata e dopo che la sventurata ebbe implorato pietà per quei

5 suoi *crimini*.

'E che dovrei fare io per tutti i crimini del genere umano? I crimini veri, intendo! Elvira aveva già languito per un anno nelle **segrete** della **Inquisizione** e fu condannata a scontarne ancora tre. Fu obbligata a portare sulle vesti la **croce gialla** dell'ignominia, che serviva ad identificare i

10 condannati del tribunale dell'Inquisizione. Per ultimo le furono confiscati i beni. Perché i beni degli inquisiti erano regolarmente confiscati e divisi tra gl'inquisitori, gli **scribi**, i **delatori**, gl'impiccatori e, beninteso, il papa. Proprio come avvenne sotto la croce.'

Seguì una lunga pausa più cupa della notte.

15 'L'Inquisizione non era un'istituzione brutale,' rilevò cauto Sua Santità, 'se rapportata alla **mentalità del tempo, alle sue fobie, alle sue angosce** e ai suoi spettri. Era il terrore di non essere **in linea con** la Tua volontà che muoveva lo zelo degli inquisitori. Io ho sinceramente pietà per le follie determinate dall'esaltazione, ma, a modo loro, quegli inquisitori furono

20 uomini devoti. Spietati, sì, ma per amor Tuo. Più ciechi che colpevoli, essi erano solo mossi da un **malinteso senso dell'ortodossia**.'

'Per amor mio!' fece eco Quello. 'Come desidero essere detestato se l'amor mio deve generare sofferenza! Quello però non era amore, era il fanatismo della cecità di esaltati, lontani dal capire che l'opera loro mirava

25 esclusivamente a rafforzare il potere del papa sulle anime.'

'Eppure, non era certo alla propria cecità che gl'inquisitori attribuivano l'annientamento degli eretici, ma alla Tua volontà. E Tu tacevi, accoglievi le lodi, i profumi degli incensi e le messe di ringraziamento...'

'Avrei dovuto intromettermi, dici tu? E disapprovi perché non l'ho fatto.

30 E se avessi reagito, quante volte credi che avrei dovuto ridurre questo mondo ad un cumulo di macerie e di carogne immonde?'

'Dopo però avresti potuto rifarlo migliore! Magari prendendoTi un po' di tempo per non avere sorprese. Che Ti costava? Hai voluto utilizzare **materiale umano** scadente e Ti lamenti se poi non **risponde**!' ironizzò Sua

35 Santità.

'Dunque avrei dovuto sottoporre la mia opera ad un **collaudo**: un esame di riparazione! Io, insomma, rimandato a settembre come uno **scolaretto**! Sappi che quello che ho creato m'è sacro, ed è irripetibile e definitivo.'

"...e **Paganini che credeva di essere originale!**" considerò di sfuggita

40 Sua Santità e replicò:

'Beh, qualche correzione l'hai fatta... col diluvio, per esempio, con **qualche intervento incendiario**.'

(Russo 1996a: 85–7)

TT

'Yes, after humiliating her and treating her like some wild beast, and stripping her down until she was barely decent; after destroying her personality and robbing her of her dignity; after continuing to torture her when she cried for mercy for her *crimes.*

5   'Tell me, what should I do about all those crimes against humanity? Real crimes! Elvira had already been locked away in prison by the Inquisition for a year and she was then sentenced to imprisonment for three more years. She had to wear the yellow cross of shame on her clothes, which served to identify those condemned by the Inquisition. Last but not least, she was deprived of all her

10   worldly goods. It was common practice for victims of the Inquisition to lose all their possessions which would be shared out among the inquisitors, pen-pushers, spies, hangmen and naturally, the pope himself. Which was precisely what happened at the foot of the Cross,' He added.

A long pause followed, gloomier than dead of night.

15   'The Inquisition was not a cruel institution,' His Holiness suggested cautiously, 'if You look at it in perspective. The period was rife with phobias, fear and paranoia. It was the terror of not doing Your will that made the inquisitors so zealous. I cannot condone the folly which derives from fanaticism but, in their way, the inquisitors were devout. Pitiless of course, but

20   for Your sake. Bigoted rather than guilty, they were moved by a mistaken sense of orthodoxy.'

'For my sake, indeed!' He repeated. 'I would really prefer to be hated if deeds committed for my sake cause such suffering! It was not for my sake at all, it was sheer bigotry by fanatics who could not see that what they were doing had no

25   other purpose than to strengthen the pope's hold over the people.'

'It was to You that the inquisitors attributed the annihilation of heretics, not to their bigotry. You said nothing, accepting their praise, frankincense and myrrh, thanksgiving masses . . .'

'So, I should have done something about it, should I? And you rebuke

30   me for not doing so? If I had intervened, I would have had to reduce the world to a heap of rubble with rotting corpses every five minutes!'

'Then You could have built a better world! Maybe You would have been more careful, so as to avoid unpleasant surprises. It wouldn't have cost You anything! You create second-rate human beings and then You complain

35   because things aren't quite ship-shape!'

'So I should have been checked out, should I? If I failed my exam I would have to re-sit it like some schoolboy! I'll have you know that what I create is sacred, unrepeatable and final.'

'. . . Like Paganini, who never repeated himself!' His Holiness quipped

40   mentally. Then he replied:

'Well, You did intervene sometimes . . . what about the Flood? Or Your tricks with fire?'

(Russo 1996b: 89–91)

10

Language variety: Translation issues in register, sociolect and dialect

In this chapter, we look at characteristics in the way the message is formulated that reveal information about the speaker or writer. These stylistically conveyed meanings are connotations: they are not normally recorded in the dictionary, but are read between the lines, on the basis of widespread associations. We shall call the information revealed 'speaker-related information', regardless of whether there is a written text or not. Likewise, to avoid cluttering the text with heavy compounds ('speaker/writer', 'reader/listener'), we shall apply the terms 'speaker' and 'listener' to spoken and written texts alike.

There are two broad categories of speaker-related information that can be revealed through the manner, or style, in which the message is formulated. The first comprises things that speakers intend to reveal, notably the effect they want their utterance to have on the listener. The second comprises things they do not necessarily intend to reveal, notably the social stereotype they appear to belong to, and their regional and class affiliations. Any or all of these things can occur together, of course, and they are sometimes hard to distinguish from one another. But, in analysing style, it is useful to keep them as clearly distinct as possible, because it helps the translator to pin down what features are textually important.

REGISTER

'Register' is a term used in so many different ways that it can be positively misleading. For our purposes, it is enough to distinguish two types of register.

Tonal register

The first is **tonal register**. Tonal register is what is often simply called 'register' in dictionaries and textbooks on style. It is the feature of linguistic expression that carries affective meaning. It is *the tone that the speaker takes* – vulgar, familiar, polite, formal, etc. The affective meaning of a feature of tonal register is conveyed by a more or less deliberate *choice* of one out of a range of expressions capable of conveying a given literal message – compare, for example, 'me ne frego della tua salute', 'non mi importa della tua salute' and 'la tua salute mi è indifferente'. The effect of tonal register on listeners is thus something for which speakers can be held responsible, in so far as they are deliberately being obscene, polite, etc.

It is clearly important for the translator to assess where the ST expression comes on the SL politeness scale, and to render it with a corresponding TL degree of politeness. But it is not enough just to have a repertoire of expressions capable of injecting various affective meanings into a literal message. Equally important is the *situation* in which the expression is used. Different sorts of social transaction – preaching in church, defending a client in court, selling a car to a male customer, etc. – all imply different tonal registers. Nor is that all. The source culture and the target culture may have different expectations regarding the appropriate tonal register(s) for a given situation: awareness of such differences is as important as awareness of situation and having a repertoire of tonal registers.

Social register

A **social register** is a style from which the listener infers what social stereotype the speaker belongs to. A stereotype by definition excludes individual idiosyncrasies of people belonging to the stereotype; but, for better or for worse, we do tend to organize our interactions with other people on the basis of social stereotypes. These stereotypes range from broad value-judgemental labels such as 'pompous', 'down-to-earth', 'chipper', etc. to increasingly specific stereotypical personality-types such as 'the henpecked husband', 'the six-pints-before-the-kick-off football fan', 'the middle-aged female *Guardian*-reading academic', etc. In so far as each of these stereotypes has a characteristic style of language-use, this style is what we mean by social register. Social register therefore differs from tonal register in that the speaker-related information is not usually *intentionally* revealed by the speaker.

Whatever information the style conveys about the kind of person the speaker is, it will often be tentative. It is generally confirmed and refined by context and situation. Once these are taken into account, social register will carry information about such things as the speaker's educational background, social persona (i.e. a social role the speaker is used to fulfilling), occupation and professional standing, and so on. In other words, a social register is a style that is conventionally seen as appropriate to both a type of person and a type of situation.

Clearly, in translating an ST that has speaking characters in it, or whose author uses social register for self-projection, a major concern is constructing an appropriate TL register. In purely informative texts, this is relatively straightforward, the main problem being to find the conventional TL style for the genre. The more journalistic or literary the ST, however, the greater the importance of characterization, and therefore of social persona. When the translator is operating between Western European cultures, social stereotypes can sometimes be matched reasonably closely – football fans perhaps, or guests at an aristocratic ball, or university students. But even such parallels are far from exact: there are discrepancies between the stereotypes of British and Italian football fans, British and Italian aristocrats, British and Italian university students. And what is the Italian translator to do with Jeeves and Wooster, for example, or the characters in *Trainspotting*? The problem is more acute still where there is no target-culture counterpart to an ST social persona. Take the *bersagliere*, the *giudice per le indagini preliminari*, the *vinificatore* in the hills: if there are social registers characteristic of these types, how is the translator going to convey them in English? Any strategy is going to involve loss, compromise and compensation. Whatever TL social register is finally decided on, it is most important to keep it consistent: if the *vinificatore* sounded like a cross between a gentleman farmer and a straw-chewing rustic, the effect could be ruined.

Social or tonal?

Social and tonal register are not always fully distinguishable. There are two reasons for this. First, it is not always clear whether a style of expression reflects social stereotyping or the speaker's intentions towards the listener. And second, characteristics of particular social registers often include features of tonal register. Both reasons are exemplified in the following outburst:

Sei solo un'egoista, ecco cosa. Una stronzetta che vuole fare un po' di esperienza con noialtri marginali. Ti eccita che mi buco, giusto? Ti eccita che un poveraccio si spara merda in vena. (Ballestra 1991a: 126)	You're totally self-centred, you are. A stupid cow that just wants to sample life with the drop-outs. Turns you on, doesn't it, me being a smack-head? Turns you on, some poor bastard shooting shit in his veins.

There are obvious features of tonal register that reinforce the initial insult ('Sei solo un'egoista'): 'stronzetta'; the belligerent 'ti eccita [. . .], giusto?'; 'poveraccio'; 'merda'. The social register is that of an aggressive and perhaps self-pitying young drop-out. The context shows that he is a specific kind of drop-out: he injects, and he uses druggie jargon ('mi buco'), together with phrases such as 'fare un po' di esperienza con noialtri marginali', typical of the stereotypical left-winger. With more of the context, it might even be possible to identify a specific left-wing social register. But there is enough here to see that part of the social register is contributed by the tonal register. Conversely, it may be that some of the features of tonal register are not actually deliberate reflections of the speaker's attitude, but are simply automatically entailed by his social persona; this could be the case with 'poveraccio' and 'merda', for example. In addition to this, it is notable that the text is not incoherent or illiterate; the social register is that of a junkie who has some education – 'marginale', for example, is typical sociological jargon. This is why, in the TT, we have 'sample life with the drop-outs' rather than 'see what life's like with the drop-outs', and 'doesn't' instead of 'don't'.

It is clear that the workings of register can be pretty complex even in a simple example like this one. Here, tonal and social register can to a great extent be distinguished from one another. In cases where it is impossible to disentangle them without lengthy analysis, it is acceptable for translation purposes simply to use 'register' as a cover-term.

SOCIOLECT

Whereas a social register belongs to a fairly narrowly stereotyped social persona, a sociolect is defined in terms of sociological notions of class. A **sociolect** is a language variety typical of one of the broad groupings that together constitute the 'class structure' of a society. Examples of major sociolects in the United Kingdom are those labelled as 'urban working class', 'white collar', 'public school', etc. These labels are noticeably vague. This is partly because British society does not have a rigid class structure, and partly because a 'class' label is often useless if not qualified by geographical reference. 'Public school' is relatively neutral to regional variation, but the further the speaker is from 'public school' on the scale, the more necessary it is to take class and regional factors together: compare 'urban working class', 'Leith urban working class', 'Bermondsey urban working class', etc. Mixed sociolectal/regional designations like these are often more helpful in recognizing language variants than purely sociological ones.

Sociolectal features can nevertheless convey important speaker-related information. If they are salient features of the ST, the translator cannot ignore them when deciding on a strategy. The first crucial factor to consider is what their function is in the ST. Thus, in translation of an eyewitness account of a crime for Interpol, sociolect (and register) would probably be subordinated to getting the facts clear. But if sociolect is not incidental, the translator may need to find a way of showing this in the TT. This is sometimes the case with journalistic texts, and often with literary texts. Even in such cases, however, a number of questions must be weighed in forming a strategy: What is the function of the ST sociolect(s)? What is the purpose of the TT? Would it not be safest to produce a TT in a bland 'educated middle-class' sociolect?

If the strategy is to incorporate some TL sociolectal features corresponding to those in the ST, the requirements are similar to those involved in choosing social register: it has to be decided what sociolects are the most appropriate, and there must be no inconsistencies in TT sociolect (assuming there are none in the ST sociolects). To return to the junkie example, 'doesn't' and third-person singular 'don't' belong to different sociolects; it might sound odd to mix '*sample life* with the drop-outs' and 'turns you on, *don't it*' – unless the context showed that the ST speaker also mixes sociolects.

DIALECT

The fourth type of speaker-related information that can be inferred from style concerns what part of the country speakers are from – where they grew up, or where they live. This inference is based on **dialect**, a language variety with features of accent, lexis, syntax and sentence-formation characteristic of a given region. In Italy, dialects are used much more commonly than in the United Kingdom. They are also so different from one another and from 'national Italian' that a speaker of one dialect may not be able to understand a speaker of another. National Italian itself is more fluid than standard British English, especially in respect of pronunciation. Very many literary texts include dialectal features that instantly identify the regional affiliations of the characters. For the Italian reader, this enriches the text with all manner of associations. The very fact of switching between dialect and national Italian may therefore convey important meanings. All these meanings are naturally lost on a foreign reader who is not thoroughly steeped in Italian culture. As far as translation is concerned, even if the translator spots such features and their significance, there is still the question of what to do about them. Apart from being able to identify dialect features in the first place, there are three main problems.

First, it has to be decided how important the dialect features in the ST are to its overall effect. Similar considerations apply as to sociolect. In purely informative texts, dialect is unlikely to be significant. But in journalism, and especially in literary texts, the ST dialect(s) may have important functions: one character may habitually be incomprehensible to another; or dialect may carry vital source-culture connotations; or it may give vital local colour to the ST.

Second, if dialect does have a function in the ST, an essential strategic decision is whether and why to use TL dialectal features. There are very obvious dangers in using TL dialect: How do you decide which – if any – TL dialects correspond to the ST ones? And will not a TL dialect sound ridiculous on the lips of Lombards or Sicilians? With luck, dropping ST dialectal features will not incur really damaging translation loss. If one is not so lucky, but prudence warns against using dialect in the TT, the important ST effects produced by dialect will probably have to be rendered through compensation. The most useful technique is to make occasional additions. The form these take will depend entirely on the context. Here, for discussion, is an example from Ugo Pirro's *Il luogo dei delitti*, with a draft translation. (*Contextual information.* The Mafia boss Don Ernesto is addressing the engineer Ficuzza, using typical Sicilianisms. These have a threatening irony in the context. Ficuzza has drawn up plans for a hotel complex in the Valley of the Temples near Agrigento, and has attempted to minimize the environmental impact by designing low buildings. Don Ernesto is not impressed. Ficuzza says nervously that they can always discuss possible changes.)

'Sì... vossia capì!' gli disse Don Ernesto e, indicando le costruzioni colorate che popolavano il plastico, aggiunse i suoi ordini, usando un tono persuasivo e insieme ultimativo.

'Come dissi a vossia fin dalla prima volta che ebbi l'onore e il piacere di incontrarla insieme alla sua gentilissima signora... e dietro raccomandazione del nostro caro amico e socio il dottor Pilato, gli alberghi bassi non mi piacquero mai... Forse che a New York sono bassi gli hotel?... No... E perché minghia vossia bassi li vuole ad Agrigento?

(Pirro 1991: 16)

'Yes Mr Ficuzza, quite right Mr Ficuzza', replied Don Ernesto in the ingratiating tone Sicilians sometimes adopt, and, pointing to the model teeming with coloured buildings, he issued his orders in a tone at once persuasive and menacing.

'As I told you the first time I had the honour and pleasure of meeting your good self and your gracious lady . . . on the recommendation of our good friend and partner Dr Pilato, low-rise hotels are not for me . . . They don't have them in New York now, do they? . . . No . . . So would you be good enough to tell me why the bloody hell you want to build them in Agrigento?'

If, as here, ST dialectal features are closely associated with other features of language variety, it is sometimes possible to use TL sociolect or register to compensate for the loss of connotations carried by the ST dialect(s). A final possibility is wholesale cultural transplantation. This is rare. It is generally only done with literary works, for box-office reasons. It often requires such extreme adaptation that it can barely be described as translation, however brilliant the TL text may be.

The third problem is one that applies to sociolect and register as well: once a decision is taken to use TL dialect, it must be accurate, and it must be consistent. Many literary TTs in particular are sabotaged by weaknesses in the translator's grasp of TL language variety. Among the many skills a translator has to have is that of pastiche.

CODE-SWITCHING

Many people are adept at switching between language varieties, and even between languages. This is known as **code-switching**. People may do this for social camouflage, to match their social persona to the particular situation they are in. Or they may do it for storytelling purposes, imitating the various characters in their story. Or it may be for persuasive purposes, sprinkling the text with expressions from different registers, sociolects or dialects – Don Ernesto does this in the passage we have just seen, and there are good examples in Practical 3.1. Any text containing characters with recognizably different styles of expression is by definition marked by code-switching. This is particularly common in literary texts. Since code-switching is a definite strategic device, translators have to be prepared to convey in the TT the effects it has in the ST. In doing this, of course, they are subject to the requirements and caveats that we have outlined in discussing register, sociolect and dialect.

PRACTICAL 10

10.1 Language variety

Assignment
  (i)   You are translating for publication in the United Kingdom the text from which the following ST is taken. Concentrating on language variety, discuss the strategic decisions that you have to take before starting detailed translation of this ST, and outline and justify the strategy you adopt.
 (ii)   Translate the text into English.
(iii)   Discuss the main decisions of detail you took; pay special attention to language variety, but do not overlook other major decisions.

Contextual information
The text is from a novella by Silvia Ballestra. Antò Lu Purk, from Pescara, in Central Italy, is a typical 1980s left-wing student. He has just found a

summer job on a building site. The foreman had challenged him to try building work, not thinking him tough enough for it. The ST mixes standard Italian, Pescara dialect, colloquial Italian and youth slang. Bettino Craxi, secretary of the Socialist Party, became Prime Minister in 1983. He fled Italy following accusations of bribery and corruption. Dialect forms not likely to be in the dictionary are: *cumpà*: compagno, amico; *jame*: andiamo; *mo'*: ora; *scì*: sì. The trickiest phrase is *'ssa su per in là*. Signora Ballestra has kindly supplied the following gloss:

> Si tratta di un ibrido tra invenzione e dialetto. Dovrebbe essere un ordine generico e confuso per indicare una direzione. ''Ssa' sta per 'là' (in dialetto 'esso-iesso-essa' significano 'là', più o meno). Dunque bisognerebbe trovare una forma contratta e musicale per rendere quest'idea di indicazione perentoria ma in realtà approssimativa verso un luogo imprecisato.

ST
Il venerdì mattina presto, senza aver chiuso occhio tutta notte per l'emozione della nuova impresa, si presentò al capomastro in tenuta da lavoro: capelli sciolti lunghi, pantaloni di velluto a coste fini e maglietta *Marijuana libera, Craxi in galera! Sarà questa, la nostra primavera!*

5   'Non ti vedo affatto in forma, ragazzo' lo apostrofò il capomastro, scrutando i lividi preoccupanti che gli cerchiavano gli occhi: 'Che ti succede, non hai dormito?'

'Tranquillo, cumpà. Sto caricato a mille' mentì Lu Purk. 'Non vedo l'ora di cominciare. Jame' disse. 'Passatemi il primo secchio 'ssa su per in là.'

10   Fece un gesto vago verso la sommità dell'impalcatura; uno dei muratori giovani lo vide dal tetto, lo salutò allegro con un cenno del braccio.

'Mo' arrivo, cumpà! Te vengo a da' 'na mano' fremette impaziente.

'Stai scherzando, figliolo?' disse il capomastro, con un filo d'inquietudine nella voce. 'Eravamo d'accordo che tu ti saresti occupato dei secchi.

15 Non è posto per te, lassù. È pericoloso' assentì gravemente. 'Sorveglierai la macchina impastatrice e darai una mano allo zoppo per i secchi, punto e basta.'

'Come volete voi, capo' disse Lu Purk, allargando le braccia. 'Non vi scaldate. Resterò di guardia alla fottuta macchina impastatrice dovesse

20 cascare il mondo.'

'Certo' assentì il capomastro. 'Se vuoi tirar su qualche soldo e non farmi rimpiangere d'averti dato ascolto, mi farai il santo piacere di obbedire agli ordini, d'accordo?'

'*Scì*' disse Antò Lu Purk. 'Non vorrei darvi grattacapi per niente al mondo'

25 aggiunse.

                                                     (Ballestra 1991b: 80–1)

10.2   Language variety

Assignment
  (i) You are translating for publication in the United Kingdom the novel
       from which the following ST is taken. Discuss the strategic decisions
       that you have to take before starting detailed translation of this ST,
       and outline and justify the strategy you adopt.
 (ii) Translate the text into English.
(iii) Discuss the main decisions of detail you took; pay special attention
       to language variety, but do not overlook other major decisions.

Contextual information
The text is from *La donna della domenica* (1971), set in modern Turin.
Commissario Santamaria is investigating a series of murders, helped by the
civilian Anna Carla, an educated lady who lives in the city. In this extract,
Anna Carla is waiting for friends she has arranged to meet.

ST
Anna Carla aspettava in mezzo alla piazza, accanto a un banco di libri e
giornali vecchi. Alzò gli occhi dal MANUALE PRATICO DI POLIZIA
GIUDIZIARIA del Cav. Luigi Valentini (*Attribuzioni degli ufficiali e agenti
di P.G. – Formulario dei rapporti e processi verbali. – Alcuni esempi di*
5 *segnalazioni dei reati più comuni e più gravi. – Terza edizione riveduta e
corretta. Roma, 1935–XIII*), che aveva appena comprato per duecento lire,
e si guardò intorno. Ma gli altri non si vedevano ancora da nessuna parte.
  'Il denunziante peraltro' – riprese a leggere affascinata – 'nessun sospetto
aveva e nessun indizio poté darci. Vestiti della nostra divisa ci portammo
10 quindi alla stazione ferroviaria, allo scopo di procedere alle indagini del
caso.
  'Avvicinato il guardasala G.M. (generalità complete) addetto al controllo
dei biglietti nella sala d'ingresso della stazione, questi ci disse di aver notato
la presenza di un individuo alto, vestito di chiaro con cappello marrone e
15 scarpe gialle, di colorito piuttosto pallido, con occhi scurissimi, baffetti
all'americana, che dai movimenti, dalle occhiate furtive che ad ogni momento
rivolgeva in qua e in là, aveva richiamato la sua attenzione. Disse inoltre
che nel forare il biglietto aveva visto che lo strano individuo era diretto a
Roma ed era partito col treno delle ore 13.45 che giunge a... alle ore...
20 Senza por tempo in mezzo, visto che alla detta ora mancavano ancora ore
1 e minuti 25, provvedemmo quindi...'
  S'interruppe di nuovo per guardare l'orologio, e vide che era già quasi
l'una e dieci. L'una e otto, esattamente. Sorrise pensando che adesso, forse,
avrebbe dovuto abituarsi a dire le tredici e zero otto. Calcolò anche, con
25 deliberata sfrontatezza, che al suo appuntamento del pomeriggio mancavano
ancora ore 3 e minuti 52. Ma era strano che qui, intanto, non si vedessero

né Massimo con Lello, né Sheila col Bonetto. Fortuna che aveva trovato una lettura dal suspense così avvincente.

(Fruttero and Lucentini 1971: 359–60)

11

Textual genre and translation issues

It has become clear from the first half of this course that different STs require different strategic priorities. In deciding which textual variables to prioritize, the translator has always to ask: what is the purpose of the ST, and what is the purpose of the TT? These questions imply two others: what kind of text is the ST, and what kind of text should the TT be? The texts we have used as examples and in practicals all illustrate the importance of these questions in deciding a strategy. At issue here is a fundamental consideration in translation: all texts are defined in terms of **genre**. By genre we mean what Hymes calls a 'type of communicative event' (quoted in Hervey 1992: 199) – that is, a category to which, in a given culture, a given text is seen to belong and within which the text is seen to share a type of communicative purpose with other texts. In this definition, the term also covers the traditionally identified genres of literature. The term **text-type** is often used in a similar sense to 'genre'. If there is a difference, it is at most one of nuance: there is perhaps a danger that 'type' has static connotations, which might lead students to overlook the element of *purpose* in the definable qualities of a text. We shall use 'genre', because the element of 'event' in its definition ensures that the definable qualities of a text are seen as dynamic, as together constituting an attempt to realize a communicative purpose.

Most texts belong to a genre or genres. Some innovative texts arguably do not, when they first appear: but even these are defined by contrast with genres to which they do *not* belong. Innovative texts aside, it can be said that any ST shares some of its properties with other texts of the same genre, and is perceived by an SL audience as being what it is on account of such genre-defining properties. Therefore, in order to assess the nature and purpose of the ST, the translator must have some sort of overview of genre-types in the source culture, and be familiar with the characteristics of relevant genres within those types.

What is true of SL texts is true of TL texts. Since the nature and the purpose of a given text imply one another, the translator has to be as familiar with target-culture genre-types and genres as with those of the source culture. Paying due attention to the nature and purpose of the TT guarantees a degree of TL bias which helps to prevent the excessive SL bias that so often defeats the purpose of the TT. In the 'Blackpool' texts on p. 24, for example, the purpose of the ST is to persuade the purchaser that she has bought wisely and should do so again. Presumably, the TT has the same purpose. But in fact, even where the TT is not unfaithful to literal meaning, it *is* unfaithful to the purpose of both ST and TT: in failing to prioritize TL connotative meanings and tonal registers in the pursuit of an appropriate commercial blarney, the translator has not produced a text in the TL genre of publicity leaflet, but what looks like a parody of English as spoken by foreigners – a very different genre. This poor grasp of appropriate TL genre features is inseparable from an equally poor grasp of TL textual variables. The 'Blackpool' text is an especially clear illustration of the fact that each implies the other.

Since translators need to consider these genre-related questions before translating a text, it is useful for them to have a framework of broad genre-types. This will help them to identify salient genre characteristics of the ST, and to check those of the TT they are producing. We are not going to attempt an exhaustive typology of genres; that would be too elaborate for our purposes. In determining the genre of a text, two essential factors need to considered. The first is the author's attitude to the treatment of the subject matter of the text. (We use 'author' to denote the originator of the text, whether it is oral or written.) The second is the question of whether the text is an oral one or a written one.

SUBJECT MATTER

Subject matter in itself is not a useful criterion for describing genres, because the same subject matter can figure in very different genres. What is at issue is the author's attitude, implicit or explicit, to treatment of the subject matter. On this basis, we shall distinguish five broad categories of genre.

The first category is that of literary genres. Literary genres have sub-divided and diversified very greatly over the centuries. There are innumerable sub-genres of poetry, fiction and drama, each with its characteristic style. However, all texts in this category have two essential features. First, they concern a world created autonomously in and through the texts themselves, and not controlled by the physical world outside. However close a literary text is to history or autobiography, it still approaches its subject matter by recreating experience in terms of a subjective, internal world, which is funda-mentally perceived as fictive, for all its similarities to the world outside the text. Second, whatever other characteristics they have, and whatever their subject matter, literary texts contain features of *expression*, on any level of textual variables, that emphasize, modify or actually create features of *content*. A simple example of this is the Tabucchi text in Practical 6.1.

The second category comprises religious genres. In terms of the author's attitude, the subject matter of religious texts implies the existence of a spiritual world that is not fictive, but has its own external realities and truths. The author is understood not to be free to create the world that animates the subject matter, but to be merely instrumental in exploring it. This category has perhaps diversified less than any of the others, but, certainly in the field of Christianity, it still has a wide range of styles, from Authorized Version to happy-clappy.

The third category comprises philosophical genres. These have as their subject matter a 'world' of ideas. Pure mathematics is the best example of the kind of subject matter that defines philosophical genres. Even in the field of metaphysics, the author is understood not to be free to develop theoretical structures at will, but to be constrained by some standard of rationality. Philosophical genres have not proliferated as much as literary ones, but they are strikingly diverse nonetheless.

The fourth category is that of empirical genres. Genres in this category deal with the real world as it is experienced by observers. An empirical text is more or less informative, and it is understood to take an objective view of observable phenomena. Scientific, technological and many scholarly texts fall into this category. It therefore goes on diversifying into new sub-genres as new scientific and academic disciplines are created.

Finally, there is the category of persuasive genres. The essence of these is that they aim at making listeners or readers behave in prescribed or suggested ways. This aim can be pursued through various means: we are classifying in a single category the entire gamut of texts from instruction manuals, through laws, rules and regulations to propaganda leaflets and advertisements. The very many sub-genres in this category have a common purpose, that of getting an audience to take a certain course of action, and perhaps explaining how to take it.

ORAL TEXTS AND WRITTEN TEXTS

Each of these five genre categories includes both oral and written texts. In truth, it is almost impossible not to distinguish an oral text as belonging to a discrete oral genre, and a written text as belonging to a discrete written genre, even where the texts share the same subject matter: the difference in medium generally entails a difference in attitude to treatment of the subject matter. Thus, a story told in a pub is in a different genre from a story printed in a magazine. A prayer on the Beatitudes, a talk on Gramsci, a tutorial explanation of quarks – each is in a different genre from any kind of written reflection on the topic. A complicating factor is that many oral genres also involve written texts: songs, plays, sermons, lectures, a salesman's patter – all may be performed on the basis of a written text that is either read out, or spoken from memory, or used as the basis for improvisation. To get an idea of the significance of these factors for translation, it is helpful first to look at some of the specific characteristics of oral texts as distinct from written ones.

An oral text is in essence a fleeting and unrepeatable event. This has important implications. First, vocal utterance is usually accompanied by visual cues, such as gestures or facial expressions, that are secondary to it but do form part of the overall text and can play a role in creating its meaning. Prosodic features that operate on the sentential and discourse levels (see e.g. pp. 56–7, 68, 78–9) are often reinforced by such visual cues. Second, on every level of textual variable, effective oral texts obey the 'rules' of a spoken language first and foremost. In particular, an effective oral text avoids information overload, elaborate cross-referencing, excessive speed, and so on, because these can make the text hard to follow. In all these respects, what is true for oral STs is true for oral TTs as well.

A third implication of orality is the appearance of spontaneity that generally characterizes oral texts. This goes not only for impromptu conversation or narrative, but also for prepared texts, such as memorized lines in a play. Even in a speech or a lecture where the speaker sticks closely to a script, the delivery may imitate that of an unscripted text. Similarly, dramatized reading, recited verse and song lyrics, if well performed, can all give the audience a chance to enter into the illusion of spontaneous vocal utterance. An oral text is, in fact, always quite different in nature and impact from even the most closely corresponding written version.

An awareness of these properties of oral texts is a necessary starting-point for translating an oral ST into an oral TT. Spoken communication has characteristics that are very much language-specific. Oral translation is not simply a matter of verbal transposition: the genre-related techniques of the target culture must be respected as well, including gestures, facial expressions, and so on. Translating a joke, for instance, will generally involve quite different genres from conference interpreting. Both, however, make it clear that an oral text in any genre is not only an utterance, but also a dramatic performance.

Another genre helps to highlight a second set of difficulties peculiar to oral translation. This is the genre of the song lyric. Assuming that the TT is to be sung to the same tune as the ST, there will be major translation problems on the phonic/graphic and prosodic levels as well as the grammatical level. We have seen that the phonic and prosodic properties of different languages are very different. This poses real problems in translating opera into English, as Michael Irwin points out:

A language prolific in short vowel-sounds, awkward consonantal clusters and sudden shifts of tempo does not lend itself easily to musical drama. No singer is likely to relish tackling a word such as 'strengths' or 'relapsed'. 'To be or not to be' could be splendidly singable; 'that is the question' would be taxing. Presumably Rodolfo was given the absurd phrase, 'your tiny hand is frozen', because the natural adjective, 'little', is a terrible throat-closer.

(Irwin 1996: 96–7)

Clearly, anyone translating a lyric or libretto needs to understand the prosodic features not only of the SL, but also of the TL. On the phonic level, the song-translator must pay attention to how vowels correspond with notes in the score: on certain musical notes, certain vowels are impossible to sing without distortion. Consonant clusters must also be attended to, not just so that the performer is not given a tongue-twister to sing, but also to avoid nonsense: in Ronald Millar's *Robert and Elizabeth*, for instance, 'while earth contains us two' can come out as 'while earth contains a stew' when sung. Given these factors, it is not surprising that translators of songs and libretti sometimes take considerable liberties with ST literal meaning.

Translators actually do a great deal of their work in a written medium, even when it involves an oral text or texts. Inevitably, metamorphoses result from the crossover from written to oral and vice versa. These metamorphoses are essentially due to the fact that writing is such a pale copy of speech in terms of expressive force. Crossover in the process of translation may take a number of forms. We shall mention four, and there will be an opportunity to try some of these out in the practical.

In the first type of crossover, the translator starts with an oral ST, and then uses a written transcript to compose a TT which is on paper, but suitable for oral performance. Song lyrics are typically translated in this way. In the second type of crossover, the translator starts with a *written* ST, considers how it might be performed orally, and then composes a TT which is on paper, but suitable for oral performance: this is generally how plays are translated. Third, the translator may start with a written script, try out the ST orally, and then produce a TT suitable either for silent reading or for oral performance, or for both. Poetry is usually translated like this – a good example is the second translation of the Scialoja poem on p. 60. In the fourth type, the translator starts with an oral ST and its transcript, and produces a TT for silent reading: this is how film subtitles are generally produced.

Subtitling is a very useful exercise in a course like this. As a form of gist translation, it has special requirements that force the student to focus especially sharply on many of the issues raised in this chapter and previous ones. And, while working in a written medium, under very tight constraints of time and space, the translator will often want to hint at some of the oral characteristics of the ST – principally features of language variety. This is especially true of feature films, where it might be misleading to suggest that the ST character 'talks like a book'.

Even without the equipment for subtitling film or videotape, it is possible to do a useful introductory exercise using an ordinary audiocassette. There will be a chance to do such an exercise in Practical 11. To help in preparation for it, here are some general notes on subtitling as practised by professionals, followed by a sample of the amateur version using an audiocassette.

NOTES ON SUBTITLING

The subtitler/translator usually has a transcript of all the verbal content of the film, known as a 'dialogue list'. The dialogue list does not include details of cuts. The subtitler runs the film on a viewing/editing table, measuring the time of each phrase, sentence and shot to determine when titles should start and stop. This process is called 'spotting'. The technicalities vary, depending on whether one is working with 35 mm film or videotape, but the essential rules are the same (throughout, subtitles are referred to as 'titles'):

- A single-line title requires at least two seconds' viewing time.
- A double-line title requires at least four seconds.
- Never show a title for less than two seconds or more than six seconds.
- Avoid carrying a title over a cut (except in newsreel with many cuts).
- Voices off, such as telephone voices or narrations, are in italics (unless the speaker is present but simply not in camera view).
- Observe the basic rules of punctuation but, where the end of a title coincides with the end of a sentence, omit the full stop.
- In two-line titles, try to make the second line shorter than the first, but do not be inflexible: the first line should read well and not end clumsily.
- Make every title a clear statement. Avoid ambiguity (unless the ST is significantly ambiguous): viewers have little time to take in the message, and cannot turn back as they can with a book or a newspaper.
- When a sentence is split over more than one title, end the first one with three suspension points, and begin the next one with three suspension points.
- Do not use telegraphese: viewers rarely have time to work it out.

When timings are short, it is sometimes helpful to have two speakers' dialogue as a double-line title (ideally for question and answer). In such cases, use a dash to introduce each line, and range left, so that the titles are not centred on the screen. For example:

– Where have they gone today?
– To the country

Here is an example of how to split a whole sentence over two or more titles. The text itself conveys the point we are making: 'In such cases, it is especially important to make each title sensible in itself, unless the speaker is rambling, delirious, or similar, so that viewers maintain a steady understanding of the dialogue.' This would be effectively subtitled as follows:

Title 1   In such cases...
Title 2   ...it is especially important to make
             each title sensible in itself...
Title 3   ...unless the speaker is rambling,
             delirious, or similar, so that...
Title 4   ...viewers maintain a steady
             understanding of the dialogue

Here is an example of how *not* to do it:

Title 1   In such cases, it is especially...
Title 2   ...important to make each title sensible...
Title 3   ...in itself, unless the speaker is rambling,
             delirious, or similar, so that...
Title 4   ...viewers maintain a steady
             understanding of the dialogue

The main weakness of this version is that breaks between titles correspond to neither the structure nor the oral phrasing of the sentence. Despite the suspension points, Title 2 looks like the end of the sentence or clause, and Title 3 like the start of one. The result is that the 'unless' clause looks like a clause parenthetically inserted in mid-sentence: the text might seem to be saying 'In itself, unless the speaker is rambling in such a way that viewers maintain a steady understanding [. . .]'. But the anticipated resolution of this apparent sentence does not materialize, so that the viewer is (at best) momentarily puzzled.

Note that the maximum number of spaces allowed for a line varies, depending on the equipment used. We shall take as an example 36, which is not untypical. This includes letters, spaces between words, and punctuation marks. So, for instance, the following title is exactly 36 spaces long:

...so that viewers maintain a steady

Sample subtitling exercise

Dialogue list
(*Contextual information*. The dialogue is part of an interview with Riccardo Pradella, director of the Teatro dei Filodrammatici, Milan. 'I' denotes the interviewer, 'P' denotes signor Pradella.)

I. Ecco, oggi mi sembra che in Italia c'è un fiorire di nuovi interessi per il teatro, specialmente tra i giovani. Voi avete programmi speciali, delle... direi quasi dei prezzi speciali per i giovani?
P. Sì. Devo dire che la... l'incremento importante, considerevole, che c'è stato
5   riguardo al pubblico teatrale che c'è stato sicuramente in questo... questi sette anni e non solo per il 'Filodrammatici' ma anche per le altre iniziative, è dovuto anche al fatto che un grosso interesse l'hanno portato gli studenti.
I. Ecco, come vi siete avvicinati agli studenti, che direi, forse inizialmente
10 avranno guardato con sospetto al teatro 'dalle poltrone rosse di velluto'?
(Adapted from Pradella 1982: 5)

Spotting
Following the taped text on the dialogue list, mark off convenient sections coinciding, if possible, with pauses and intonational cues in the spoken delivery. Each of these sections will subsequently form the basis of a subtitle. (The more spontaneous the speech, however, the more likely it is that the pauses will sometimes clash with those implied by grammar. This happens here, especially in signor Pradella's reply. As we shall see, this may entail redistributing the message between the sections created by spotting.) At the end of spotting, the dialogue list will look something like this:

I. Ecco, oggi mi sembra che in Italia / c'è un fiorire di nuovi interessi per il teatro, / specialmente tra i giovani. / Voi avete programmi speciali, delle... / direi quasi dei prezzi speciali per i giovani? /
P. Sì. Devo dire che la... l'incremento / importante, considerevole, che c'è
5   stato / riguardo al pubblico teatrale che c'è stato sicuramente in questo... questi sette anni / e non solo per il 'Filodrammatici' ma anche per le altre iniziative, / è dovuto anche al fatto che un grosso interesse l'hanno portato gli studenti. /
I. Ecco, come vi siete avvicinati agli studenti, / che direi, forse inizialmente
10 avranno guardato con sospetto / al teatro 'dalle poltrone rosse di velluto'? /

Timing
The sections marked off in spotting are numbered, and the time between the start of one section and the start of the next is measured (with a stop-watch if possible, but the second hand on a watch will do for our purposes).

The timing of the subtitles is based on these measurements. (*Remember that any pauses in and between sentences are part of the overall time the text lasts.* These are useful allies for the subtitler, because they give extra time for the viewer to digest the titles.) The timed list should look like this:

Title 1	4.0 sec	Ecco . . . Italia
Title 2	4.5	c'è . . . teatro,
Title 3	2.5	specialmente . . . giovani.
Title 4	7.0	Voi . . . delle...
Title 5	5.0	direi . . . giovani?
Title 6	5.0	Sì . . . incremento
Title 7	4.0	importante . . . stato
Title 8	6.0	riguardo . . . anni
Title 9	4.0	e non solo . . . iniziative,
Title 10	6.0	è dovuto . . . studenti.
Title 11	4.5	Ecco, come . . . studenti,
Title 12	4.5	che direi . . . sospetto
Title 13	4.0	al . . . velluto'?

Creating subtitles

Each of the spottings into which the dialogue list has been divided is translated into English, observing the following constraints:

(i) Not more than two lines can be shown on the screen at once.
(ii) Lines cannot be longer than 36 spaces.
(iii) The maximum time available for displaying each subtitle is given by the timing measurements above; allow *at least two seconds for a single-line title*, and *at least four seconds for a two-line title* (but not more than six seconds for any title).

Here is a possible TT (the times given in brackets are moments during which no title is shown):

Title 1	4.0 sec	I get the impression that in Italy today...
Title 2	4.5	...there's been a great upsurge in interest in the theatre...
Title 3	2.5	...especially among young people
Title 4	(3 +) 4.0	Do you put on special programmes...
Title 5	5.0	...with special cut-price tickets for young people?
Title 6	(2 +) 3.0	Yes. There has certainly been...
Title 7	4.0	...a great increase in attendances over the last few years, not just...
Title 8	4.5 (+ 1.5)	...here at the Filodrammatici, but in theatres everywhere

Title 9	4.0	I should point out, though, that a major factor in this has been...
Title 10	6.0	...the great interest shown by school and university students
Title 11	4.5	How did you approach the student public?
Title 12	(2.5 +) 2.0	I would have thought...
Title 13	4.0	...they'd regard 'posh' theatre with a certain suspicion!

There are two reasons for having the brief periods with no title on screen. First, the speakers sometimes speak very slowly. Second, more problematically, signor Pradella's reply (titles 6–10) is relatively complex. The two 'che c'è stato' clauses and the parenthetic 'e non solo [. . .] iniziative' greatly delay the arrival of 'è dovuto' and obscure the function of 'anche'. In addition, the second 'che c'è stato' is an untidy insertion, one of those sudden afterthoughts so common in spontaneous oral texts. Of course, reading the printed transcript, one can spend time over it and make sense of it. And watching the interview, a speaker of Italian will be able to filter out the grammatical fractures and follow what is being said, especially with the help of facial and gestural cues. The subtitle viewer, however, is unlikely to pick these up, and cannot go back and puzzle the text out. This, together with the severe constraints on time and space, is why the text has been recast, avoiding the relative clauses and the parenthesis, and inserting an explicit cohesion marker, 'though', in title 9. The 1.5-second gap after title 8 reinforces this cohesion, announcing a new stage in the argument.

For comparison, here is a version of Signor Pradella's reply which matches the ST structure more closely. The risk of confusion for the viewer is clearly much greater:

Title 6	5.0	Yes. I ought to say that the very considerable increase...
Title 7	4.0	...that has occurred...
Title 8	6.0	...in theatre attendance, that has occurred in these seven years...
Title 9	4.0	...and not only at our theatre but at others too...
Title 10	6.0	...is also due to the huge interest that students have shown

Consideration of the two factors we mentioned at the outset – the author's attitude to treatment of the subject matter, and whether the text is an oral or a written one – concentrates the translator's mind on four groups of vital strategic questions. First, what are the salient features of the ST? What do these features imply about its purpose? What genre do the features and purpose suggest it belongs to? Second, does the ST have recognizable genre-specific characteristics that require special attention? If so, which of them should be retained in translation? Third, what TL genre(s) provide a match for the ST genre? What do existing specimens of these TL genres suggest regarding formulation of the TT? Fourth, what genre should the TT ultimately belong to, and what genre-specific features should it have?

Two words of caution are needed here. First, it is easy for student translators to begin their strategic considerations something like this: 'This text belongs to genre A, therefore it has characteristics x, y and z.' This is putting the cart before the horse. It is much more useful to identify the text's characteristics first, and then, on that basis, to assign it to a genre. This results in a more sensitive appraisal of the true purpose of the text, which in turn makes it easier to be flexible and to recognize cases where, as very often happens, the ST actually has a blend of features – it may be predominantly typical of one genre, but also have features from other genres or even other genre categories. So, for example, instruction manuals may vary in character between the empirical and the persuasive categories. Advertising commonly shares features with literary texts, as do religious and philosophical texts. The same is even true of some empirical texts, such as Goethe's scientific treatises in verse. Religious texts, such as sermons, often share features with persuasive texts. Many legal or administrative texts – contracts or memoranda of agreement, for instance – combine empirical and persuasive genre-features. Texts often contain quotations from texts that belong to other genres – for example, the biblical extract in the empirical text on Chernobyl in Practical 2.1.

Such 'hybridization' in genre is common in journalism, and in parody and satire, which can make wholesale use of a mixture of features from various genre categories – the ST in Practical 10.2 is an example. Such blends may theoretically constitute sub-genres and subdivisions of sub-genres, but that is not our concern: our aim here is to encourage and enable students to isolate the salient features and the purpose of an ST, so that they can relate these to the purpose of the TT and thus be in a position to develop an appropriate translation strategy.

The second word of caution is that it is essential for translators to be familiar with the characteristic features of the TL genre or genres that they decide correspond most closely to the ST genre(s). If in doubt, sample texts from the chosen TL genre should be carefully examined before the translation is started. Professional translators tend to specialize in particular fields, and one of the first things they do is acquire an awareness of relevant TL genre characteristics. Before embarking on any of the exercises in Practical 11, the student should where necessary do some of this preliminary TL genre-sampling.

PRACTICAL 11

11.1 Genre and translation

Assignment
(i)   You are translating the following ST for publication in a British broad-
      sheet newspaper in a regular digest of the Italian football scene.
      Discuss the strategic decisions that you have to take before starting
      detailed translation of this ST, and outline and justify the strategy you
      adopt.
(ii) Translate the text into English.
(iii) Explain the main decisions of detail you took.

Contextual information
The ST was published in 1997, the day after Lecce's shock win over AC
Milan. The game is actually reported elsewhere in the paper; this article is
more a reflection on its implications. Lecce had lost all their games prior
to this one. Milan had been supreme in Italian football for several years,
but had got off to a poor start in 1997–8, and there was already talk of a
crisis at the club. Kluivert, Savicevic, Taibi, Boban and Ba were playing
for Milan, Casale for Lecce. Fabio Capello was Milan's manager. Signor
De Santis was the referee; he sent Savicevic off after six minutes; he allowed
five extra minutes for the first half, and in that time awarded Lecce two
penalties, one of them conceded by Taibi, the other by Boban. It may be
relevant that the Milan logo is a devil.

ST
       CAPELLO, MA TU CHE FAI PER UN POVERO DIAVOLO?

Il Milan non c'è. In questo vuoto pneumatico, il caso infierisce. Così monta
il piagnisteo. Per rimanere a ieri: un rigore non rilevato su Kluivert e ben
due concessi al Lecce in 90", nei minuti di recupero del primo tempo; solo
2' di prolungamento alla fine, 84' in 10 contro 11.
5   Sull'assenza di una squadra, il signor De Santis non sembra avere responsabilità: Savicevic ha dato un calcio da tergo a Casale, con la palla lontana;
il rigore provocato da Taibi è netto; sul fallo di Boban è stato certo fiscale,
ma quello subito da Kluivert sembra molto più dubbio, quasi inesistente; le
recriminazioni sul recupero finale sono ridicole. Più in generale: è avvilente
10 che una società come il Milan insegua appigli per spiegare la sua disastrosa
posizione in classifica.
       I cinque punti in sei partite sono il (misero) frutto di una campagna
acquisti discutibile; della difficoltà di inserimento dei nuovi; dell'insuffi-
ciente   rendimento   di   qualche   vecchio;   di   una   condizione   fisica
15 incredibilmente deficitaria.

Ma c'è anche qualcos'altro, più profondo e più preoccupante. Forse i problemi del Milan derivano dalle incertezze di colui che invece aveva sempre dimostrato di saper adattare il proprio gioco ai giocatori a disposizione, e vice-versa. Non è che il caos di cui fa mostra la squadra in campo
20 rispecchi la confusione di Fabio Capello?

Questo Milan nasce per il 5-3-2 (o 3-5-2, se si vuole) con Ba e Ziege sulle fasce e tre difensori centrali. Dura una partita di precampionato, a Monza. Diventa prima un 4-4-2. Poi, con l'arrivo di Leonardo, un 4-3-1-2. Ieri, perfino un 3-4-3. Quattro moduli in due mesi non hanno senso.
25 Soprattutto quando sembrano suggeriti solo dall'angoscia di fare risultato. Non era questo il Capello che conoscevamo.

(Vaccari 1997: 1)

11.2   Genre and translation

Note. The song is easily obtainable on CD, e.g. on *L'album di Successi degli anni '60* (R.C.A. 74321-30807-2 (2)).

Assignment
  (i)   The singer Gino Paoli is planning a farewell tour of Britain, and wants to sing the following song in English. You are to produce a singable TT. Listen first to the song, without following the printed text. *Treating it as an oral text*, discuss its genre, content and impact.
  (ii) Examine the words of the song, and discuss its salient features *as a written text*.
  (iii) Listen to the song again, following it on the text, and discuss the relation between the words and the music.
  (iv) Discuss the strategic decisions that you have to take before starting detailed translation of this ST, and outline and justify the strategy you adopt.
  (v)   Produce a translation of the text that can be sung to Paoli's music, in his style and by him.
  (vi) Explain the main decisions of detail you took.

Contextual information
Gino Paoli (b. 1934) is perhaps Italy's best-known singer-songwriter. This song, 'Sapore di sale', was one of the 1960s' biggest hits, and is still frequently heard today.

ST

                    Sapore di sale, sapore di mare
                    che hai sulla pelle, che hai sulle labbra
                    quando esci dall'acqua e ti vieni a sdraiare
        4   vicino a me, vicino a me.

Sapore di sale, sapore di mare
un gusto un po' amaro di cose perdute
di cose lasciate lontano da noi
8   dove il mondo è diverso, diverso da qui.
Qui il tempo è dei giorni che passano pigri
e lasciano in bocca il gusto del sale.
Ti butti nell'acqua e mi lasci a guardarti
12   e rimango da solo nella sabbia e nel sole.
Poi torni vicino e ti lasci cadere
così nella sabbia e nelle mie braccia
e mentre ti bacio sapore di sale
16   sapore di mare, sapore di te.
(Adapted from Paoli 1981: 20)

11.3 Genre and translation

Note. The audio cassette containing this ST is obtainable from Drake Educational Associates, St Fagan's Road, Fairwater, Cardiff, CF5 3AE, UK, tel. 01222–560333. It is the first in a set: N. Messora and L. Quartermaine, *Italia, anni '80. Corso di lingua e cultura*, Exeter Tapes, 1982, and it can be bought separately. The ST is taken from Unità N. 1 of the course.

Assignment
  (i)   You are producing subtitles for a television documentary featuring the interview from which the following ST is taken. Listen to the recording of the ST. Listen to it again, following it in the printed transcript (the dialogue list). Discuss the strategic decisions that you have to take before starting detailed translation of this ST into subtitles, and outline and justify the strategy you adopt.
  (ii) Use a stopwatch or wristwatch to convert the dialogue list into spottings. (Remember that pauses are part of the overall time that the text lasts. And remember that a title should not be carried over a cut.)
 (iii) Translate the text into subtitles, observing a maximum of 36 spaces for each line. Lay your TT out as shown on pp. 122–3. Remember to indicate any gaps during which no title shows.
 (iv) Explain the main decisions of detail you took.

Contextual information
The text is the continuation of the interview from which the specimen text on p. 121 is taken. Signor Pradella is replying to the interviewer's second question.

ST

Ma, prima di tutto cercando di avvicinarsi ai loro ambienti, quindi al loro mondo, che è la scuola, interessando gli insegnanti più attenti, invitando i capigruppo a visionare gli spettacoli – tutte le volte che noi facciamo uno spettacolo lo discutiamo con loro – e soprattutto facendo una politica di
5   prezzi all'altezza delle finanze e delle tasche degli studenti. Siamo passati dalle cinquecento lire dei primi anni, alle mille lire per gruppi di questi anni; toccheremo quest'anno forse le millecinquecento lire. E praticando ad esempio degli abbonamenti specialissimi ai cinque spettacoli che noi offriamo tutti gli anni, proprio per le università, per i licei, per gli studenti
10 in genere. Per acquistare questo abbonamento *è sufficiente che lo studente o si presenti in certi casi con la sua età, che non ha bisogno di tessera o, nel caso di universitari, **presentando il libretto universitario e acquistando questo... questo abbonamento speciale.

(Adapted from Pradella 1982: 5)

* cut to interviewer
** cut to signor Pradella

12

Scientific and technical translation

All texts can be categorized in terms of genre. There is no a priori reason for giving special attention to any one genre rather than any other. However, since most language students are not trained in science or technology, they are often in awe of 'technical' texts. Yet many professionals earn their living translating such texts. This is why we are devoting a whole chapter to the main translation issues they raise.

The 'technical' is not confined to science and technology, of course. It is simply to avoid repeating 'scientific and technological' that we shall be using the term 'technical texts' to denote texts written in the context of scientific or technological disciplines. In fact, of course, *any* specialist field has its own technical terms and its own genre-marking characteristics: a look at a hobbies magazine, or a review of the rock scene, or the business pages in the paper, quickly confirms this. Texts in these and any other specialized field are properly speaking 'technical' texts. Nevertheless, the fact that scientific and technological texts are so very unfamiliar for many language students makes them clear illustrations of two important points in the translation of all specialist texts. First, the translator must be just as familiar with technical terms and genre-marking features in the TL as in the SL. Second, the problems met in translating specialist texts are mostly no different from those met in translating in any other genre, specialized or not. A textual variable is a textual variable, a hyponym is a hyponym, whatever the genre and whatever the subject matter; and the relative merits of literal and free translation need to be considered in translating any text.

Taking 'technical' in the narrow definition we have given it, we can say that most technical texts are relatively inaccessible to the non-specialist reader. There are three main reasons for this inaccessibility. One is lexical, the others are conceptual. In illustrating them, we shall refer to the following text:

Un'altra importante applicazione del Bilobalide riguarda l'azione sul Pneumocystis carinii, microorganismo di incerta localizzazione tassonomica (protozoo per i più, fungo per alcuni) ma di certa responsabilità nel sostenere polmoniti mortali negli immunodepressi e quindi di particolare attualità. La 5 coltura di questo parassita, di recente introduzione, si presta allo studio di nuovi farmaci e per il confronto con quelli esistenti. Il Bilobalide in questi esperimenti è stato confrontato con il Cotrimossazolo verso il quale presenta vantaggi utili ai fini terapeutici. *In vitro* a concentrazioni superiori a 12 μg/ml (concentrazione attiva) il Bilobalide esplica un'azione pari a quella 10 della sostanza di riferimento, mentre a dosi superiori esplica un'attività decisamente superiore, indicando che la curva dose-effetto non è parallela a quella del Cotrimossazolo ma superiore. *In vivo* la dose massima tollerata del Bilobalide è di 100 mg/Kg per 5 giorni per via i.p. La dose di 10 mg/Kg è ben tollerata ed induce nell'animale da esperimento una sensibile dimin-15 uzione della malattia.

Il Bilobalide è stato così testato:

Saggio su Schizomiceti – Soluzioni del composto a varie diluizioni sono state aggiunte in parti uguali a terreno Mueller-Hinton agartizzato mantenuto fuso a 56°C, versato poi in piastre Petri. Dopo solidificazione le piastre 20 sono state seminate in superficie con sospensioni di Schizomiceti di recente isolamento da materiale patologico ed incubate a 37°C in atmosfera di CO_2 per 18 ore.

(Test-piece set by work-provider for new translators)

There are three sorts of lexical problem arising from the specialized use of technical terms. First, there is the obvious problem of terms not used in everyday, ordinary language, and which are therefore totally unfamiliar to the lay translator. The text given above contains a simple example of this problem in 'Schizomiceti' (l. 17). Fortunately, the translator would be able to find the term 'Schistomycetes' in a medical dictionary. Another typical feature in some scientific fields (e.g. medicine, natural history) is the frequent use of Latin names, such as 'Pneumocystis carinii' (l. 2), and Latin phrases such as '*in vitro*' (l. 8) and '*in vivo*' (l. 12). Such terms are usually left in Latin in the TT, and do not cause a translation problem. Even here, though, Latin nomenclature is sometimes revised in botany and zoology, so it is always advisable to check whether the ST term is the one current among TL specialists. If in doubt, it is safest to add the alternative term in brackets after the ST one.

The second problem is that of terms whose everyday uses are familiar to the translator, but which look as if they are being used in some techni-cally specialized way in the ST. An example in the above text is 'localizzazione' in the collocation with 'incerta' and 'tassonomica' (l. 2). The everyday meanings of this term are not self-evidently inappropriate. The collocation itself may give the translator a clue as to the correct interpretation of the term in this pharmacological context – something like 'of uncertain taxonomic affiliation/classification'. But only a specialist will be able to confirm whether 'localizzazione' is indeed a technical term here, or whether it is simply an example of nominalization. In the former case, the appropriate TL specialist noun will do; in the the second, a relative clause would be acceptable – 'which is difficult to place taxonomically'.

Third, a term may have an everyday sense that is not obviously wrong in the context. This is the most dangerous sort of case, because the translator can easily fail to recognize the term as a technical one, and mistakenly render it in its ordinary sense. For example, only a specialist will think of translating 'versato' (l. 19) in this context as 'plated', and not 'poured'. Another example is 'piastre' (l. 19). If the translator has done some science at school, the term 'petri *dish*' may come to mind; but even then, it is impossible to know, without specialist confirmation, that there is not something called a 'petri slab'. Likewise, specialist knowledge is needed for 'seminate in superficie' (l. 20) to be rendered as 'inoculated', instead of 'sown'. 'Sensibile' (l. 14) is a similar example. It looks straightforward enough: 'considerable' or 'marked'. In this field, however, the specialist term is 'detectable'. In some of these cases, there may well be little empirical difference between the different TL versions – to *plate* a petri dish with liquid material, you perhaps have to *pour* the liquid in anyway; but the specialist reader would immediately identify the TT as the work of a non-specialist, and therefore as potentially unreliable.

As these examples show, access to up-to-date specialist dictionaries and data banks is essential for technical translators. Of course, even the most recent materials will by definition be slightly out of date, because scientific and technological fields are constantly developing. In any case, even the best reference material does not always give a single, unambiguous synonym for a particular technical term. This means that the normal caveats concerning use of dictionaries also apply to technical translation. That is, translators can only select the appropriate TL term if they have a firm grasp of both the textual context and the wider technical context. The problem is not lessened, of course, by the fact that some of the context may remain obscure until the correct sense of the ST terms has been defined! This brings us to the two conceptual reasons why technical texts may be difficult to translate.

The first type of conceptual problem in technical translation arises from ignorance of underlying knowledge taken for granted by experts, but not understood by non-specialists and not explicit in the ST. The last paragraph of the Bilobalide text contains some good examples of this. Only an expert will know that 'saggio su' in this context (l. 17) is not a 'test on', but an 'assay against'. The phrase 'terreno Mueller-Hinton agartizzato' (l. 18) is impenetrable to the lay person. Even if intelligent guesswork suggested that it meant something like 'agarized Mueller-Hinton growing medium', the tyro translator would have no idea whether this was the correct TL rendering.

The correct translation, 'Mueller-Hinton flasks containing agar', requires specialist knowledge of what sort of experiments are needed in this field, and how they are carried out. Similarly, 'in parti uguali' (l. 18) should be translated here as 'in equal volumes', not 'equal parts' (which could refer to volume or weight) – but the non-specialist has no way of knowing this. Another example of the importance of first-hand knowledge of the subject can be seen in an expert's rendering of 'animale d'esperimento' (l. 14) as 'experimental animal' (versus 'laboratory animal'). As we have already suggested, it is important to use the exact terms required by the TL genre, so that the TT does not seem potentially unreliable to the specialist reader.

The conceptual unfamiliarity of technical texts makes it easy to misconstrue the syntax. A single such mistake can make the TT factually nonsensical. There is a simple example in the Bilobalide text. In 'la coltura di questo parassita, di recente introduzione' (ll. 4–5), the uninitiated translator may not be sure whether it is the 'coltura' or the 'parassita' that is recent.

The second conceptual problem concerns what might be called the 'logic' of a discipline – methods of argumentation, the development of relations between concepts. There may be problems that hinge specifically on that logic. The need for reformulation in the last paragraph of the Bilobalide text is a good example. This type of problem is the most intractable of all in technical translation. Non-specialists are always likely to reach a conceptual impasse from which no amount of attention to syntax or vocabulary can rescue them. In that case they have only two options: learn the concepts of the field in which they wish to translate, or work in close consultation with experts. In practice, trainee technical translators generally do both, quickly becoming experts themselves with the help of specialist supervisors. However, not even expert translators can expect to keep abreast of all the latest research while at the same time doing translation, and they will sooner or later come up against problems that can only be solved by consulting other experts or, where possible, the author of the ST.

These remarks about the need for consultation are not to be taken lightly. They raise the important question of the responsibility – and perhaps the legal liability – of the translator. There is a difference here between literary translation and technical translation. It is not that literary translators are not held responsible for their work, but the implications of mistranslation are generally less serious for them than for technical translators, where one mistake could cause financial damage or loss of life and limb. This is another respect in which technical translation is exemplary, bringing out extremely clearly a golden rule which is in fact essential to all translation: *never be too proud or embarrassed to ask for help or advice.*

The spectre of legal liability is a reminder that even the minutest error of detail on any level of textual variables is typically magnified in a technical text. It is all too easy in translation to confuse similar words. Take the Calvino texts in Practical 4.1: 'sotto la pelle' (l. 6) is translated as 'over his skin'. This is wrong, and spoils the image, but it does not make nonsense of the text. Now look at 'sospensioni' in the Bilobalide text (l. 20): translating this as 'solutions' instead of 'suspensions' is wrong, and nonsensical – yet even professionals have been known to make this mistake. An even bigger danger is that of confusing closely similar technical names in chemistry. Consider how similar are some of the prefixes and suffixes that can be attached to the root 'sulph', and how many possible permutations of them there are:

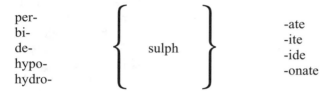

per-
bi-
de-   sulph   -ate
hypo-   -ite
hydro-   -ide
                                -onate

The slightest error in affixation here will be a major factual error, whereas, in non-technical language, affixation may sometimes be a matter of style. For example, in Italian, there is a subtle distinction between 'continuo', 'continuato' and 'continuativo' – compare 'un rumore continuo', 'orario continuato' and 'in via continuativa'. Depending on context, the translator often has a choice between 'continu*ous*' and 'continu*al*'. Similarly, there is generally little difference in practice between '*dis*believing' and '*un*believing', or between '*in*excusable' and '*un*excusable'. In literary texts, the choice between affixes can often depend on context or questions of euphony or style. But with technical terms in specialist texts of any kind, the temptation to be guided by such considerations must be resisted absolutely.

Another temptation students often succumb to is that of 'improving on' the ST. This is risky in any genre, but disastrous in technical translation. A translation of 'misure' as 'quantification' instead of 'measurements', or of 'composizione' as 'structure' instead of 'composition', may or may not sound 'better' or 'more technical', but that is *irrelevant*. Similarly, in a text on nuclear radiation, 'un equivalente di dose efficace' is 'an effective dose equivalent', whether you like it or not – too bad if you think it would sound more elegant or make more sense to say 'an effectively equivalent dose' or 'an equivalent effective dose'!

Some parts of technical texts may be formulated in mathematical symbols. These need minimal effort in translation, although they cannot always be literally transcribed. Careful attention must be paid to any differences between SL and TL convention. For example, where English has a decimal point in figures, Italian has a comma.

The technical translator's paramount concerns, then, are accuracy and conformity with the requirements of genre. In so far as the requirements of genre imply style, register is also important: the wrong tonal register may alienate the reader and undermine confidence in the TT; the wrong social register may misrepresent a social persona that the ST author has been at pains to project.

The relation between accuracy and style is not always straightforward, however. If an ST is badly written or ungrammatical, should this be reflected in the TT? The question applies to all translation, of course. In our view, translators are not in principle responsible for 'improving' defective STs. However, this is sometimes necessary with purely informative texts, because the crucial thing is factual accuracy. If there is any potentially misleading or dangerous ambiguity or obscurity in the ST, there is every reason to keep it out of the TT – if necessary after consultation with the author or an expert. In the Bilobalide text, there are two terms which, although not ambiguous in context, are not ones normally expected in this subject area in this genre: instead of 'localizzazione' (l. 2), 'classificazione' is more usual; and instead of 'malattia' (l. 15), the expected term is 'infezione'. In some genres (in literary texts for instance), these slight departures from usage might have significant implications; but this is not the case here, and the translator is well advised to use terms expected in the TL genre. Thus, even if 'di incerta localizzazione tassonomica' means nothing more complicated than 'hard to place taxonomically', it is safer to translate it as 'of uncertain taxonomy/taxonomic classification', in order not to undermine the reader's faith in the authority of the TT as a whole.

Before embarking on the Practical, it will be useful to note some of the characteristics of technical texts in English. First, the language is usually informative, and often includes expressions denoting purpose or role, and explanations of method or process. Second, in accounts of experiments or research programmes, the passive is used extensively, which keeps the style impersonal. This is also true of Italian technical texts – see, for instance, the Bilobalide text, ll. 7 and 16. The logic and development of technical texts is crucial, and formulations of cause and effect are normal, including connectors such as 'consequently', 'hence' and 'thus', verbs such as 'cause', 'determine' and 'result in', and the use of 'by + -ing' to signal method. (Note, however, that such connectors are usually less prominent in *abstracts* of reports: to keep things brief, abstracts tend to list the main areas of investigation and the main conclusions, without linking them explicitly.)

Italian texts tend to use a variety of formulations to express a single concept; for instance, 'rappresentare', 'assicurare', 'costituire' and 'presentare' often simply correspond to the verb 'to be'. They are sometimes repetitive and over-precise by English standards; as a rule, technical translation into English prioritizes economy of language, precision and clarity.

Another typical feature of technical texts is the frequent use of compound nouns (e.g. 'web site design', 'fine-coal dewatering centrifuge') and indeed of nominalization in general. Nominalization as such is discussed in Chapter 16; we shall just note here its prevalence in technical texts. The Bilobalide text contains good Italian examples of nominalization and some of its effects. Here, for discussion, are ll. 4–6 and a plausible English TT:

La coltura di questo parassita, di recente introduzione, si presta allo studio di nuovi farmaci e per il confronto con quelli esistenti.	Recently introduced methods for the culture of this parasite are useful in the study of new medicines and in their comparison with existing ones.

The nominalized compactness and impersonality of this TT match those of the ST, and meet TL genre requirements. It must be remembered, however, that even non-technical Italian makes much more use of nominalization than non-technical English does. So, in translating technical texts, it should not be assumed that all ST nominal structures have to be rendered with TL nominal structures. The sentence we have just looked at contains an example: even the technical TT renders 'di recente introduzione' as 'recently intro-duced', not as 'of recent introduction'. There are other examples in the Bilobalide text. In context, it makes more sense to translate 'Dopo solidifi-cazione' (l. 19) as 'When the agar has solidified' than as 'After solidification', which could be ambiguous. And 'di recente isolamento' (ll. 20–1) is more idiomatically rendered as 'recently isolated' than as 'of recent isolation'.

The examples we have been looking at illustrate the features of scien-tific and technological language that Pinchuk neatly categorizes as follows:

1. [Technical language] is specialized and tends to become more and more specialized in contrast to the versatility of ordinary language. [Everyday] language tends towards liveliness and multiplicity of meaning, but the controlled language of science is manipulated in the direction of insipidity and colourlessness.
2. It seeks the most economic use of linguistic means to achieve stan-dardization of terms and usage.
3. It seeks to avoid ordinary language associations and endeavours to define terms accurately.

(Pinchuk 1977: 165)

As Pinchuk points out (246–51), before embarking on a translation it is important to ascertain whether the work has already been translated. He provides a list of organizations which have registers of available transla-tions, including Aslib (The Association of Special Libraries and Information Bureaux). And of course technical translation, like translation in any genre, requires familiarity with SL and TL material of a similar type, to serve as a source of information and as a stylistic model. Translators may well need some time to find the information (e.g. concepts or lexis) they are seeking. Useful sources of information include monographs, abstracting and indexing journals, periodicals, yearbooks, textbooks, encyclopedias, standards and trade literature, theses and dissertations. Some organizations, like the European Commission, keep databases containing centrally agreed translations of technical expressions. These databases are continually added to, and translators are expected to conform to the agreed renderings, in the interests of organization-wide consistency and clarity.

We have quoted a number of times from the text on p. 130. In preparation for Practical 12, the problems it poses should be analysed, and a translation attempted. This exercise and the others in Practical 12 will show that, apart from the lexical and conceptual problems outlined above, technical translation is not essentially different from most other sorts of prose translation: as long as specialist help can be called on, there is no reason why anyone should not confidently tackle technical translation in any field.

PRACTICAL 12

12.1 Scientific and technical translation

Assignment
After class discussion of problems encountered in translating the Bilobalide text, compare your TT with that of an expert, which will be given you by your tutor.

12.2 Scientific and technical translation

Assignment
  (i) You are translating the following ST for publication in a monthly journal of abstracts of recent research. Discuss the strategic decisions that you have to take before starting detailed translation of this ST, and outline the strategy you adopt.
 (ii) Translate the text into English.
(iii) Explain the main decisions of detail you took.
 (iv) Discuss the published TT (Carbosulcis 1997b), which will be given you by your tutor.

Contextual information
The unsigned text was published in 1997 by Carbosulcis, an Italian firm. (NB Misprints in the original have been corrected here.)

ST

LOGISTICA DEL TRASPORTO DI MATERIALE TRAMITE MEZZI GOMMATI IN MINIERE DI CARBONE

La ricerca è stata svolta presso la miniera di Monte Sinni, una miniera di carbone sub-bituminoso situata nella Sardegna sud-occidentale (Italia). L'obiettivo della ricerca è stato quello di sviluppare un sistema di controllo del flusso del materiale e del traffico dei mezzi gommati destinati a tale
5 trasporto idoneo per miniere di carbone. In particolare si è cercato di simulare il controllo di tutte le fasi di approvvigionamento dei materiali dal magazzino esterno fino ai cantieri nonché il ciclo inverso. Le apparecchiature hardware sono state fornite dalla Montan Forschung (Germania) mentre il software di gestione è stato prodotto dalla Tele Data Software di Cagliari
10 (Italia). La strumentazione è costituita da due parti fisicamente separate. La prima ha il compito di controllare il percorso del carro a trolley e permette di effettuare lo scambio di dati e voce tra il conducente del carro ed una stazione centrale di ricevimento. La seconda, invece, controlla il flusso di ogni singola unità di trasporto tramite targhette porta dati (T.P.D.), conte-
15 nenti un codice numerico fisso di identificazione, che vengono applicate su tali unità. Tutto il ciclo di trasporto è controllato dal software di gestione installato in un personal computer che rappresenta la 'stazione centrale'. Il sistema di controllo del flusso di materiale ha fornito risultati soddisfacenti che hanno consentito alla ricerca di raggiungere gli obiettivi prefissati.
20 L'applicazione futura nella miniera porterà sicuramente dei vantaggi, anche in termini economici, soprattutto per la riduzione dei tempi di approvvigionamento e per l'impossibilità di smarrimento od errori di smistamento del carico o di parte di esso.

(Carbosulcis 1997a: 24)

13

Official, legal and business translation

For the lay translator, the many genres of official, legal and business text can be just as disconcerting as scientific and technological ones. Here is an example of one such genre. It is the first part of an agreement on cultural exchange between Italy and Namibia. Before going on to the rest of the chapter, draft a translation of the text and make notes on its most striking features.

PREMESSA

Nell'ambito dell'accordo di scambio culturale tra l'Università della Namibia e la Seconda Università degli Studi di Napoli – approvato dal Senato Accademico il 16.12.94 e dal Consiglio di Amministrazione il 21.12.94 – per la migliore definizione dei programmi e degli impegni reciproci final-
5   izzati alla formazione di un'ipotesi di lavoro di ricerca su temi specifici e con la conseguente applicazione di tali ricerche attraverso la realizzazione di Laboratori Sperimentali Inter-disciplinari;

- riconosciuta la necessità di una concreta cooperazione culturale Nord/Sud;
- riconosciuto il beneficio derivante dallo sviluppo di rapporti di lavoro basati
10   sul rispetto reciproco, rendendo ambo le parti eguali nella pianificazione, nello sviluppo, nell'esecuzione e nella verifica dei programmi;
- confermando la necessità di allargamento a tutte le aree disciplinari ritenute reciprocamente indispensabili al migliore risultato della cooper-azione culturale internazionale per la crescita della intera Università della
15   Namibia;
- riconosciuta l'opportunità di avviare l'inizio delle attività di ricerca più urgenti;

appare indispensabile l'invio di una missione culturale finalizzata a:

1. Definizione e sottoscrizione della convenzione e del contratto;
20 2. Definizione del progetto generale, dei tempi e dei modi di attuazione;
3. Identificazione delle risorse economiche e dei canali di finanziamento attivabili;
4. Definizione delle risorse umane disponibili.

The biggest problem is the difference in style between a legal type of text and a text written in more everyday language. It is usual for an agreement or a contract to begin with the recitals, which introduce the subject of the text and put it into focus. However, Italian texts of this type often do not start with a clear unambiguous reference to the issue, either structurally or semantically. In fact, in this text, the grammatical focus only becomes clear after the bullet points: 'appare indispensabile l'invio di una missione culturale'. This makes it difficult at first to follow the logic of the ST argument. Faced with complex syntax and discourse in a less specialized type of text, the translator would obviously consider a degree of textual reorganization. However, translators of texts like this one, where the format is almost as important as the content, have no opportunity for large-scale reorganization, but only for local grammatical transposition. They therefore have to carry out a careful 'reconnaissance' of the ST, undertaking an exercise in orienteering in order to get their bearings.

In the first part of this ST, up to the bullet points, the mass of information somehow has to be coherently rechannelled into an acceptable form in the TT, using appropriate lexis and register. Moreover, the translator is normally required to respect the original formulation in terms of layout. Reconciling these aspects is what makes translating such texts a real challenge.

One approach is to produce a framework as a starting-point which can subsequently be fleshed out into the full TT. This framework could consist of a summary of the different constituent parts in note form, so as to gain a clear overall picture – or, returning to the reconnaissance metaphor – an aerial view of the ST in terms of coordinates.

The next problem is understanding the coordinates themselves. The ST contains nouns such as 'programmi', 'ipotesi di lavoro', 'opportunità' and 'ricerca' which are unaccompanied by detail in the ST context, thus making it difficult to know exactly what is intended. The difficulty stems in part from the fact that English often tends to use verbal constructions in cases where Italian uses a more static, conceptual, nominalized style. (See Chapter 16 for discussion of this question.)

The emphasis in this ST on concepts rather than instances of them in practice requires the translator to interpret contextual references in a rather general conceptual framework. What is more, no matter how complex or confusing the ST, the TT reader will expect a translation that is presented in the form of an official agreement, and which clearly defines the parameters, so that all parties concerned will know what their respectives roles and functions are.

Another commonly translated genre is the chairman's report and letter to shareholders. These are usually accompanied by accounts, often in summary form. Here are two extracts from such texts, for comment on salient features and draft translation. Which elements constitute translation problems, and how can they best be tackled? (The STs are based on an existing report and part of a balance sheet, but the company name and details are fictitious.) ST 1 is the beginning of the chairman's report.

ST 1

ASTRA COSTRUZIONI S.R.L.

Sede in Prato – Via del Commercio, 41
Capitale Sociale L. 215.000.000 interamente versato
Iscritta nel registro delle Imprese di Firenze al n. 6294/FI
5 Codice Fiscale n. 00395719305

RELAZIONE DELL'AMMINISTRATORE UNICO SULLA GESTIONE
DELL'ESERCIZIO 1996

Signori Soci,
Viene sottoposto al Vostro esame ed approvazione il Bilancio al 31.12.1996
10 composto dallo Stato Patrimoniale, dal Conto Economico e dalla Nota Integrativa che ne costituisce parte integrante e nella quale risultano indicati i principi di formazione del Bilancio ed i relativi criteri valutativi e sono fornite tutte le informazioni richieste dall'art. 2427 C.C. e dalle altre disposizioni di Legge.
15 Con la presente Relazione, che accompagna ed illustra l'attività ed il Bilancio del trascorso esercizio, diamo ai Soci le informazioni richieste dall'art. 2428 del C.C.

The following items are extracts from the accompanying balance sheet. They provide a good example of the standard terminology and layout. What reference materials would you consult before translating this part of the text? (The items in bold and italic are section headings.)

ST 2

BILANCIO AL 31.12.96

STATO PATRIMONIALE

Attivo

Crediti vs. soci per versamenti ancora dovuti
5 *Immobilizzazioni*
Immobilizzazioni immateriali
Immobilizzazioni materiali
Immobilizzazioni finanziarie
Partecipazioni in imprese controllate
10 Crediti:
• verso imprese collegate
Altri titoli
Attivo circolante
Rimanenze
15 Crediti:
• verso clienti
• esigibili entro l'esercizio successivo
• esigibili oltre l'esercizio successivo
Disponibilità liquide
20 Ratei e risconti
Totale attivo

Passivo

Patrimonio netto
Capitale
25 Riserve statutarie
Fondi per rischi e oneri
Trattamento di fine lavoro subordinato
Debiti
Totale passivo

Documents of this type are generally set out in a standard format, which varies with the nature, size and business of a company. However, there are basic differences in types of company across the world, and this variety is a problem. If it is necessary to translate a company type, a decision will have to be taken based on advice from the firm that has commissioned the translation.

Take, for example, 'Srl': 'società a responsabilità limitata'. In Britain, there are several types of limited company: a limited liability company, a private limited company (Ltd) and a public limited company (plc). Therefore, the translator may have some difficulty in deciding which, if any, of these types is broadly equivalent to the ST company. The problem of translation does not arise when the abbreviation is used, as this can be transcribed as it stands, e.g. SpA in Italy, GmbH in Germany or SA in France.

As with any genre, translators need to have some familiarity with texts of similar type written in English, so that the appropriate register, terminology and conventions are used in the TT. It must be borne in mind, however, that Italian accounts are often much more complex than English-language ones, and contain a plethora of items which in English may be subsumed under a single entry. Bugbears which assail inexperienced translators are terms like 'crediti' and 'debiti', which may appear under both assets and liabilities, initially causing some confusion. Another point which is often a problem in accounts is the use of very lengthy figures, frequently billions of lire, which have to be copied down in columns beside the entries. Where different years' performances are compared, there may be three or four columns of figures.

Problems with interpreting abbreviations and conventions loom large in this kind of translation. It is not difficult to see that 'Cod. fisc.' is 'codice fiscale', but what about the abbreviations in the following example? What could the translator do if 'REA' could not be found in a dictionary or reference work? And what about 'bis'?

> Nuova Astra SRL
> Sede legale in Torino – Via Cavour, 93bis
> Cod. fisc. 00793216805
> Iscritta al tribunale di Torino n. 247351 vol. 7831 fasc. 49
> C.C.I.A.A. di Torino n. 349810
> Capitale sociale: L.125.000.000 i.v.
> Iscritta al REA al n. 247351

Difficulties of a similar type and some of the tendencies noted above can be seen in legal documents. The following text comes from the 'Testo unificato sui rifiuti: Decreti attuativi' (published in 1992/3). Draft a translation of it, and make notes on the types of problem encountered and the decisions taken in tackling them.

1.3.22 DECRETO 25 MAGGIO. – INDIVIDUAZIONE DEI RIFIUTI OSPEDALIERI DA QUALIFICARE COME ASSIMILABILI AI RIFIUTI SOLIDI URBANI (IN G.U. N. 137 DEL 14 GIUGNO 1989)

Il Ministro dell'ambiente di concerto con il Ministro della sanità

5 • visto il decreto del Presidente della Repubblica 10 settembre 1982, n. 915;

- visto il decreto-legge 14 dicembre 1988, n. 527, convertito, con modificazioni, nella legge 10 febbraio 1989, n. 45;
- visto l'art.1, comma 2-*quater*, del decreto-legge 14 dicembre 1988 n.
10 527, convertito, con modificazioni, nella legge 10 febbraio 1989 n. 45, che affida al Ministero dell'ambiente, di intesa con il Ministero della sanità, il compito di individuare le frazioni dei rifiuti ospedalieri da qualificare come assimilabili ai rifiuti solidi urbani nonché le eventuali ulteriori categorie che abbisognano di particolari sistemi di smaltimento; [. . .]
15 - viste le risultanze delle audizioni effettuate con i rappresentanti della Federazione nazionale degli ordini dei medici, dell'Ordine nazionale dei biologi e dell'Ordine nazionale dei veterinari, nonché dell'Associazione italiana patologi clinici e con i direttori sanitari di alcune strutture ospedaliere;

decreta:
20 Art.1 [etc.]

A number of the challenging features in this text include specific references to legislation. Though legal systems and legislation share common features, there is a distinct lack of equivalence between different countries as regards legislative bodies and instruments. The terms of reference in this text differ substantially from those used in British legislation. For example, Italy is a republic, and has a legal system based on the Napoleonic Code. Hence terms such as 'DPR' ('Decreto del Presidente della Repubblica'), 'decreto-legge', 'decreto regionale', and so on. One can even find 'DR' ('decreto regio'), referring to laws passed under the monarchy (before 1948). The formulations also appear far more complex than in English contexts, as in the text above.

The search for legal equivalence is therefore sometimes fruitless. The translator's objective is to convey as clearly as possible the concept in question, so that it is both accurate and understandable to the target readership, which may be specialized, lay, or both. The language adopted will also need to be in current use. Looking through a legal dictionary will show just how many historical terms are still currently used in the English legal system – 'lien', 'tort', 'estoppel', 'garnishment', 'chattels', etc. The translator must find out if and when such terms may be used when translating from the language of a country whose institutions and precepts differ from TL ones. Certain differences are taken for granted. In England and Wales law is based on precedent, while in Italy it is enshrined in the Codes: Codice Civile (C.C.), Codice di Procedura Civile (C.P.C.), Codice Penale (C.P.), etc. Such terms are best translated, especially where the original contains an abbreviation.

Legal language also typically uses Latin expressions, many of which are specific to a particular legal system. Translating into Italian is less problematic than into English, as Italians are more likely than their English-speaking counterparts to be able to understand Latin expressions. Often, a Latin expression in an Italian ST, though retained in the TT, will require a footnote or gloss by the translator to explain its sense in the context.

In translating Italian legal texts, then, the accent will be on accuracy, clarity and avoidance of ambiguity. Where necessary, footnotes or translator's notes will be used. Technical terms used in the United Kingdom will often be unacceptable, because too culture-specific. Take even such an apparently uncomplicated term as 'legge'. The parallel instrument in the United Kingdom is an Act (of Parliament), but using this term to denote an Italian law would cause cultural confusion. Similarly, the term 'avvocato' has a number of parallels, according to the legal system in question and the specific context: it may denote a solicitor, barrister, advocate, attorney or counsel.

Translating Italian legal texts therefore requires at least a basic knowledge of the SL and TL legal systems, as well as research into the specific area in question – criminal law, commercial law, contract law, etc. And, with experience, it will become second nature to the translator to use 'will' and 'shall' accurately in conveying function and obligation, to use passive forms, and to insert initial capital letters correctly, as the example below from a draft contract shows to good effect:

CONTRACT

Between   and

(represented by ....)   hereinafter referred to as **the Interpreter**

hereinafter referred to as
5 **the Client**

It is agreed as follows:
The client requires the services of the Interpreter for an international conference/meeting between .... 200.. and .... 200.. at .... for interpreting duties from .... and into ....

10 **1. Interpreter's Duties**
The Interpreter will be available at the venue from .... to .... 200.. for .... days of simultaneous/consecutive interpreting work for a period not exceeding an eight-hour day. (Where the working day exceeds eight hours, additional hours shall be subject to overtime, at a rate to be agreed.)

15 **2. Fees**
The Client shall pay the Interpreter a fee of £.......... for each half day worked (up to three hours), and £.......... for each full day worked. The hourly rate for overtime shall be £.......... per hour. Expenses as outlined below shall also be charged.

Last, but not least, recent changes in the Italian legal system have engendered new abbreviations, such as 'g.i.p' ('giudice per le indagini preliminari'), a function which used to be the responsibility of the *giudice istruttore*. In this case, both may be translated as 'examining magistrate' or 'investigating magistrate', but translators have to keep up to date with any changes.

As with any area, the debutant translator should build up for reference purposes a portfolio of 'parallel texts' in both languages, such as contracts and tenders, balance sheets, certificates and official documents. This makes it possible to get a feel for different types of document and register, to understand how they work, what they are for and the specialist language used. The conventions used in both languages will gradually become apparent, and can be automatically applied in translation. There is no model translation for documents. The essential requirement is that the translation should accurately reflect the purpose for which the ST was written, that the TT format should accurately correspond to the ST format, and that the TT should take into consideration any cultural gaps which the reader may not be able to bridge without assistance. A good example of such a gap is the translation of a degree, A-level or Scottish Higher certificate: degree courses have a different structure in Italy, and there is no exact equivalent to British school exams. The *licenza liceale* in Italy follows a completely different pattern from A-levels or Highers: any translation will necessarily reflect the cultural and educational differences. Similarly, translating birth, marriage and death certificates causes a series of problems in layout, content and terminology, due to the physical and legal differences between the documents in the respective languages. Consequently, when translating a birth certificate, for example, it is always useful to have a British one to hand, for broad terms of reference.

Finally, as with any text in any genre, it is important to bear in mind the purpose and readership of the TT when translating documents, as this will inform the strategy adopted in tackling cultural issues, such as lack of equivalent institutions or instruments, lack of equivalent terminology, presence or absence of features such as capitals, abbreviations, notes, Latinisms, etc. The TT of a legal or financial text created for information purposes is potentially more flexible as a medium than one which will be used in court or in a legal action. It is also important to gain as much information as possible about the situation in which a text has originated, particularly if it is being used in a legal action or is the subject of controversy or dispute. Texts are never produced in a vacuum: the more that is known about the subject matter of the ST, the better the TT will be.

PRACTICAL 13

13.1   Official and legal translation

Assignment
After class discussion of problems encountered in translating the 'Namibia–Napoli' text on pp. 138–9, compare your TT with that of an expert, which will be given you by your tutor.

13.2   Official and legal translation

Assignment
After class discussion of problems encountered in translating the 'Decreto' text on pp. 142–3, compare your TT with that of an expert, which will be given you by your tutor.

14

Translating consumer-oriented texts

All texts, including translations, are produced for a purpose. The purpose is always a major factor in deciding a strategy. Translating consumer-oriented texts makes the importance of purpose especially clear. This, together with the fact that many translators earn their living with these sorts of text, is why we are giving them a chapter to themselves.

By 'consumer-oriented texts', we mean texts which try to persuade the public to buy something, or tell purchasers how to use what they have bought, or advise on commodities that might be bought or courses of action that might be taken. The range thus includes advertisements, tourist brochures, user manuals, consumer magazines, recipe books, CD booklets, public notices, information leaflets, etc. – even a lot of propaganda can be classified under this heading. Consumer-oriented texts may therefore fall into the category either of persuasive or of empirical genres, or both. Often, they have literary, religious or philosophical genre-features as well. Sometimes, they are so specialized that they are given to technical translators; even then, the translator has to keep target-culture consumers' specific needs in mind.

The most extreme instance of consumer-oriented translation is translating advertisements. This is often as much a question of writing original copy as of translation. In fact, big firms are most likely to ask an agency to produce a tailor-made advertisement for the target culture. But it is not rare for translators to be asked to translate advertisements, and intra-trade publicity is commonly translated. For our needs in this course, translating advertisements is certainly a good way of focusing attention on the dimension of purpose in textual genre. If you did not do Practical 5.2, we recommend that you do it for this chapter. The texts on pp. 24 and 72–3 are also useful reference points.

Translating advertisements also obliges the translator to consider carefully the central question of cultural differences between SL public and TL public:

nowhere more clearly than in advertising may inter-cultural differences make literal translation unwelcome, even where it is possible. Different cultures value different things, and have different taboos. There is also evidence that different cultures stereotype consumers differently. It is impossible to generalize on the basis of one example, but, as a sample of possible differences in cultural stereotyping that might influence translation choice, here is a pair of texts for analysis and comparison (and not necessarily imitation!). The texts are from the leaflet supplied with a coffee-maker:

Consigli per un buon caffè
Una volta riempito il filtro ad
imbuto di caffè forate la superficie
di polvere 3 volte con uno stuz-
5 zicadenti.
Per un caffè ancora più buono
aggiungete un granello di sale
all'acqua nella caffettiera.
Ed inoltre mescolando energica-
10 mente 3 cucchiaini di zucchero con
le prime gocce di caffè che fuori-
escono dalla caffettiera otterrete
una gustosa crema da aggiungere
al caffè in ogni tazzina.
15

Simple to use
The 'Moka System' is so simple!
Any type of cooker is perfectly
suitable for the MOKA as it has a
thick, hollow ground base.
Quick.
It takes only 3–6 minutes
depending on the size of your
coffee maker and the intensity of
the heat to set the coffee pleasantly
bubbling to the top, ready to serve.
Impossible.
If freshly roasted and ground beans
are used it is virtually impossible
to make 'bad' coffee.

One wonders who produced the English text, and why! It may just be an editorial oversight, the TT being an accidental relic from an earlier leaflet. Perhaps it was written by someone who thinks the British do not appreciate the subtleties of coffee-making, or that the Italian text is empty affectation. Whatever the answer, the difference between the two texts implies assumptions about cultural differences between Italy and the United Kingdom. One may not accept the implied assumptions, but the fact is that the Italian manufacturer has published texts that do imply them. This extreme example illustrates particularly clearly that purpose and audience-stereotyping are as crucial in consumer-oriented texts as in any other.

The point is that, as ever, part of the translator's preparation must be to study examples of appropriate TL texts, so as to become familiar with the requirements and assumptions of the genre that is intended for the TT. It is just as important, of course, to be aware of stylistic features and cultural assumptions that are *not* characteristic of the intended TL genre. Even intralingually, if the style of the *Brownie Cookbook* were used in Mrs Beeton, her readers would be insulted, and would not not take her seriously;

conversely, Mrs Beeton's style might mystify the Brownie. Either option would be commercial suicide. The trendy twenty-something niche requires something else again. In translation, putting notes for a Schubert CD booklet into *New Musical Express* style would be an act of commercial sabotage – as would translating Zucchero notes into the English of Schubert criticism.

All these sorts of consideration will apply in Practical 14. It is, however, also important to remember that changes in structure, vocabulary and register are as much a matter of standard differences between languages as of genre-specific cross-cultural differences. This point can be exemplified from an Italian bath and shower gel carton. It may be that the English text is not actually a translation of the Italian, but they do correspond to one another very closely. The differences are not differences of genre, but of characteristic idiom and grammatical structure. A literal translation of either text would be unidiomatic. Here they are, for comparison and discussion:

Aveeno olio detergente, a base di avena colloidale e di un sistema equilibrato di olii selezionati, deterge accuratamente la pelle
5 sensibile, svolgendo inoltre una spiccata azione emolliente, idratante e condizionante. Si disperde uniformemente nell'acqua, formando un'emulsione lattea
10 finissima che agisce su tutta la superficie cutanea senza privarla dei costituenti protettivi e migliorandone le caratteristiche dopo la detersione.
15 **Uso: Bagno:** versare circa 30 ml (5 cucchiai) nell'acqua del bagno. **Doccia:** applicare direttamente sulla cute, massaggiare e risciacquare.

Aveeno Bath & Shower Oil, with colloidal oatmeal and a balanced mixture of softening oils, thoroughly cleanses, moisturizes, and conditions sensitive skin. Aveeno Bath & Shower Oil evenly disperses throughout the water, forming a delicate milky emulsion which acts on the entire surface of the skin. It safeguards the skin and helps to maintain natural moisturizing oils.
Instructions for use: Bath: add approximately 30 ml (5 Tablespoons) to bath water. **Shower:** massage directly onto skin and then rinse.

Finally, the same point can be made 'negatively', by comparing an ST with a TT that, for whatever reason, has not taken grammatical and idiomatic differences between SL and TL sufficiently into account. However scrupulous the attention to genre, the TT suffers somewhat from excessive SL orientation. The texts are from *Torino Cultura 1997*, a brochure published by the city of Turin:

Suds	**Souths**
Museo della Fotografia Storica e Contemporanea 21 marzo/4 maggio	Museum of Historical and Contemporary Photography 21st March/4th May
La mostra è il risultato di un progetto che ha radunato 8 fotografi francesi uniti da un certo modo di guardare i vari sud del mondo, rifiutando le lusinghe dei facili esotismi.	The show is the result of a project which gathered eight French photographers united by their particular way of looking at the various souths of the world, refusing the flattery of banal exoticisms.

PRACTICAL 14

14.1 Consumer-oriented texts

Assignment
(i)   You have been commissioned to translate the owner handbook for the Fiat Cinquecento, from which the following ST is taken. Discuss the strategic decisions that you have to take before starting detailed translation of this ST, and outline and justify the strategy you adopt.
(ii)   Translate the text into English. (If you know anyone with a Fiat, resist the temptation to look at the handbook: the published TT will be discussed in class.)
(iii)   Explain the main decisions of detail you took.
(iv)   Compare your translation with the published TT (Fiat 1993b), which will be given you by your tutor.

Contextual information
The handbook was published in 1993. The text is in a section entitled 'Cosa fare se si scarica la batteria'. It explains how to use the battery on another vehicle to start a car with a flat battery. It is accompanied by a diagram showing how to connect the two batteries. The most useful contextual advice is to look at the battery section in a couple of handbooks for British-built cars; this will give you an idea of typical content, style and terminology.

ST
Avviamento con batteria ausiliaria
Qualora, accidentalmente, la batteria si fosse scaricata, è possibile effettuare l'avviamento del motore con una batteria ausiliaria che abbia caratteristiche elettriche equivalenti o di poco superiori a quelle della batteria scarica
5   (pagina 93), agendo nel modo seguente:
• collegare i morsetti positivi delle due batterie con un cavo sussidiario;

* collegare un secondo cavo al morsetto negativo della batteria carica ed al terminale metallico del cavo di massa, indicato in figura, della vettura con batteria scarica;
10 * a motore avviato, rimuovere i collegamenti **iniziando dalla pinza collegata con il terminale metallico lontano dalla batteria.**

Non usare un caricabatterie per effettuare l'avviamento d'emergenza!

Ricarica della batteria
Per effettuare la ricarica della batteria, operare nel modo seguente:
15 * scollegare i morsetti terminali dell'impianto elettrico della vettura dai poli della batteria;
* collegare ai poli della batteria i cavi dell'apparecchio di ricarica ed accendere quest'ultimo;
* ad operazione di ricarica ultimata, disinserire l'apparecchio prima di scol-
20   legarlo dalla batteria;
* prima di ripristinare il fissaggio dei morsetti ai poli della batteria, spalmarli con vaselina pura o altri appositi protettivi.

Vedere al capitolo MANUTENZIONE E CONSIGLI PRATICI le precauzioni per prevenire la scarica della batteria e garantirne una lunga funzionalità.

25 *Attenzione*   **La soluzione elettrolitica contenuta nella batteria è velenosa e corrosiva; evitarne il contatto con la pelle o con gli occhi.**
            L'operazione di ricarica della batteria deve essere effettuata in ambiente ventilato e lontano da fiamme libere o possibili fonti di scintille.
30   **È preferibile una ricarica lenta della batteria (basso amperaggio ed almeno 24 ore di carica).**
            Prima di qualsiasi intervento sull'impianto elettrico, staccare il cavo del polo negativo della batteria.

(Fiat 1993a: 59–60)

14.2   Consumer-oriented texts

Assignment
   (i)   You have been commissioned to translate *Piemonte dal vivo*, a lavish brochure from which the following ST is taken. The brochure gives details of events combining 'cultura e turismo' throughout Piedmont. Discuss the strategic decisions that you have to take before starting detailed translation of this ST, and outline and justify the strategy you adopt.
  (ii)   Translate the text into English.
 (iii)   Explain the main decisions of detail you took.
  (iv)   Compare your translation with the published TT, which will be given you by your tutor.

Contextual information
The ST was published in 1997. Vignale Monferrato is a town in Piedmont.
The Festival of Dance takes place each year in July and August. It is orga-
nized by the Fondazione Teatro Nuovo per la Danza of Turin.

ST

VIGNALEDANZA

Dal 1979, anno della prima edizione, Vignale Monferrato è diventata la
'capitale della danza estiva', animata da momenti di grande suggestione
spettacolare seguiti da un pubblico che, nel corso di questi anni, si è rive-
lato numeroso, attento, entusiasta. Nel corso delle successive edizioni il
5   Festival monferrino ha sperimentato un felice abbinamento di proposte spet-
tacolari e didattiche che, alternando in un brillante calendario ospiti-étoiles,
compagnie che presentano prime internazionali, creazioni in esclusiva,
concorsi e stage, ha catalizzato l'interesse di un pubblico crescente, prove-
niente dal Piemonte, ma anche da tutta Italia. Gruppi storici figurano accanto
10 a gruppi emergenti, vengono proposti laboratori coreografici e proiezioni di
film sulla danza, in un intreccio intenso di proficua interazione fra profes-
sionismo e pratica scolastica.
     La manifestazione, realizzata su un'idea di Gian Mesturino e Germana
Erba, tuttora direttori artistici, ha visto succedersi nel corso di diciotto
15 edizioni solisti e complessi di indiscutibile prestigio internazionale. Tra essi
i Pilobolus, il Mudra di Béjart, il Nikolais Dance Theatre, Lindsay Kemp,
Antonio Gades, Roland Petit con il Ballet national de Marseille, Alicia
Alonso, Luciana Savignano, che ha dato lustro a tanti appuntamenti e Pompea
Santoro, attuale preziosa collaboratrice della Fondazione Teatro Nuovo.
20   Il Festival riesce inoltre a inventare un rivitalizzante clima di festa, susci-
tando entusiasmi e curiosità negli spettatori, permettendo loro di accostarsi
ai diversi linguaggi e modi espressivi, dai più consolidati e tradizionali ai
più informali, innovativamente aperti alla ricerca artistica contemporanea.
Uno stimolante risultato dunque, frutto di una positiva, continua crescita
25 della manifestazione che ogni volta, con un'offerta di spettacolo sempre
nuova e sempre di alto livello, concorre a comporre un'immagine articolata,
sfaccettata e composita della realtà e dei percorsi della danza, oggi.

(Chiriotti et al 1997: 32)

15

Revising and editing TTs

Throughout the course, we have considered translation sometimes as a process, and sometimes as a product. The assessment of existing TTs has been an important feature in practicals. In this chapter, we turn our attention to the final stage of translation as a process, where the proposed TT is actually examined as a product.

Any form of post-translation process is an operation carried out in writing on a pre-existent text. Revision is concerned with ensuring accuracy by eliminating errors and inconsistencies. Errors of accuracy can be relatively minor, such as spelling mistakes or punctuation, but they can also include ungrammatical or misleading constructions. And it is not only the language of the TT which may be wrong or unsuitable: the concepts themselves may have been distorted in transmission. The TT is the sum not only of a translator's ability in the two linguistic systems concerned, but also of knowledge of the subject matter in question. So, for example, a translator may be equipped linguistically to tackle a text on computer software, but not have the expertise necessary to make the right terminological and practical decisions, thereby undermining the TT's authoritativeness.

In this chapter we shall refer to **revision** where the task concerns checking a TT against the ST for accuracy, and to **editing** where the TT requires 'polishing' after the revision process. The two overlap to some extent, especially where TT peculiarities are not so much errors as features of style and/or register.

As a preliminary exercise, it will be useful to assess the quality of the following three TTs and point out where the faults lie. They are all taken from the same collection of articles. It is obvious from the varied quality of the translations in this volume that several different people were commissioned to translate it.

ST 1

Disfunzioni odierne. Napoli è, a giudizio unanime, una città invivi- bile. I problemi posti dalla odierna condizione metropolitana hanno
5 determinato il collasso della città. La patologia derivante da una 'concentrazione senza sviluppo' si manifesta in un diffuso fenomeno di 'calcuttizzazione' della struttura
10 urbana. Gli effetti macroscopici di tale degenerazione sono:- *paralisi del traffico*: vi sono solo 3 strade di attraversamento est-ovest della città bassa (via Partenope, tunnel
15 della Vittoria, via Chiaia); questa è collegata alla città alta mediante 3 strade.

TT 1

Today's misfunctionings. Naples living standard is unanimously considered extremely poor. The problems posed by the present metropolitan way of life caused the city collapse. The pathology, deriving from a 'concentration without any improvement', shows a 'Calcutta-like' urban structure. The main effects of this degenera- tion are:- *The City traffic paralysis*: there are only three roads available crossing the lower town from east to west (Via Partenope, the Vittoria tunnel, via Chiaia); three roads connecting the lower part with the upper part.

(Loris Rossi 1987: 175)

ST 2

Densità. Non è determinata da fi- gure astratte di progettazione, ma dalla qualità di vita raggiunta attra- verso una concezione urbanistica.
5 *Economia.* Una densità più alta riduce i costi del progetto di un suolo, dei servizi pubblici. *Spazi aperti.* Montecalvario è uno spazio aperto, grande, verso il
10 quale ogni cosa concorre. Piccoli spazi aperti definiti dalla geometria dei palazzi sono raggruppati lungo i viali pedonali lontano dal traffico. I percorsi, lungo e sotto gli aggetti
15 dei palazzi, forniscono una protezione contro le intemperie per la circolazione attraverso il luogo.

TT 2

Density. It is not determined by abstract planning figures but by the quality of life achieved through an urban concept. *Economics.* Higher density reduces the project's cost of land, public utilities and services. *Open spaces.* Montecalvario is the large open space toward which everything concurs. Small open spaces defined by the building's geometry are grouped along pedestrian malls away from traffic. The malls, along or under building's overhangs, provide a weather protected circulation across the site.

(Catalano 1987: 107)

ST 3

La collina ed il mare. L'area interessata è la fascia che va dal Vomero (via Cilea) fin giù al mare.

TT 3

The Hill and the Sea. The area we are concerned with is a piece of land which descends from the

Il tema è quindi la collina ed il mare, i due poli entro cui si muove la vicenda della città.

È prevista su via Cilea una piazza su cui si innesta l'asse visivo e pedonale che continua con Calata San Francesco; si recupera così un tessuto di recente formazione, privo di qualità urbane.

L'asse geometrico dritto verso Capri attua quella osmosi visiva che è il primo contatto con la formidabile presenza paesistica del golfo, le cui acque sono intrise di miti.

Vomero (Via Cilea) right down as far as the sea. Thus the theme is the hill and the sea. The nerve-centre of the city's life is here, in the area lying between these two focal points.

A square is planned on Via Cilea, on to which a visual and pedestrian axis will be grafted, continuing down Calata San Francesco. In this way a fabric of recent formation and lacking in urban quality will be recovered.

The geometrical axis which continues on to Capri, performs that visual osmosis which is the first point of contact with the formidable presence of landscape in the bay, whose waters are saturated with myths.

(Dalisi 1987: 117)

TT 1 looks like the work of a non-native speaker of English. There is poor lexis and syntax ('misfunctionings', 'the city traffic paralysis', 'caused the city collapse', 'Naples living standard'). Restructuring the text has distorted the ST meaning – it is not so much that the 'living standard' of Naples is 'extremely poor' as that Naples is an impossible place to live in. In the rendering of 'strade di attraversamento', 'available' is an arbitrary addition.

ST 2 is possibly more challenging than ST 1. The TT is certainly no better than TT 1. In addition to problems of lexis ('astratte figure', 'concorre'), the poor translation of 'costi del progetto di un suolo' shows that the translator does not understand this concept. The wrong use of the apostrophe in 'building's' downgrades this TT even further.

Reading TT 3 is something of a relief. The ST contains certain idiosyncrasies, which could cause interpretation problems. There is an example in 'i due poli entro cui si muove *la vicenda* della città'. Here the translator has restructured the phrase by splitting it into two sentences, but cohesion perhaps suffers from this inversion of the 'due poli' and 'vicenda' units. While 'the formidable presence of landscape in the bay' does suggest the renowned (if stereotyped) view of the Bay of Naples evoked by 'formidabile presenza paesistica del golfo', it has far less impact than the ST expression. As this translator is given to restructuring the ST, any revision of the article as a whole will have to involve careful evaluation of the accuracy and appropriateness of departures from ST structures.

Unusual translations may also be thrown up in technical translation, as for example in the following excerpt from a trade brochure:

ST	TT
L'estrusione a freddo dell'alluminio ha trovato un'importante applicazione nei particolari per filtri carburante (nafta e benzina). L'alluminio è 5 preferito al ferro zincato per il suo migliore comportamento nelle prove in atmosfera salina. I pezzi da noi realizzati fino ad oggi sono le vaschette ed i tubetti interni. [. . .] 10 Sempre per l'alimentazione carburante produciamo oggi carcasse per pompe di diverso tipo. Dove particolari esigenze di durezza e resistenza lo richiedono, abbiamo realizzato 15 l'applicazione di inserti in acciaio.	The cold extrusion of the aluminium has found an important application in the parts for fuel filters (Diesel oil and petrol). The aluminium is preferred to the galvanized iron for his better behaviour for the tests in the saline atmosphere. The pieces we have realized till now are the cans and the inside tubes. [. . .] Always for the fuel's feeding we are now manufacturing frames for pumps of various type. Where particular exigences of hardness and resistance request it, we have realized the application of steel inserts.

A peculiarity of this TT is that some appropriate technical terms have been used, but are stitched into a practically meaningless fabric.

In the literary field, a survey of published translations of Italian classics shows that not all translators are of the stature of a William Weaver. Here is an example:

ST	TT
Ma sul punto di uscire, abbracciò con lo sguardo la chiesa intera con le sue file di colonne, il suo soffitto a cassettoni, il suo pavi- 5 mento deserto, il suo altare e gli sembrò di dare addio per sempre all'immagine antica e sopravvissuta di un mondo come lo desiderava e sapeva che non era più possibile 10 che fosse. Una specie di miraggio alla rovescia, ritto in un passato irrevocabile, dal quale i suoi passi lo allontanavano sempre più. (Moravia 1981: 111)	Just as he was on the point of going out, however, he cast a glance round the church, with its rows of pillars, its coffered ceiling, its deserted floor, its great altar, and it seemed to him that he was saying farewell for ever to an ancient survival of a world such as he longed for and such as he knew could never exist again. It was a kind of mirage in reverse, based on an irrevocable past from which his steps carried him further and further away. (Moravia 1952: 114)

Using 'however' instead of 'but' slows the sentence down needlessly. The addition of 'great' to 'altar' is redundant, or at least inappropriate – one normally refers to an altar as 'high', if this quality is specified or implied. More importantly, 'immagine' has not been rendered, so that Moravia's picture is simplified and weakened. The mirage simile is also weak in the TT, as 'reverse' does not capture 'alla rovescia'; worse still is the anodyne 'based' for 'ritto'.

Of course, it is one thing to criticize a translation, but another thing entirely to revise and edit it. How does one go about such a complex task? The revision and editing process comprises several activities, which broadly speaking fall into two stages. The first is checking the TT for adherence to the ST in terms of accuracy: the reviser focuses on errors, omissions, additions, names and titles, figures and tables, etc. The second stage focuses on the end-user of the TT, and attempts to achieve the 'optimum orientation of the translated text to the requirements of the target readership' (Graham 1983: 104).

At the revision or checking stage, greater emphasis is usually placed on accuracy than on terminology. The objectivity of the reviser should ensure that any ambiguities or unclear phrasing are dealt with before passing on to the editing stage. There are no hard and fast rules for editing, though critical factors are certainly appearance, appeal, impact, harmony, taste, register and style. If revision is concerned with the 'bare bones' of the TT, the editing process will perform 'remedial surgery' (Graham 1983: 103), which should consist of 'upgrading the terminology, clarifying obscurities, reinforcing the impact, honing the emotive appeal to suit the target reader'. A final 'cosmetic' stage should be to ensure that the appearance and layout of the TT respect the requirements as stated by the client.

A knotty issue is style, as style and language-use obviously vary from one translator to another. Care must be taken that changes are only made to items which are in some way incorrect or unsuitable, not those which are merely phrased differently from the way the translator/reviser would phrase them. For example, there is an enormous difference in legal English between 'will' and 'shall' used in the third person, particularly in the context of contracts and agreements, but in the first person these forms are interchangeable. In a text containing direct speech, there would be little point in changing 'I shall go out later' to 'I will go out later', unless there was a particular contextual reason. However, if the TT of a contract contained the words '[The contractor] *will* complete the work by August 10th' instead of '*shall* complete' (for 'dovrà completare i lavori entro il 10 agosto'), the reviser would have to intervene: the former TT implies that it is a foregone conclusion that the work will be completed by 10th August, whereas the latter puts the onus fairly and squarely on the contractor to finish the work by the deadline.

Some texts are passed on to an editor before publication, and here the translator or reviser will often play no further part: in reality, it is unlikely that they will be consulted about changes to the TT. An editor may wish to prune what are considered to be irrelevancies from the TT, or to reduce the length of the text due to typographical or impagination constraints.

In effect, the editor is responsible to the translator for any changes made to the TT, whether or not the translator is consulted about them. If the TT is subsequently judged defective in some way by readers, it is the translator who will automatically be held responsible by readers or reviewers, rather than the author, the editor or the printer. It must therefore never be forgotten that revision and editing are part of the 'quality control' procedure that all translators should implement on completing their translating (or during and after translating, depending on how the translator works). Whether or not the TT will be revised and edited by a third party, it is essential that translators have their own system for careful self-assessment of the work, and that even when completing a rush job careful reading and checking is carried out to repair errors and omissions. (Excellent advice on checking can be found in Anderson and Avery 1995.)

PRACTICAL 15

15.1 Revising and editing

Assignment
  (i)   You have been asked to revise and edit the following TT. Discuss the main types of revision and editing challenges it poses.
 (ii)   Revise the TT.
(iii)   Report on your revisions, saying what criteria you adopted for assessment of the TT, and explaining the main changes you made.
 (iv)   Exchange the revised text for another student's, and edit it.
  (v)   Explain your edits.

Contextual information
The ST and TT are taken from 'Stagioni d'Italia' 2/90, published in Italian and English by Electa Napoli for the Ente Nazionale del Turismo – ENIT.

Turn to p. 160

ST

CILENTO DA SCOPRIRE

L'Italia è davvero il paese delle meraviglie nel senso che – oltre ai tesori d'arte ed all'incanto dei paesaggi – offre continue scoperte di territori che per secoli furono ignorati dalle grandi correnti turistiche, e che costituiscono oggi preziose riserve. Ieri fu la volta della Sardegna, balzata alla ribalta
5   internazionale con le sue coste stupende, o delle Isole Eolie o delle Tremiti o della classica serenità della Puglia: oggi è la volta delle zone interne della Campania, e precisamente quel vasto territorio del Cilento, che va dalla costa di Palinuro e di Paestum ai monti dell'Appennino, fino al vallo di Diano ed alla straordinaria Certosa di Padula. Una zona rimasta secoli fuori
10   delle grandi vie del turismo, priva di agevoli arterie, isolata e povera: ma proprio per queste ragioni negative, rimasta intatta con il suo paesaggio, le città d'arte, le sue tradizioni di folklore, di gastronomia.

    Lungo la costa della Campania, pareva che l'incanto finisse con la Costa Amalfitana, per avere poi una eccezionale fioritura nella piana di Paestum
15   con i celebri templi, e quindi offrire le cale e le spiagge di Agropoli, Santa Maria di Castellabate, Ascea e Camerota, per riaffiorare lungo la costa della Calabria. [. . .]

    Oggi il Cilento si affaccia con prepotenza al turismo, nel quadro di una politica regionale dell'Assessorato che intende esaltare le zone interne della
20   regione, sia per decongestionare la fascia costiera sia per obiettive condizioni di interesse paesistico e monumentale, che caratterizzano l'interno della Campania, pochissimo conosciuto e capace di provocare straordinarie emozioni nel turista. [. . .]

    Per troppo tempo la Campania ha costituito un insieme di attrattive colle-
25   gate all'immagine delle isole, di Pompei, della costa da Sorrento ad Amalfi: qui si è affollato il maggior interesse, qui si è avuto il massimo, ed ormai non più espandibile, accrescimento delle attrezzature ricettive, a danno della stessa godibilità delle attrattive stesse, a detrimento della giusta conoscenza, ricca di nuove sorprese, del cuore della regione.

(Colucci 1990a: 82–3)

TT

THE CILENTO: AN AREA TO EXPLORE

Italy is indeed the land of wonders: in the sense that – besides the art trea-
sures and the beauty of its countryside – it continually offers the chance to
discover areas which for centuries have been off the tourist-beaten track
and which now constitute valuable reserves. A short while ago it was
5 Sardinia's turn, which leapt into the international limelight with its superb
coasts; then there were the Eolian Islands and the Tremiti Islands, and the
classic peace and quiet of Apulia.

Now the interior of Campania is having its turn, or to be precise, the
vast area of the Cilento which runs from the coast of Palinuro and Paestum
10 to the Appennines, right up to the valley of Diano and the extraordinary
Carthusian Monastery of Padula. An area which for centuries remained cut
off from busy tourist routes, devoid of good roads, isolated and poor: but
it is for these negative reasons that the Cilento has remained intact, with
its countryside, the art of its towns, its traditions of folklore and gastronomy.

15 Along the coast of Campania the magic spell looked as though it was
going to finish with the Amalfi Coast. But it then blossomed in the plain
of Paestum with its famous temples, and after that offered the coves and
beaches of Agropoli, Santa Maria di Castellabate, Ascea and Camerota, and
then flowered again along the Calabrian coast. [. . .]

20 Now the Cilento is facing up to tourism assertively: the Regional Council's
policy is to give the interior a boost, both to take the load off the coastal
strip and because of the conditions of natural and historical interest which
characterise Campania's interior, little known and capable of stirring great
excitement in the tourist. [. . .]

25 For too long Campania has been a set of attractions connected with the
image of the islands, of Pompei, of the Sorrento and Amalfi coasts. This is
where interest has been focused, where the greatest growth, up to saturation
point, has been seen in the hotel industry, to the detriment of the very enjoy-
ment of those attractions, and to the exclusion of the unexpected riches of
30 the heart of the region.

(Colucci 1990b: 113)

Contrastive topics and practicals: Introduction

The next four chapters deal with topics from the 'contrastive linguistics' of Italian and English. Each chapter is self-contained, and can be used as the basis of a practical at whatever stage of the course seems most useful. There are two aims in these chapters. The first is to focus attention on some of the structural differences between Italian and English which most commonly offer obstacles to literal translation. The second is to increase awareness of the range of options open to translators confronted with these constructions.

There are very many such systematic discrepancies between Italian and English usage. Many have already been encountered in practicals, usually where grammatical transposition or compensation has been necessary. The choice of just four contrastive topics for special attention is therefore rather arbitrary. We have chosen four of the most common sources of translation difficulties, and illustrated each with a variety of exercises. Chapter 16 focuses on nominalization – that is, expressions which consist of a noun or have a noun as their nucleus and which, in either the same language or another one, could be replaced by a different part of speech. On a related topic, Chapter 17 deals with some of the more problematic types of determiner – articles, demonstratives, possessives, relatives and quantifiers. Chapter 18 deals with problems posed by differences between Italian and English in respect of adverbial expressions. Finally, in Chapter 19, we look at some of the biggest differences between how the two languages express condition and future in the past.

The contrastive exercises differ in two ways from the other practicals. First, students will often be translating individual sentences taken out of context. This is so that attention can be focused on the contrastive problems themselves – problems which, in textual context, can be masked or blurred by considerations of style or genre. Obviously, we are not suggesting that context is after all not as important as we have insisted. On the contrary, where context and register are significant factors, attention is drawn to this fact. However, the aim in these chapters is to help the student develop a comprehensive contrastive awareness of available options in translation. The availability of potential options can only be properly assessed by taking sentences out of context.

Second, in the contrastive chapters the direction of translation is sometimes reversed, to translating from English into Italian. This is in order to bring into the open certain possibilities in *English* which it is easy to overlook when translating from *Italian*. For some Italian sentences, it is possible to translate into English without significant grammatical transposition, but at the cost of significant translation loss in terms of idiomaticity or register. Many of the English STs in the contrastive chapters contain constructions which cannot pass into Italian without grammatical transposition. These are instances of precisely those idiomatic English constructions which it is easiest to overlook when translating an Italian ST containing constructions which can be replicated in English. Our hope is that, having stumbled over these constructions as obstacles in translation *into* Italian, students will remain aware of their existence as options in translating *from* Italian.

16

Contrastive topic and practical: Nominalization

This chapter constitutes the material for all or part of a practical. It focuses on translation issues raised by nominal expressions. A **nominal expression** either consists of a noun or has a noun as its nucleus. Here are some examples, each with an alternative avoiding use of a noun:

With shocking speed.	Shockingly quickly.
A matter of great importance.	A very important matter.
That's within anyone's capability.	Anyone can do that.
He walked up the street with long strides.	He strode up the street.

We shall use the term **nominalization** to denote the use of a nominal expression which, in the same language or another, could be replaced by an expression not containing a noun. Italian often uses nominal expressions where English would not. An English TT that matches an Italian ST noun for noun tends to read unidiomatically, having a static and abstract quality at odds with the English-speaker's habitual way of expressing the world. Whether such exoticism is or is not desirable depends, of course, on the purpose of the TT. Our aim here is simply to show that nominalization can have implications for idiomaticity, register and genre.

We can start the discussion with a sentence from the pharmacological text in Chapter 12 (p. 130):

> *La coltura* di questo parassita, *di recente introduzione*, si presta *allo studio* di nuovi farmaci e *per il confronto* con quelli esistenti.

The expressions in italics are examples of nominalization. Here is a 'technical' TT, observing TL conventions for scientific and technical texts:

Recently introduced methods for *the culture* of this parasite are useful in *the study* of new medicines and *in their comparison* with existing ones.

The nominalizations give the technical TT similar compactness and impersonality to the ST. These are absent from this more conversational version:

Scientists have recently introduced methods for growing this parasite that are useful if you want to study new medicines and compare them with ones that already exist.

In this TT, turning 'introduzione' into an active verb has required adding an agent, 'scientist'. This personalization could be avoided with a passive, although the result is awkward to read:

Methods for growing this parasite that are useful if you want to study new medicines and compare them with ones that already exist have recently been introduced.

The TT can also be made slightly less conversational by avoiding 'you'. Here are permutations of a few possibilities, which it is useful to compare in class discussion:

. . . if one wants to study new medicines . . .

. . . for those who want/need to study new medicines . . .

. . . for specialists/researchers/anyone/someone studying new medicines . . .

Despite the differences in register and message content, these variants do all have one thing in common: all are particularizations, in that they add details that are, at most, implicit in the ST – person, time, and sometimes modality ('want to', 'need to'). In fact, transposing a nominal expression into a verbal one almost inevitably results in either particularizing translation or partially overlapping translation with a strongly particularizing bias. This is often a significant consideration in translation. The issue can generally be avoided if the ST nominalization is copied in the TT, as in the 'technical' TT above, in rendering 'coltura' as 'culture', 'studio' as 'study' and 'confronto' as 'comparison'. But if a decision is taken not to render noun with noun, particularization is often inevitable. For instance, 'di recente introduzione' gives no indication of who introduced the new methods. Rendering it with a verb forces the translator to narrow the focus from the general abstraction 'introduction' to a particular act performed by a particular someone. At this point, an element of surmise comes in: was it one person or more? were they researchers or technicians? pharmacologists?

biochemists? bacteriologists? Sometimes, the context gives the answer; sometimes the translator will know, or be able to find out, from other sources. Often, the particularization will not matter; but particularization there will usually be.

This particularization is not confined to the subject of the verb. Supposing the verb of our ST sentence were in a different tense: 'si prestava/sarebbe prestata', etc. The verb 'introduce' would then have to be in the appropriate TL tense: 'had introduced/have *or* had introduced', etc.

Note that, in this example, the temporal adjective 'recente' restricts the number of available tenses. With a different adjective, the range of possible particularizations could be wider. For instance (depending on the tense of 'prestarsi'), the noun in 'd'opportuna introduzione' could be rendered in many ways: 'introduce/are introducing/introduced/have introduced/had introduced/were introducing/will introduce/would introduce', etc. Which of these was chosen would depend on context, the translator's knowledge of the field, and whether the translation loss incurred was significant.

There are two main implications for translators in the discussion so far. The first is that nouns, especially abstract nouns, typically have a generic quality. Such a noun contains many different potential particularizations; in most cases, these cannot be predicted from the noun itself, but can only be inferred from context or extratextual factors. Second, the generic nature of nouns, especially abstract nouns, also gives them a kind of static quality. So, 'introduction' is a concept, an abstraction frozen outside time; but any finite form of the verb 'to introduce' ('I'm introducing', 'you introduced', etc.) is dynamic, as well as particularizing, in that the referent is an event happening in time and performed by an agent. Arguably, this is even true of gerunds: compare 'preparing vegetables' and 'the preparation of vegetables'.

These considerations are relevant for translation when there is choice between retaining ST nominalization and abandoning it. The choice has implications for genre, register and idiomaticity. This is clear in the pharmacological example: as we have already said (p. 135), even non-technical Italian makes much more use of nominalization than non-technical English does. So, even in translating technical texts, it should not be assumed that all ST nominal structures have to be rendered with TL nominal structures. Our specimen sentence contains an example: the technical TT renders 'di recente introduzione' as 'recently introduced', not as 'of recent introduction'. Two other examples from the pharmacology text are discussed on p. 135.

If the translator is aiming to produce a TT that does not draw attention grammatically to its Italian origin, then as a rule of thumb it can be said that, the less scientific, technical or academic the ST, the more the nominalization will need to be rendered through grammatical transposition. Even in user manuals, which are sometimes quite technical, rendering noun with noun would often give comic results. To get the measure of this, the following extracts from the handbook for a portable CD player should be analysed and discussed in class; a literal translation of either would be heavily marked by exoticism:

Inserting the CD	**Inserimento del CD**
Push gently on the CD center so that it fits onto the hub.	Esercitare una lieve pressione in corrispondenza del centro del CD in modo che si inserisca correttamente sul supporto.
Removing the CD	**Rimozione del CD**
Hold the CD by its edge and press the hub gently. [. . .]	Tenere il CD per il bordo ed esercitare una lieve pressione sul supporto. [. . .]
Deactivating all buttons	**Disattivazione di tutti i tasti**
Slide the switch to the right to deactivate all buttons (except the button OPEN).	Portare l'interruttore sulla destra per disattivare tutti i tasti (ad eccezione di OPEN).
• Display indication: HOLD.	• Indicazione su display di: HOLD.
• Now, the set is protected against accidentally activating the buttons when you are carrying the CD player around.	• In questo modo, l'apparecchio è protetto dall'eventuale azionamento accidentale dei tasti durante il trasporto del lettore.

A good way of showing that nominalization is more characteristic of Italian than of English is to take an ST and TT from a genre very distant from scientific writing or hi-fi handbooks. Here is an extract from Irvine Welsh's *Trainspotting*, with its published translation. The ST is very colloquial; it is striking how much more nominalized even this colloquial TT is. These nominalizations should be identified and discussed before going on to the rest of the chapter. (It would also be useful to discuss the mistranslation in TT ll. 13–16.)

ST

Sick Boy tourniqued Ali above her elbow, obviously staking his place in the queue, and tapped up a vein oan her thin ash-white airm.

– Want me tae dae it? he asked.
She nodded.

He droaps a cotton ball intae the spoon n blaws oan it, before sucking up aboot 5 mls through the needle, intae the barrel ay the syringe. He's goat a fuckin huge blue vein tapped up, which seems

TT

Sick Boy stringe forte un laccio sopra al gomito di Ali, prenotandosi chiaramente il posto in fila, e si mette a darle dei colpetti sul braccio, sottile e bianco come la cenere, per tirar fuori la vena.

'Te lo faccio io, se vuoi', le dice.
Lei fa segno di sì.

Lui lascia cadere nel cucchiaino un batuffolo di ovatta e ci soffia sopra, poi con l'ago risucchia nel cilindro della siringa 5 ml. di

tae be almost comin through Ali's
airm. He pierces her flesh and
15 injects a wee bit slowly, before
sucking blood back intae the
chamber. Her lips are quivering as
she gazes pleadingly at him for a
second or two. Sick Boy's face
20 looks ugly, leering and reptilian,
before he slams the cocktail
towards her brain.

    She pulls back her heid, shuts
her eyes and opens her mooth,
25 givin oot an orgasmic groan. Sick
Boy's eyes are now innocent and
full ay wonder, his expression like
a bairn thit's come through oan
Christmas morning tae a pile ay
30 gift-wrapped presents stacked under
the tree. They baith look strangely
beautiful and pure in the flickering
candlelight.

                         (Welsh 1996a: 8–9)
35

liquido. Ha una vena del cazzo che
gli sporge, enorme, blu, così grossa
che sembra quasi di vederla
attraverso il braccio di Ali. Le fa
un buco e gliene inietta un goccio
piano piano, prima di risucchiare
un po' di sangue nella siringa. Lei
lo guarda fisso per un istante o
due, le labbra che le tremano, lo
sguardo implorante. Sick Boy ha
una faccia brutta, un'espressione
malefica, da serpente, prima di
schiaffarle in corpo quel cocktail
che le arriva dritto al cervello.

    Lei getta la testa all'indietro, e
con gli occhi chiusi e la bocca
semiaperta tira fuori un verso da
orgasmo. Sick Boy adesso ha gli
occhi pieni di stupore e di inno-
cenza, ha l'espressione di un
bambino che si sveglia la mattina
di Natale e trova ammucchiati
sotto l'albero un sacco di regali
impacchettati. Hanno un'aria strana
tutti e due, belli e puri alla luce
tremolante della candela.

                      (Welsh 1996b: 15)

In the pharmacology text, we saw potentially major changes that can be
entailed in transposing a nominal expression into a verbal one. Often, there
is little or no option but to do this. The translator of *Trainspotting* had to
do it in reverse in the first sentence of our extract, 'tourniqued' becoming
'stringe forte un laccio'. Here are some examples from Italian STs:

Mi trovavo nell'impossibilità di far fronte ai debiti.

[*From the instruction leaflet for an espresso machine*] Premere il tasto
caffè. Al raggiungimento della quantità desiderata premere nuovamente
il tasto per disinserirlo.

[*On jacking up a car, from an owner's handbook*] Procedere al solleva-
mento della vettura sino a quando la ruota risulta sollevata da terra di
alcuni centimetri.

[*On football coaches' problems with new signings*] La difficoltà d'inserimento dei nuovi.

Where the translator does have a choice, the deciding factors will usually be contextual considerations such as genre and register, as in the following examples:

Un mercato in continuo sviluppo.	A market in constant evolution/A constantly evolving market.
Nell'esercizio delle proprie funzioni.	In the performance of one's duties/While carrying out one's duties.
Non sono in grado di dirlo.	I'm not in a position to say/I can't say.
Rimozione del CD.	Removal of the CD/Removing the CD.
[Il fungo atomico levatosi nel cielo] al momento dello scoppio del reattore.	[. . .] at the moment of the explosion of the reactor/when the reactor exploded.

As the last example shows, using a TL verb is not the only grammatical transposition open to the translator faced with ST nominalization. Rendering '*al momento* dello scoppio del reattore' as '*when* the reactor exploded' is a typical instance of translating a noun-based ST adverbial phrase with a conjunction-based TL one. There is another example in the same text (the 'Cernóbil' text in Practical 2): 'zone distanti migliaia di chilometri dal luogo del disastro'. Again, the choice depends on the contextual constraints of genre and register. Here are three possibilities for comparison in class:

areas thousands of miles from the place/site of the disaster.

areas thousands of miles from the disaster site.

areas thousands of miles from where the disaster occurred.

Many noun-based Italian adverbial expressions are regularly translated with simple adverbs in English. Sometimes there is little or no choice but to do this, as in:

Non si vedeva da nessuna parte.	She was nowhere to be seen.
La casa di fronte.	The house opposite.

We shall concentrate on cases where there is a degree of choice, because this is where the translator has to make a reasoned decision.

Very often indeed, an Italian adverbial phrase will have a *preposition + noun* structure. The structure is usually also possible in English; but English nearly always has a choice between it and a simple adverb, even where Italian does not. As we shall see, the fact that choice is possible raises important translation issues. Here are two examples of this type of phrase:

| Accogliamo senza esitazione la vostra proposta. | We accept your proposal without hesitation/unhesitatingly. |
| Parlava con agitazione delle lettere. | She was talking in agitation/agitatedly about the letters. |

In comparing the pairs of TTs, most English-speakers will feel that there is a difference in register between the alternatives. But there may also be another difference. In the second example, certainly, the adverb 'agitatedly' is arguably more dynamic and concrete than 'in agitation', in so far as it invites the reader to *picture* her behaving in an agitated way – looking distraught, fidgeting, breathing unevenly, etc. It is like an excerpt from a film. In contrast, the version with a noun expresses more of a detached discernment and definition of what is involved: 'agitation' is an abstraction, more an *inference from* how she was behaving than a *description of* it. The distinction is a fine one, and some people will be more sensitive to it than others. Nevertheless, a whole TT can be affected by how the translator renders the many such expressions as:

con cortesia	with kindness/kindly
senza complessi	without (any) inhibition(s)/ uninhibitedly
con ragione	with reason/rightly

Nor must it be forgotten that the choice is often not purely one of register, but has semantic implications as well. This is clear in the last example, where in many contexts there will be a significant difference between the two TL possibilities.

An expanded form of this structure, and just as common, is *preposition + noun + adjective*. Here again, English often has a choice between this and a structure that is usually denied to Italian, this time *adverb + adjective*:

| È d'importanza decisiva. | It's of crucial importance/crucially important. |
| Un'invenzione melodica di dolorosa dolcezza. | A melodic invention of painful sweetness/A painfully sweet melodic line. |

Here again, there is more than just a difference in register between the alternative TTs. Take the second example, from a text on a piano sonata. Leaving aside the question of what 'invenzione' means, 'of painful sweetness' is not just more donnish, it is also more abstract and static. As in the 'agitation' example, the sweetness is a quality that has been intellectually inferred from the physical experience of hearing the music – the listener has analysed the experience, discerned sweetness in it, and then discerned pain in the sweetness. In 'painfully sweet', the sweetness is described as actively hurting the listener. Whereas the adverb expresses an immediacy of sensation, the nominalization implies that one has stood back from one's reactions, assessed them and allotted them to a category. (This may be why nominal expressions so often strike English-speakers as academic or even pedantic.)

In translating *preposition + noun + adjective*, there are more registers open to the English-speaker than to the Italian-speaker: it is unlikely that the Italian author would have written 'un'invenzione melodica dolorosamente dolce'! The main deciding factors in choosing the TL register will be genre and context. And, as the musical example shows, translators should always remember that even elementary syntax is a relevant contextual factor: 'invention of painful sweetness' is in fact ambiguous, but 'painfully sweet invention' would not be.

Two more examples of this same structure show another possibility open to the translator, that of using one adverb to qualify another, in juxtaposition:

Fu eletta quasi all'unanimità.	She was elected virtually unanimously.
Suona con delicatezza sbalorditiva.	He plays amazingly delicately.

Whereas English readily juxtaposes adverbs ending in -*ly*, Italian rarely if ever does it with adverbs in -*mente*. In the second example, there is again a choice between keeping the ST nominalization and using the two adverbs; and again, the deciding factor is probably that of genre: 'He plays with amazing delicacy' would be completely unexceptionable in a critical review or a lecture.

There are two lessons for translators in these adverbial examples. First, the grammatical transpositions are likely to affect register. In English, noun-based adverbial phrases can sound formal or pretentious. But because the structures do exist in English, it is easy to produce TT expressions calqued on ST expressions of this type. The result is often a TT that is more formal or pompous than the ST, where these structures are unexceptional, stylistically unmarked, and do not strike SL readers as formal. Second, it seems almost inevitable that these transpositions will entail partially overlapping translation, with explicit things being left to inference and implicit things being made explicit. A decision has to be made in each case as to whether the translation loss entailed needs to be compensated for.

Sometimes, an Italian nominal structure lends itself to more than one possible grammatical transposition. Here is an example from Practical 7, followed by the published TT and then by an alternative:

Le due classi, dei pessimisti e degli ottimisti, non sono peraltro così ben distinte: non già perché gli agnostici siano molti, ma perché i più, senza memoria né coerenza, oscillano fra le due posizioni-limite, a seconda dell'interlocutore e del momento.

The two classes of pessimists and optimists are not so clearly defined, however, not because there are many agnostics, but because the majority, without memory or coherence, drift between the two extremes, according to the moment and the mood of the person they happen to meet.

And yet the two types, the pessimists and the optimists, are not so very different: not so much because a lot of us are agnostic about it, but rather because, forgetfully and inconsistently, most swing between the two extremes, depending on whom they are talking to and when.

The ST expression 'senza memoria né coerenza' invites translation with adverbs: 'forgetfully and inconsistently'. Keeping the ST structure, 'without memory or consistency', would suggest chronic amnesia, and perhaps softness (hence no doubt the use of 'coherence' instead of 'consistency'). However, translating with adverbs necessitates reordering the sentence. If they were placed between 'most' and 'swing', this might distort the message, because they could be describing the manner of swinging more than the minds of the people. Even the second TT is open to this criticism. Fortunately, a close approximation to the ST can be achieved by using adjectives instead of adverbs: 'but rather because, forgetful and inconsistent, most swing between the two extremes'.

This example is useful for three reasons. First, it shows that choosing whether to abandon noun-for-noun translation is not a one-dimensional affair; multiple factors are involved in any grammatical transposition. Second, it raises the question of what translation loss the use of adjectives rather than adverbs incurs in respect of dynamism and concreteness – this is something worth discussing in class. And as such, third, it is a good introduction to another common transposition, from Italian noun to English adjective.

Of course, there are many cases where the translator has little choice: 'Ho fame/sete/ragione'; 'fa un freddo terribile'; 'nel bene e nel male', etc. This is also true of the common *preposition + noun* structure, as in:

ruota di scorta	spare wheel
passaggio a livello	level crossing
pezzo di ricambio	spare part
le indagini del caso	the appropriate investigations

Very often, English uses nouns as adjectives where Italian more clearly preserves their nominal status with a preposition: 'uscita/cintura/misure di

sicurezza'; 'motore a scoppio'; 'locomotiva a vapore'; 'i lavori di fatica', etc.
More challenging for the translator are cases where there is a genuine choice:

La freschezza dei vostri pesci lascia a desiderare.	The freshness of your fish leaves something to be desired/Your fish are less than fresh.
Un mascalzone di prim'ordine.	A scoundrel of the first order/prime scoundrel.
Che larghezza ha?	What's the width/How wide is it?
Neanche pensare a presentarsi semplicemente a Bianchi, implicitamente concordando sulla sua bruttezza.	No question of simply introducing himself to Bianchi and implicitly agreeing he really is ugly.

This last example calls for comment! Rossi has to meet Bianchi, but
doesn't know him. Bianchi said over the phone that there'd be no problem:
'Io sono bruttissimo.' Now, of course, assuming Rossi does recognize
Bianchi, he is agonizing over how to approach him. The translation problem
is that rendering noun with noun – 'agreeing on/about/over his ugliness' –
would not ring true. The adjective 'ugly' is the only realistic option. However,
Italian does have a choice here between a nominal construction and a verbal
one ('che era/fosse brutto'), whereas English has no unmarked idiomatic
alternative. In its context, the ST formulation is slightly more emphatic
than the verbal construction would be. The TL adjective 'ugly' loses this
emphasis, but the loss is compensated for with the added intensifier 'really'.

As all these examples suggest, there may be less difference, in respect
of dynamism, between a noun and an adjective than between a noun and
an adverb: compare 'forgetful and inconsistent' and 'forgetfully and inconsistently', or 'with amazing delicacy' and 'amazingly delicately'. There is
a stronger implication in the adjectives that the things described have been
scrutinized and allotted to appropriate categories before the sentence is
uttered. Even so, the element of analysis, categorization and abstraction
is often still more evident in the use of a noun as opposed to an adjective:
compare 'incoherent' and 'without coherence', or 'concordando che fosse
brutto' and 'concordando sulla sua bruttezza'. As with the other grammatical transpositions discussed in this chapter, the translator has to decide each
time whether the translation loss incurred is serious enough to require
compensation. And, of course, this can only be done in terms of the purpose
and genre of the ST and the TT.

A fourth category of nominalization involves prepositions. There are two
sorts of translation issue here. The first is that Italian prepositions are often
reinforced with a noun in cases where their English counterparts stand on
their own, as in these examples:

Agisco per conto del signor Paoli.	I'm acting for Signor Paoli.
È molto gentile da parte tua.	That's very nice of you.
Non è all'altezza del proprio compito.	He's not up to his job.

In prepositional phrases like these, the noun is generally not translated. Sometimes, there is a real choice. In Italian as in English, technical texts and user manuals are sometimes marked by *needless* nominalization, as if the greater abstraction gave the text more dignity or authority. The first four of the following sentences are typical examples of this in Italian – in each case, a preposition could have been used on its own, or with an adjective. In some of these cases, nominalization seems very unlikely in English; in others, the deciding factor will be genre and register:

Inserire il martinetto nel lungherone, in prossimità della ruota [cf. vicino alla ruota].	Insert the jack into the side member, near the wheel.
Disattivare tutti i tasti (ad eccezione di OPEN) [cf. eccetto OPEN].	Deactivate all the buttons (except OPEN).
Lei è esperto in materia di religione [cf. in religione].	You're an expert on the subject of religion/on religion.
A basso contenuto di colesterolo [cf. con poco colesterolo].	With a low cholesterol content/low in cholesterol.
Diglielo da parte mia.	Tell him on my behalf/Tell him from me.

The second issue is that of prepositional and phrasal verbs. A prepositional verb is one that forms a combination with a preposition, for example *refer to*, *apply for*, *live off*, *call on*, *hint at*. A phrasal verb forms a combination with an adverbial particle, for example *turn down*, *call up*, *dust off*, *catch on*. These adverbs are generally identical in form to prepositions, which is why we are considering phrasal and prepositional verbs together. The following examples bring out clearly constructions which are very common in English but hard to achieve in Italian. Translating from Italian, the problem is that it is usually possible to keep the Italian structure and use a noun in English, although it is often more idiomatic to substitute a prepositional or phrasal verb for the noun. Sometimes, the decision is a matter of nuance or register, as in:

Vive a spese della madre.	She's living at her mother's expense/off her mother.

Mi sono fatto largo a forza di gomitate.	I used my elbows to get through/ elbowed my way through.
Tornò col pensiero alla sua infanzia.	She went back in her thoughts to her childhood/thought back to her childhood.
Lo rispedisce nel casone con un calcio.	He sends him back into the hut with a kick/kicks him back into the hut.
Alzò gli occhi dal suo libro.	She raised her eyes from her book/ looked up from her book.
Scomparirà una volta passato l'effetto del vino.	It'll go away once the wine's worn off.

Often, however, if the TT is not to be marked with exoticism, there is no choice but to drop the noun:

Le ho fatto cenno col braccio di venire.	I waved her over.
Lei mi mandò via con la mano.	She waved me away.
A dare un colpo di spugna al passato e al futuro si impara assai presto.	You pretty soon learn to wipe away/ erase the past and the future.

In all the examples we have looked at, the versions with prepositional or phrasal verbs are more concise, arguably more concrete and dynamic, but also more impressionistic, less precise. The nature and degree of translation loss has to be assessed for each individual case. Where there genuinely is a choice, a crucial factor (as well as genre and register) is how idiomatic a noun-for-noun translation would be. What is certain is that if there were no prepositional or phrasal verbs at all in an English text, it would read somewhat oddly, even if the reader could not quite pin down why.

We have been talking in this chapter about a notable contrast between Italian and English. But this does not mean that the translator has mechanically to strip an English text of nouns, or pack an Italian one with nominalization! The sensible starting-point is always to try rendering noun with noun, adverb with adverb, and so on. It is just that, in the many cases where nominalization does after all turn out to require grammatical transposition, the translator is statistically more likely to transpose *from* a noun in translating into English, and *to* a noun in translating into Italian.

There are, of course, plenty of exceptions to the statistical norm. Here, to conclude this warning word of common sense, are some examples for discussion:

Ogni congettura è arbitraria ed esattamente priva di fondamento reale.	All conjecture is arbitrary and utterly without foundation in reality.
Gli altri lo scappellottano.	The others clap him on the back.
Costruire nel rispetto delle norme più restrittive per essere in grado di rispondere produttivamente alla domanda espressa dai mercati.	Observe the strictest constructional standards and thus be able to match production to the specific demands of the market.
Ci sentiamo telefonicamente.	We'll talk on the phone.
Lo studente che non conosce una lingua straniera è nettamente svantaggiato.	A student who does not know a foreign language is at a clear disadvantage.
È meglio prevenire che curare.	Prevention is better than cure.
Sono misure che tradiscono clamorosamente gli impegni presi dal partito.	These measures are a blatant betrayal of the commitments undertaken by the party.
Una missione culturale finalizzata a [. . .].	A cultural mission with the following aims [. . .].
Un momento culminante del suo originale rapporto con le forme classiche.	A climactic point in the originality of his approach to classical forms.
Neanche pensare a presentarsi semplicemente a Bianchi.	No question of simply introducing himself to Bianchi.

17

Contrastive topic and practical: Determiners

This chapter constitutes the material for all or part of a practical. It concerns five of the many types of determiner in Italian and English. A **determiner** is an expression which specifies the range of reference of a noun. We have chosen determiners which often pose problems in translation. The five types are: definite and indefinite articles (*the*, *a*); demonstratives (*this*, *that*, *those*); possessives (*my*, *your*, etc.); relative pronouns, a subset of the *wh*-determiners (*what(ever)*, *which(ever)*, *whose*); and quantifiers (*some*, *any*, *each*, etc.). We shall give most attention to cases where there tends to be asymmetry between English and Italian usage – that is, where one type of determiner tends to be rendered with a different type, or where a determiner is present in one language but not in the other.

We begin with articles. In general, the way articles are used in the two languages does not usually cause translation problems. However, there are significant differences in their use, which do need to be borne in mind. For instance, in Italian the definite article is used in some cases where it would be omitted in English:

I cani sono *gli animali domestici* più   *Dogs* are the most intelligent (of) *pets.*
intelligenti.

L'amore è una cosa meravigliosa.   *Love* is a many-splendoured thing.

Generic plurals are unaccompanied by 'the' in English as a rule, as the first example shows. And, as the second example shows, English does not require the definite article before normally uncountable nouns (i.e. nouns like 'violence', 'obstinacy', 'furniture'), unless they are followed by modifiers in the form of prepositions or relative clauses (e.g. '*The* furniture (*which is*) *in* this room is antique'). In Italian, modifiers of this type often have consequences for translation, as in the following example. (*Contextual information.* The protagonist lives alone in a house with a beautiful view of the harbour and the sea. She rarely goes out, and often stands gazing out of the window.)

> La bellezza dalle sue finestre era la bellezza; i rumori che salivano dal porto erano i rumori.

This sentence contains two different SL uses of the definite article. The first 'la bellezza' is modified by 'che': it is the particular beauty she sees from her window. The second is generic beauty (i.e. beauty as a class, as in e.g. 'la bellezza è una specie di armonia', '[all] beauty is a kind of harmony'). Similarly, the first 'i rumori' are the particular ones she hears, and the second are generic (as in e.g. 'questa camera è isolata contro i rumori').

Clearly, the generic expressions cannot be translated using the English definite article:

> The beauty from her windows was *the beauty*; the noises that rose from the harbour were *the noises*.

The immediate response to this sentence is to assume that the expressions italicized refer to things already mentioned in the text – *which* beauty? *which* noises? The trouble is that if the articles are omitted, as English grammar demands, then it is not clear that the second 'beauty' and the second 'noises' are not TL partitive constructions – i.e. that the reference is not to a part or sample of beauty or noises, as one might say '(some) milk and (some) eggs':

> The beauty from her windows was beauty; the noises that rose from the harbour were noises.

Here, for discussion, are three possible ways round the problem; which is preferable will depend on the register, the emphases and possibly the prosodic features of the immediate context.

(a) The beauty from her windows was Beauty; the noises that rose from the harbour were Noise.

(b) The beauty from her windows was all of/the whole of beauty; the noises that rose from the harbour were all of/the whole of noise.

(c) The beauty from her window was what beauty was; the noises that rose from the port were what noise was.

One reason why the differences between Italian and English definite articles are important is that Italian is so much more heavily nominalized than English, as we saw in Chapter 16. Where there is a noun, there either is or is not an article; and significant instances of the presence or absence of articles are more numerous in a typical Italian text than in a typical English one. A good illustration of both points is found in expressions involving parts of the body. Here is an example for discussion, from the translation of *Trainspotting*. Compare it with (a) the interlinear back-translation and (b) the original English:

Lei lo guarda fisso per un istante o due, le labbra che le tremano, lo sguardo implorante. Sick Boy ha una faccia brutta, un'espressione malefica, da serpente, prima di schiaffarle in corpo quel cocktail che le arriva dritto al cervello.

(a) She looks at him fixedly for a moment or two, the lips which tremble to her, the look imploring. Sick Boy has an ugly face, a maleficent expression, of a serpent, before flinging to her into body that cocktail that arrives to her straight to the brain.

(b) Her lips are quivering as she gazes pleadingly at him for a second or two. Sick Boy's face looks ugly, leering and reptilian, before he slams the cocktail towards her brain.

As this example shows, the differences between English and Italian in respect of parts of the body are also a simple reminder that translating definite articles is not just a matter of keeping or omitting the article, but of deciding whether to exchange definite and indefinite articles, or even whether to use a completely different part of speech, such as a possessive adjective.

It is not only parts of the body that attract the characteristic choice between article and possessive. Here are two simple examples:

Sono nell'impossibilità di far fronte ai debiti.	I just can't cope with my debts.
Non chiudere i quaderni.	Don't close your books.

Sometimes, the three-way option (omit the article, swap definite and indefinite, use a possessive) is insufficient. Here is an example from the Vittorio Russo text in Practical 9.1; the reference is to all human souls, not those of specific individuals: 'Rafforzare il potere del papa sulle anime'. In context, 'strengthen the pope's power over the souls' is not an option; 'strengthen the pope's power over souls' sounds unconvincing, and is in any case potentially ambiguous – it could mean just *some* souls. A more accurate and idiomatic version would seem to involve a different option, such as the partially overlapping translation 'the pope's power over people's souls'. If the alliteration here is unacceptable, an alternative might be 'the pope's power over the human soul' – but this is significantly different from the ST.

We have seen that the translator's choice may sometimes be between definite and indefinite article. As with the definite article, use of the indefinite article is broadly similar in the two languages, but there are certain variations. For example, the same form in Italian corresponds to English 'a/an' and 'one', and generalizations show divergent tendencies:

Lo studente che non conosce almeno *una* lingua straniera è nettamente svantaggiato.	*A* student who does not know at least *one* foreign language is at a definite disadvantage.

Although 'the student' could be used here, it may sound unnatural. In some contexts, it might be even more natural to express the concept in the generic plural in English ('Students who . . .'). Some of the simplest everyday constructions are reminders of the possible asymmetry of definite and indefinite articles, as in:

Tre volte al giorno.	Three times a day.
2500 lire il pacchetto.	2,500 lire a packet.

It is one thing to spot how to translate an Italian article. It is another to spot cases where an idiomatic translation requires using an article in the TT where a different determiner is used in the ST. Particularly troublesome in this respect are the demonstratives *quello* and *questo*. In particular, ST demonstrative will often best be rendered with TT article and vice versa, or sometimes even by a pronoun. Here are some simple examples:

[*Choosing a green shirt in preference to a red one*] La preferisco a quella rossa.	I prefer it to the red one.
[*Shopping for clothes with a friend*] Mi sta bene questa gonna? – Sì, ma quella rossa ti starebbe meglio.	'Does this skirt suit me?' 'Yes, but the red one would suit you better.'
Non è più quella di prima.	She's not the woman she was.
In questi giorni l'Onu discute sulla criminalità transnazionale.	Over the last few days UNO has been debating transnational crime.

Very often, the Italian demonstrative is best dropped altogether. Sometimes, an English demonstrative is preferable to an Italian article. Sometimes 'the . . . one', 'the latter', etc. will be odd in context, and it will be more idiomatic to repeat the noun. Sometimes it is more idiomatic to render 'questo' with 'that' and 'quello' with 'this'. Here are some examples of TTs that may need revision. Revising them in discussion is a good way of sharpening awareness of these asymmetries between Italian and English determiners, and of the need to use sometimes considerable grammatical transposition in translation.

[. . .] segue i discorsi e ride e gira intorno gli occhi verdi. E ogni volta i suoi occhi s'incontrano con quelli ombrati del Dritto [. . .].
(Calvino 1993: 87)

[. . .] she is following what's said and laughing and swivelling her green eyes around the room. And every time her eyes meet the shadowed ones of Dritto [. . .].
(Calvino 1976: 77)

[*In reply to someone boasting that he has stolen a sailor's pistol*] Una pistola marinaia: sarà di quelle a acqua!
(Calvino 1993: 76)

A naval pistol; it must be one of those water ones.
(Calvino 1976: 68)

[. . .] le parole enigmatiche di Tancredi, quelle retoriche di Ferrara, quelle false ma rivelatrici di Russo, avevano ceduto il loro rassicurante segreto.
(Tomasi di Lampedusa 1963a: 29)

[. . .] the enigmatic words of Tancredi, the rhetorical ones of Ferrara, the false but revealing ones of Russo, had yielded their reassuring secret.
(Tomasi di Lampedusa 1963b: 34)

[*Looking at paintings of ancestral lands and castles, the protagonist reflects on the fading of wealth and feudal power*] E di già alcuni di quei feudi tanto festosi nei quadri avevano preso il volo e permanevano soltanto nelle tele variopinte e nei nomi. Altri sembravano quelle rondini settembrine ancor presenti ma di già radunate stridenti sugli alberi, pronte a partire.
(Tomasi di Lampedusa 1963a: 26)

Already some of the estates which looked so gay in those pictures had taken wing, leaving behind only bright-coloured paintings and names. Others seemed like those September swallows which though still present are already grouped stridently on trees, ready for departure.
(Tomasi di Lampedusa 1963b: 31)

The fifth type of determiner is the relative pronoun. The most common problems are posed by Italian relative clauses beginning with expressions corresponding to *whose/of which* or *preposition + whose/of which + noun* (e.g. '(on) the sides of which/(on) whose sides'). Often, a relative clause turns out to be unidiomatic or cumbersome in an English TT, and grammatical transposition is needed. Here are two typical examples. (*Contextual information*. The narrator is looking into a coach-house from the doorway. The building has also been used as a makeshift gymnasium in the past.)

All'interno del vasto stanzone, in fondo al quale, nella penombra, tralucevano le sommità di due lustre, bionde pertiche da palestra, alte fino al soffitto, aleggiava un odore strano [. . .]. Il centro della rimessa era occupato da due vetture affiancate: una lunga Dilambda grigia, e una carrozza blu, le cui stanghe, rialzate, risultavano appena più basse delle pertiche retrostanti.	Inside the enormous room, at the end of which, in the half light, there gleamed the tops of two pale polished gymnasium poles that reached the ceiling, an odd smell hung about [. . .]. The middle of the coach-house was taken up with two vehicles, side by side: a long grey Dilambda and a blue carriage, the shafts of which, standing on end, were only slightly lower than the gym poles.
(Bassani 1991: 92)	(Bassani 1989: 116)

Grammatically, there is nothing wrong with the TT, even if 'at the end of which' and 'the shafts of which' sound bookish and a bit old-fashioned. In academic or technical texts in English, such structures are not unusual, but in most genres a TT containing more than an occasional instance would be off-puttingly leaden. Many translations from Italian do render relative pronoun with relative pronoun; this can have the advantage of preserving the ST sequential focus (and thus focus of attention), but at the cost of idiomaticity. As with so many grammatical structures, it often happens that this loss of idiomaticity actually disrupts the reading process, drawing attention less to what the text is saying and more to how it is trying to say it. There is therefore often less serious translation loss in restructuring the sentence than in keeping the ST relative pronouns and sequential focus. Here is a revised version of the Bassani TT which does this; compare the three texts in respect of grammar, idiomaticity and translation loss:

> In the half-light at the end of the enormous room gleamed the tips of two pale, polished gym poles that reached the ceiling. Inside, an odd smell drifted in the air [. . .]. The middle of the coach-house was taken up with two vehicles, side by side: a long grey Dilambda and a blue carriage, its upturned shafts only slightly lower than the gym poles behind it.

Note that Bassani's translator has *added* a relative clause where there is none in the ST: 'alte fino al soffitto' is translated as 'that reached the ceiling'. In context, this surely reads better than a literal translation of the adjectival phrase would. The example is a reminder that translating from Italian is not simply a matter of getting rid of as many relative pronouns as possible! Indeed, it very often happens that a relative clause is inserted in English when translating an Italian past participle used quasi-adjectivally. Here is an example adapted from the text in Practical 2.1:

Il fungo atomico levatosi nel cielo al momento dello scoppio del reattore.	The mushroom cloud that rose into the sky when the reactor exploded.

A particular feature in Italian relative clauses is that Italian has a choice between two different forms of the relative pronoun: sometimes, 'che' could be ambiguous, referring to either of two antecedents. This ambiguity is easily avoided by using 'il quale', 'la quale', 'del(la) quale', etc., instead of 'che'. Here is a good example, adapted from the ST in Practical 2.1:

> Una località in cui il 26 aprile del 1986 esplose – con conseguenze devastanti – un reattore della centrale nucleare, la quale era in funzione dal 1978.

If 'che' were used here instead of 'la quale', it would be unclear whether it referred to 'reattore' or to 'centrale'. English does not have such a choice: the only possible literal translation of the ST relative pronoun is 'which', but this would be ambiguous. The simplest idiomatic solution is to repeat 'power station':

> A city where a reactor in the nuclear power station exploded on 26 April 1986 with devastating results. The power station had been in service since 1978.

(This TT incidentally also contains a good example of the use of 'where' to render 'in cui'; as so often, 'where' seems more idiomatic in this case than 'in which'.)

To conclude these comments on relative pronouns, here are two more examples with alternative TTs for discussion:

Un mare tutto trine di spuma, sul quale galere imbandierate caracollavano.	(a) A sea of white-flecked waves on which pranced beflagged galleons. (b) A sea with beflagged galleons prancing on the white-flecked waves. (c) A sea where beflagged galleons pranced on the white-flecked waves.

Si addormentò, in una sorta di disperata euforia, cullato dal trotto dei bai, sulle cui natiche grasse i lampioncini della vettura facevano oscillare la luce.	(a) He dozed off into a kind of tense euphoria, lulled by the trotting of the bays on whose plump flanks quivered the light from the carriage lamps. (b) He dozed off, in a kind of despairing euphoria, lulled by the trotting bays and the light from the carriage lamps flickering on their plump flanks.

It is clear from the foregoing that although English and Italian share some types of determiner, they often use them in different ways. Some of the grammatical transpositions entailed in translating them are standard, others are optional and depend on context. Often, there are subtle differences which are imperceptible on first reading an ST, but which become very significant during the translation process. This is particularly true of articles, which can assume a stylistic, rather than a purely grammatical, role; in these cases, problems may arise in the reformulation, because of the whole context in which the ST was written and published.

Some of these considerations are illustrated in the following example. It presents a range of features which presuppose not only alertness to the ST context but also some familiarity with the people mentioned (public figures), the place (Rome) and the issue (Roman dialect). It is in this wider context that the articles play their role, between grammar and style. Before reading our comments on the text, translate it as if for publication in a broadsheet supplement on contemporary Italy. Then, in class, discuss how far the use of articles in student TTs mirrors that of the ST:

LINGUA E LINGUACCE

Perché il romanesco è diventato sinonimo di volgarità

Il Novissimo Ceccarelli Illustrato

'A Fra', che te serve?' Tutto cominciò con questa frase, anno 1980. Anzi, non semplicemente 'frase': slogan, tormentone giornalistico per sintetizzare un tic, un malcostume, un modo di vivere e di essere dei politici romani, faciloni, arroganti, smaccatamente corrotti. 'Fra'' era Franco Evangelisti,
5 corrente andreottiana, cardine di quella Dc strapotente che deteneva un regno a suo modo assoluto, ma che cominciava già a scricchiolare. Evangelisti raccontò senza remore (questi erano i tempi) all'intervistatore Paolo Guzzanti il piccolo aneddoto che fece epoca, nel senso proprio che segnò un'epoca: i Caltagirone, inaffondabile schiatta di 'palazzinari' romani, erano pronti a
10 esaudire ogni richiesta degli alleati politici. E si esprimevano in romanesco puro, prontamente riportato da Guzzanti sulla *Repubblica*.

E questo romanesco è moneta corrente, ingrediente giornalistico inevitabile, ogni volta che si vuole screditare, simpaticamente o meno, un qualche personaggio pubblico col vezzo di esprimersi nel colorito gergo della capitale. Non succede con altri dialetti. Dal Nord al Sud, un lombardo o un siciliano difficilmente diventa macchietta come invece succede per direttissima ad un romano. Ultimo in ordine di tempo il pittoresco avvocato Aldo Ceccarelli, che sembra un'invenzione di Carlo Verdone.

(Petrignani 1997: 168)

For 'il romanesco' in the title one could retain the article ('the Roman dialect'), although it may be better to eliminate it, as the term appears in a headline. It is also possible to reduce the expression simply to 'Roman', because the words 'Lingua e linguacce' give an idea of the subject matter. The reference to 'Il Novissimo Ceccarelli Illustrato' is both a paronym and a pun. The title of the well-known dictionary alluded to is 'Gabrielli', not 'Ceccarelli' (the latter reference appears in l. 18). Dealing successfully and succinctly with headlines/titles often requires a decision to prune the ST material; in this case, one is at the very least likely to omit the pun – it can be assumed that the TL reader does not know of the dictionary alluded to.

A particular feature of style in this passage is the suppression of indefinite articles by the author in the title, in lines 2, 5, 12 and 16. Though it *may* be possible to do the same in translating line 2, it would certainly be hard to do so with the other lists. This is largely due to English grammar: the lists are not all single words, and some may need expansion for clarity. Thus, the translator will probably use the indefinite article ('not simply a "phrase", but a "slogan"', etc.). Mixed lists like this, where the items do not all have the same grammatical structure, can cause problems for reasons of consistency. This is likely to arise with any translation of 'tormentone' (l. 2), which denotes an endlessly repeated catch phrase or slogan, whether in advertising, entertainment or politics. In this case, the translator will need to find the hyponym which will most suitably lead into the list of traits which follows. It is of course the nominal units themselves that suggest whether or not using articles with them is appropriate, and this appropriateness is dictated by the grammar, semantics and logic of the text as a whole.

A reference problem appears in line 8, with 'il piccolo aneddoto'. Reading on, this can only really refer to the information following the colon ('i Caltagirone, etc.'), but the way the ST is formulated hardly suggests translating it as 'the little anecdote'. In effect, the author is *hinting* at the story, rather than telling it, so using 'anecdote' with the definite article would appear odd. Linked to this problem is 'schiatta' (l. 9): we are obviously dealing with a large family of 'contractors', but, interestingly, reference in the 1980s was usually to 'i *fratelli* Caltagirone' rather than to a 'famiglia'. In fact, given the business they were in, it appears far more logical that the male side of the family should be more important here. However, without this knowledge the translator is obliged to allude to 'the Caltagirone family', as 'the Caltagirones' is unclear.

In lines 13–14, the generic form 'un qualche personaggio pubblico' requires an equally generic translation, while 'col vezzo di esprimersi' (l. 14) may benefit from grammatical transposition to a relative clause: 'any public figure who is in the habit of expressing himself'. In line 16, the absence of an article before 'macchietta' adds a little difficulty to the issue of lexical choice. As in the case of 'tormentone', a suitable phrase will have to be found, and one which will capture the author's indignation: 'a figure of fun', for example. '[Processo] per [via] direttissima' (ll. 16–17) is an out-of-context legal reference to a trial under criminal law where the preliminary stage is bypassed and the trial proper goes ahead with extreme urgency. In this context it assumes an adverbial, rather than a nominal, aspect, as the author is implying that Romans immediately (i.e. automatically) become figures of fun when they speak in dialect: the issue of whether to use a TL article therefore does not arise.

It is clear that style and grammar are closely interwoven. The following passage admirably shows how the use or suppression of articles plays a significant role in realizing and interlinking different registers, as in the 'comunicazione interna' drafted by Inspector Santamaria's secretary, Pietrobono ('P.b.'), which is in her own personal, comic shorthand. In the previous section the Inspector has been interviewing a suspected mafioso, while in this scene he is speaking to the daughter of the mafioso's woman. After Pietrobono's brief memo, the narrative continues. Translate the passage, as if you were translating the whole novel for publication, and discuss the translations in class:

Comunicaz. interna: S.m. avvertemi che sta tornando su con figlia; ordina pertanto spostare madre in uff. attiguo, con pretesto verbalizzare sue dichiaraz. – O.K. (*P.b.*)

    – Lui non c'entra niente. Lasciatelo andare.

5   – È un bravo ragazzo? – disse Santamaria.

Contrariamente alle sue meccaniche aspettative, la brava ragazza non aveva niente di traviato, di perduto, di degradato. Abiti sul casuale, tutti diversi da quelli della madre, ma in ordine. Capelli idem e mani, collo, orecchie lavate. Fronte chiara, occhi luminosi. E l'aveva seguito in ufficio

10 con una docilità da scolara giudiziosa, s'era guardata intorno con equanime interesse, come in un museo o laboratorio forse un po' squallido, ma da cui si può sempre imparare qualcosa.

Vedi la freschezza, pensò il commissario assistendo ora all'apparizione di due fossette, la dolcezza.

15   – Bravo ragazzo no, sorrise lei, – almeno non nel senso corrente. Io credo che sia della malavita.

Vedi il candore, pensò il commissario, l'irresponsabilità, l'intangibilità...
(Fruttero and Lucentini 1979: 243–4)

The memo is a challenge in itself. Here is a possible TT:

Memo (internal): SM warns me: coming back + daughter. Wants mother moved office next door with excuse taking her statement. OK. (PB)

Almost the same length as the ST, the TT falls short of it in stylistic effect, because the telegraphic style is generic rather than specifically police-like. To ensure coherence, no words are truncated, though articles, pronouns and some verb forms are removed. If the translator is willing to risk compromising absolute clarity, the following TT might have more of the required atmosphere:

SM warns: coming back + daughter. Move mother nxt office, to 'take statement'. OK. (PB)

The rest of the text is less enigmatic, but the articles require careful attention. For instance, when Santamaria's reactions are expressed in telegraphese, the sociolect is that of the detached, observant professional (a detachment which may not last very long . . .): does the absence of articles have any implications for translation? Does it, for instance, affect the decision whether to translate 'fronte chiara, occhi luminosi' as 'pale forehead, bright eyes' or as 'forehead pale, eyes bright'? Does the further change in register in ll. 13–17 affect these decisions?

Here, finally, is a text which is typically heavily nominalized. This may seem to make it more factual. As is often the case, however, some of the abstract nouns have 'blurred contours' – that is, they have a range of possible hyponyms, but the determiners are not in themselves enough to make it clear which to choose. Like the 'romanesco' text, this one is a reminder that no text exists in a void: translators are no different from other readers, they can only unlock a text by applying to it their knowledge of the fields of experience it relates to. So, sometimes, the determiners in a text will indeed 'determine' the right interpretation; but at other times, it is the translator's experiential baggage that will indicate how to interpret them. This text is no different. Translate it as if for publication in a weekly survey of the European press, and write notes on problems posed by determiners and by nouns. The text was published in *La Stampa* on 1 May 1999.

UN MONDO IMBOTTITO DI MAZZETTE

In questi giorni a Vienna l'Onu discute sulla criminalità organizzata transnazionale, per arrivare a una convenzione che garantisca la cooperazione, l'adozione di standards omogenei nei diversi Paesi, l'integrazione degli impegni presi a Napoli nel 1994.

5   A prima vista sembrerebbe facile l'ironia sulla coincidenza. A pochi chilometri dal teatro della guerra nei Balcani, che segna per ora tra i primi suoi risultati proprio l'assenza e la sconfitta dell'Onu, quest'ultima si dedica a esercitazioni di diritto, tanto belle quanto teoriche e riduttive su come combattere la criminalità.

10   Troppo facile: perché il discorso di Vienna – sulla convenzione e sui protocolli aggiuntivi per il traffico di clandestini, per la fabbricazione e commercio illegale di armi, per il commercio di donne e bambini – è in realtà importante per il futuro dei diritti umani, del 'buon governo', della stabilità delle società civili e del funzionamento delle istituzioni.

15   Che si tratti di un discorso concreto, lo dimostra un'altra coincidenza: quella fra le vicende giudiziarie italiane di questi giorni, che ripropongono il rapporto fra mafia, appalti e corruzione e l'analisi emersa a Vienna.

La corruzione è usata dalle organizzazioni criminali per raggiungere e consolidare profitti e potere. Perciò occorre combatterla sia sul versante clas-

20   sico del riciclaggio e della aggressione ai patrimoni mafiosi sia su quello globale dell''integrità' dei sistemi nazionali e delle relazioni internazionali commerciali, come dice Transparency International.

Il mondo della corruzione si articola su tre livelli: lo 'street level' dei funzionari pubblici; quello degli affari; il 'top level' dei grandi centri di

25   potere politico, economico e finanziario. Ed è un mondo influenzato dalle variabili dello stato dell'economia, dello sviluppo nazionale e internazionale degli affari, della stabilità politica, dell'efficacia e della credibilità delle amministrazioni pubbliche, dell'etica nelle professioni.

La risposta alla corruzione, sia nazionale che internazionale, non può

30   perciò che tener conto di tutte quelle variabili. Accanto alle misure repressive, diventano fondamentali quelle fondate sulla prevenzione e sulla educazione; per dirla in breve, misure che assicurano la 'good governance' e considerano la corruzione come un fattore di degenerazione della stabilità democratica e dell'integrità delle istituzioni.

35   Ed è un bene che questo discorso sia venuto fuori a Vienna: perché, dovremo svilupparlo anche a Bruxelles e a Roma.

(Flick 1999: 1)

18

Contrastive topic and practical: Adverbials

This chapter constitutes the material for all or part of a practical. As a preliminary exercise, here are three texts which should be translated before the chapter is read.

ST 1. 'Non è di mia competenza.' [. . .] La più italiana delle frasi [. . .] viene pronunciata da un dipendente dello Stato (per la precisione del Ministero dei beni culturali e ambientali); e subito rimediata, altrettanto italianamente, da una gentile predisposizione a rendersi comunque utile; in via amichevole naturalmente. Per simpatia e buona volontà, giammai per dovere.

ST 2. 'Ma allora è vero!' sospettò col cuore in tumulto. 'È proprio Dio! Esiste veramente!'

ST 3. [Un concorrente per il concorso di professore associato che] ha già superato l'esame di laurea, ed eventualmente quelli di dottore di ricerca e ricercatore, ha ancora davanti ben 4 prove [. . .] e non mancano giudizi di conferma ogni 6 anni per i professori ormai di ruolo.

The three preliminary texts contain typical examples of Italian adverbials. We use 'adverbials' as a cover-term for any expression having adverbial function. There are many sorts of adverbial. We shall simply talk of either 'adverbs' (e.g. 'well', 'recently') or 'adverbial phrases' (e.g. 'in fine fashion', 'a few days ago', 'once you're there'). This chapter focuses on a range of issues and problems that commonly arise in translating adverbs and adverbial phrases between Italian and English, in either direction.

In ST 1, not all the adverbials appear problematic: 'subito' and 'naturalmente' are easily dealt with. However, the nominalized 'per la precisione' would be more idiomatic in the TT as 'to be precise' than as 'for (the sake of) precision' or even 'more precisely'. 'Altrettanto italianamente' is a bigger problem, because no English adverb can be derived from 'Italian'. Grammatical transposition will be needed to convey the sarcasm, as in: 'again in typical Italian fashion'. The sarcasm is completed by the reference to the Italians' inclination for 'making themselves useful'. The problem here is assessing just how the concept is modified by 'comunque'. Adding 'if at all possible' may be a way of retaining the ST irony. The archaic 'giammai' ('never') also raises the question of tone and emphasis. If the stinging irony is to be preserved, a simple 'never' is inadequate. The loss of ironic archaism might be compensated for with something like 'God forbid' or 'Heaven forfend', as in: 'never – God forbid! – in the line of duty'. A plausible TT might be:

'That's not my department.' [. . .] This most Italian of phrases [. . .] is uttered by a civil servant – to be precise, from the Ministry of Culture and the Environment. However, the rebuff is immediately softened, again in typical Italian fashion, with a willingness to help, if at all possible, though as a favour, of course. Out of the goodness of his heart; but in the line of duty? – God forbid!

ST 2 presents the translator with a common problem: how to deal with adverbial emphasis incorporating repetition. The problem here arises because Italian and English differ in respect of where the adverb is placed. 'Ma allora è vero!' can be rendered as 'So it's true!', but the repetition arises in the use of 'proprio [. . .] veramente'. It is possible to find two English adverbs to correspond to the ST ones, as in 'It really is God! He actually exists!' But the second sentence in this TT stresses 'exists' rather than 'really', whereas the ST stresses 'veramente'. Copying the ST word order is not a solution: 'He exists actually/really/genuinely' is unidiomatic. One possibility is a structure specific to English, the use of stressed 'do' as an auxiliary: 'He (really) does exist then!' This is a regular, and very useful, grammatical transposition in translation into English. Here is a possible TT:

'So it's true! he thought, his heart pounding with apprehension. 'It really is God! He *does* exist!'

In ST 3, a typical translator's bugbear appears, the literal meaning of 'eventualmente'. Sometimes the problem is easily solved, as in this example, where it can safely be translated as 'possibly':

Candidates for the post of assistant lecturer who already have a degree, and possibly even a PhD or research qualification, still have another four tests to undergo.

The intensifier 'ben' requires a translation that highlights the complexity of the competition stages; 'another' does nicely. The 'professori ormai di ruolo' needs amplification for clarity:

And on top of that, there is an appraisal every six years for lecturers who have permanent posts.

'Ormai' can be jettisoned here, as the paraphrase clarifies the lecturers' status through a relative clause. If the translator needed to convey the marked ST distinction between full and assistant lecturer status, 'ormai' could be rendered as 'even when' or 'and once': 'even when/and once lecturers have permanent posts, they still face a six-yearly appraisal'.

As can be seen from the above examples, adverbs and adverbial phrases play an important role in cohesion, emphasis and tonal and social register. They may vary from a single word to a much longer unit. They should never be taken for granted. Control over these items can make all the difference between a barely acceptable TT and a good one.

The relationship between ST and TT adverbials goes far beyond questions of synonymy. Translating in either direction, it often happens that there is no simple TL adverb corresponding to the ST one. Sometimes the problem is morphological, sometimes semantic. Take the following example, from a text on the film actor-director-producer Nanni Moretti:

È il più pragmatico e operoso, fa film, li recita, li produce, li lancia, li distribuisce, li proieta, marxisticamente consapevole della necessità di usare il sistema [. . .] con la maggiore indipendenza e autonomia.	He is highly pragmatic and energetic; he makes films, acts in them, produces, markets, distributes and projects them, aware in true Marxist tradition of the need to exploit the system [. . .] with as much independence and freedom as possible.

The text makes the point about Moretti's versatility rather heavy-handedly, via the repetition of *pronoun* + *verb* and the unusual coinage 'marxisticamente' followed by 'consapevole'. Just what does the author mean by this adverb? What is the tone? There is no ducking the issue, as 'Marxistically' would be morphologically and idiomatically grotesque, especially with 'conscious/aware'. So the translator has to interpret the value of this adverb using contextual clues and cultural awareness.

A similar morphological challenge is found in the following example:

– Mi dispiace, non ci possiamo vedere oggi. – D'accordo. Allora ci sentiamo telefonicamente.	'I'm sorry, we can't meet up/I can't see you today.' 'O.K. We'll talk on the phone.'

Fortunately, in this case, the adverb has the same value as the adverbial phrase 'per telefono', so it will not be a problem for the translator.

The main problem in translating some of the -*mente* adverbs is that they have so many possible meanings. In fact, several quite common adverbs have a semantic range that goes well beyond the scope of suggestions given for them in bilingual dictionaries. Typical examples are 'squisitamente' and 'assolutamente'.

'Squisitamente', according to the Sansoni–Harrap two-volume dictionary, has three standard sets of equivalents in English: '1. deliciously, exquisitely, delicately, delightfully; 2. extremely, absolutely; 3. typically'. The choice is relatively straightforward in this example: 'Uno humour squisitamente inglese'. Here, there would generally be no problem with using 'typically'. At other times, however, 'exquisitely' would be better, as an emphatic value-judgement. The decision has to depend on context. The next example throws up a different problem: it is not so much a question of which dictionary meaning to choose, but whether any of them is adequate:

Il ragionamento del presidente della Bundesbank, accusato di essere troppo tecnico, è invece squisitamente politico.	The Governor of the Bundesbank has been accused of being too technical, but in fact his language is entirely political.

The implication here is not that the argument is *delightfully* political, or *typically* political (although one might speak, ironically, of a *deliciously* political argument). The basic nuance is *extremely* or *absolutely* political, but 'extremely political' and 'absolutely political' are not convincingly idiomatic. 'Squisitamente' in this context contains an emphasis which can be conveyed by a more idiomatic collocation, such as 'entirely/utterly political' – two possibilities not offered by the dictionary.

'Assolutamente' is a very common Italian adverb, particularly in more colloquial contexts, and it has an even wider range of meanings than 'squisitamente', among them: '1. absolutely (not); 2. definitely; 3. completely; 4. generally [a rare use]'. The following example raises a typical translation problem: 'Sono fatti che hanno una rilevanza assolutamente marginale.' There is a seeming paradox here: 'marginale', like English 'marginal', connotes low intensity, while 'assolutamente' connotes high intensity. In English, this discrepancy may need to be reconciled with a collocation specifying the correct degree of marginality. One solution could be: 'These facts are definitely of marginal importance.' The use of 'definitely' sets 'marginal' in an appropriate dimension, and provides the correct balance to the utterance. Of course, it would be possible to use a similar formulation to the ST: 'These facts are utterly marginal.' Here, as in the ST, a high degree of intensity ('utterly') is collocated with the reductive value of 'marginal'. This TT is more emphatically dismissive than the first; only careful assessment of the ST context will show whether the scornful tone is appropriate.

A common colloquial use of 'assolutamente' is vehement negation:

– Hai copiato all'esame, vero?
– Assolutamente!

The reply must be translated with something like an indignant 'Certainly not!' The English 'Absolutely!' would be rendered in Italian by expressions of certainty, like '(Ma) certo/certamente'.

Clearly, an adverb is just as likely as any other textual feature to require an imaginative, but precise, departure from what the dictionary suggests. Here, for discussion and translation in class, are more examples:

1. È difficile convincere gli anziani ad andarsene degnamente in pensione.
2. Gli insegnanti rappresentano una figura professionale socialmente mortificata.
3. Difficilmente si riuscirà ad ottenere il risultato prima di domani.
4. I deputati si sono schierati decisamente a favore del disegno di legge sull'ambiente.
5. Il mosto viene fatto fermentare accuratamente.
6. Il Dott. Rossi aveva offeso il suo superiore, indipendemente dalla propria volontà.

English has an astonishingly flexible system for creating adverbs from adjectives. English adverbs cause just as many problems as the Italian ones we have examined, though more often for morphological reasons than for semantic ones. A few examples at random: 'importantly', 'significantly', 'sadly', 'annoyingly', 'irritatingly', 'depressingly', etc. They are particularly tricky when they begin a sentence. Rather than rendering adverb with adverb in such cases, Italian normally uses a paraphrase. Here are two typical examples:

More importantly, the Inland Revenue did not know about the secret bank account.	Più importante ancora si rivelò il fatto che il fisco britannico non sapeva della esistenza del conto in banca segreto.

Rendering adverb with adjective requires underpinning with a noun, followed by the subordinate clause. This lengthens the sentence, but at least the meaning is clear.

In the second example, the Italian again opts for a ready-made idiom:

Depressingly, statistics show that crime is on the increase.	È triste ma vero che i crimini sono in aumento.

'Triste ma vero' neatly incorporates the nuance of 'depressing/ly'. Another possibility is: 'Un dato che deprime è l'aumento dei crimini ...'. This combination of *noun* + *'absolute' verb* (i.e. transitive verb with no object) is a common grammatical transposition where an adverb cannot be used in Italian.

In order to sharpen awareness of possibilities in *English* which it is easy to overlook in translating from *Italian*, here are some typical English sentences, for discussion and translation in class:

1. Pol Pot's career is drawing to an end in the hideously brutal style he employed to reshape his country.
2. This is a population that had timorously welcomed victorious Khmer Rouge fighters in 1975.
3. [*Of school education*] The existing system has an exhaustingly lengthy Autumn term.
4. The Government has been quietly making this point.
5. The judge robustly defended his decision.
6. Shareholders will benefit handsomely from the new management of the company.
7. These are preposterously high levels of corruption.
8. This company has a highly respected sales force.

In addition to adverbs ending in *-mente*, Italian has plenty of others, of course. Many have a range of possible meanings, which can cause problems of interpretation in context. The ones we shall examine are 'anzi', 'proprio', 'sempre' and 'ormai'.

'Anzi' tends to raise issues not of meaning, but of idiomaticity and flow. According to the dictionary, it can mean: '1. as a matter of fact, on the contrary; 2. or rather; 3. better still; 4. indeed'. In both the following examples, one could argue that 'on the contrary' is an appropriate choice:

Ma l'appuntamento non è esattamente di tipo carbonaro. Anzi.	The meeting was hardly a closely guarded secret. Quite the contrary, in fact.

In this example, 'Quite the contrary, in fact' fits the bill perfectly, because it stands alone. In the second example, 'in fact' on its own would be less obstructive to the flow of the TT:

Quel che non c'è più [. . .] è lo sdegno per le posizioni preconcette e scontate che anzi si sono consolidate.	What has disappeared [. . .] is the indignation about preconceived ideas and stereotypes, which have in fact blossomed.

Here, an alternative to 'in fact' is 'actually'.

For 'proprio', the dictionary suggests: '1. just, precisely, exactly; 2. really; 3. that's right, quite'. The list shows how versatile 'proprio' is, in both written and oral contexts. We saw an example of one use of the word in ST 2 on p. 189. There is another in the following example, a sarcastic comment on alleged war criminal Erich Priebke's bid to interest Amnesty International in his case:

Incredibile, si rivolge proprio all'organizzazione che si batte contro qualsiasi violazione che calpesti la dignità umana.	Incredible though it may seem, he even has the effrontery to appeal to the organization that investigates serious infringements of human rights.

The writer's indignation implies that 'addirittura' could have been used instead of 'proprio'; this would translate easily into English with 'even' or 'actually'. However, our more emphatic version, 'He even has the effrontery to . . .', captures more effectively the tone of indignation and irony. An alternative is to omit 'even' and transfer the emphasis to 'organization': 'the very organization'. (This ST also offers another example of a possibility in English that we have already seen, that of opening the sentence with an adverb: 'Incredibly, he even/actually . . .'.)

There is a third use of 'proprio' in the next example:

Berisha non è proprio del tutto estraneo alla colossale truffa in Albania.	Berisha is not entirely uninvolved in the colossal financial scam in Albania.

The double modification of 'estraneo' laces the comment with irony, hence our double negative. A positive reformulation of this sentence would perhaps state the writer's opinion more explicitly, but the ST irony would be lost: 'Berisha is clearly implicated in the colossal financial scam in Albania.'

'Sempre' has nuances based on 'always' and 'still'. A common formulation is the comparative 'sempre più', which often neatly translates as 'increasingly'. The standard uses of 'sempre' can be seen in comparing the following two sentences:

Ci teniamo in contatto, sempre per via fax.
Ci teniamo sempre in contatto via fax.

In the first, 'sempre' assumes previous contacts by fax; 'again' or 'as usual' would be appropriate, if the translator thought an adverbial qualification necessary. In the second, 'sempre' clearly has the value of 'always'.

'Ormai' is another interesting adverb. It implies conclusion of a period, act or event. The most appropriate rendering will depend on the temporal framework of the ST. The aspects range from 'now/by now' to 'then/by then'. Sometimes, as in ST 3 on p. 189, the TT can dispense with an adverb corresponding to 'ormai'. In some contexts, it will be clearer to refer to the start of a period rather than the end of the previous one. A few examples will give an idea of the range covered by 'ormai' and of various ways of translating it:

Ormai era sicuro di vincere la gara.	By then/By that time he was sure he would win the race.
Ormai avrà già finito l'esame.	By now/By this time he'll (already/probably) have finished his exam.
Ormai siamo quasi arrivati.	We're nearly there now.
Ormai tutto è collegato, intrecciato, interconnesso.	Everything has now become/is now connected, interrelated and correlated.

To finish this practical, here are some sentences containing a variety of adverbials, for discussion and translation in class:

1. Una vera corte di giustizia internazionale mette tutti sullo stesso piano. Già in questo modo si sfiora l'utopia.
2. Le società dell'ENI sono sempre state ben piazzate all'estero.
3. I costi di natura straordinaria ammontano a ben 140 miliardi.
4. [*Advert showing Italy the size of a CD*] Abbiamo ridotto l'Italia così.
5. La scena era assai suggestiva.
6. [*From an article on the handover of Hong Kong*] L'assorbimento da parte della Cina viene visto sempre più non come una minaccia ma come un'opportunità.
7. Ecco allora che arrivano i provvedimenti anti-turista e anti-pendolare.
8. Ha parlato male di noi, anzi malissimo.
9. Devo partire, comunque vadano le cose.
10. Più interessante, anzi stupefacente al confronto, era la stanza da letto attigua, che l'ospite volle mostrare assolutamente al suo giovane visitatore.

19

Contrastive topic and practical: Condition and future in the past

This chapter constitutes the material for all or part of a practical. As a preliminary exercise, here is a short text which should be translated before the chapter is read.

Intanto, però, c'era un problema, piccolo ma angoscioso: dovevo telefonare per primo o dovevo aspettare che lei mi telefonasse? Cecilia aveva l'abitudine di telefonarmi tutti i giorni sempre alla stessa ora, la mattina verso le dieci, per salutarmi e confermarmi l'appuntamento del pomeriggio. Io
5 potevo dunque certamente aspettare anche quel giorno la sua telefonata, ma al tempo stesso temevo che non si facesse viva e uscisse, e così, quando mi fossi deciso a telefonarle io stesso, non ci fosse e io avessi a rimanere tutto il giorno nell'incertezza [...] . [...] io volevo che Cecilia mi telefonasse per prima per poter continuare a considerarla inesistente appunto
10 perché disponibile; se invece fossi stato io a telefonarle, avrei dovuto pensare a lei come a qualche cosa di reale, appunto perché problematico e sfuggente.
(Moravia 1989: 500–1)

The preliminary text shows how complex multiple hypotheses can be in Italian past-tense narrative texts. Any hypothesis naturally involves some degree of conjecture and doubt. In this text, conjecture and doubt are especially prominent because of the modal verbs ('dovere', 'potere', 'volere'), the use of 'avere a', and the subjunctive, which all to some extent draw attention to the narrator's uncertainty about what action to take. The difficulty of translating such a text into English lies in accurately interpreting the order of events and transmitting it logically (whether the events are real or hypothetical), while retaining the tone used in the ST. A major issue is understanding and conveying the nuances implicit in the use of the subjunctive. We shall analyse a number of the expressions in the text, as a way of introducing the difficulties of translating conjecture and hypothesis, especially in indirect speech (also known as 'reported speech'). These issues will then be developed and discussed in the rest of the chapter.

The first example contains two occurrences of the verb 'dovere'. Used in the imperfect tense, this verb can denote either some kind of duty, or past obligation ('had to'), or future in the past ('was to'). In the following example the meaning of 'dovevo' is each time clearly that of duty; hence the use of 'should' in the TT:

dovevo telefonare per primo o dovevo aspettare che lei mi telefonasse?	should I phone first or should I wait for her to phone me?

The second 'dovevo', however, is followed by 'aspettare che'. The interrogative 'dovevo' in itself automatically entails a degree of uncertainty, of course, but in this case a further element of conjecture and doubt is introduced by the literal meaning of 'aspettare che' – as long as one is expecting or waiting for something to happen, one does not know that it actually will. The subjunctive after 'aspettare che' confirms the uncertainty implied in this look into the future. English, on the other hand, implies the futurity and uncertainty simply through the literal meaning of 'to wait for someone to do something'. However, since it is standard practice to use a subjunctive after 'aspettare che', the subjectivity and uncertainty are not unduly emphasized in the ST sentence. This means that the disappearance of the nuance in the TT is not a significant translation loss.

In l. 5, 'aspettare' is used differently, the subjunctive being avoided by means of a noun:

Cecilia aveva l'abitudine di telefonarmi tutti i giorni [. . .]. Io potevo dunque certamente aspettare [. . .] la sua telefonata.	Cecilia used to phone me every day [. . .] so I could certainly expect her to phone/expect a call from her [. . .].

Using a noun instead of the subjunctive introduces a nuance which English *syntax* cannot create. The TT does, however, convey it *lexically*, using 'to expect' instead of 'to wait for'. This example also contains a good instance of the danger of accidentally introducing unwanted and misleading conditional forms into an English TT. Whereas the ST uses 'aveva l'abitudine', English usually expresses past habit more simply than Italian. For the verb 'to do', for example, it can use either 'did', or 'used to do', or 'would do'. The third option is generally only used when qualified by an adverbial expression of time (e.g. 'every year', 'all that autumn'). As it happens, in this ST there is just such an expression – 'tutti i giorni'. But using 'would phone' in this case, where the whole text is speculating about the future, could easily mislead the reader into thinking that this is some kind of a conditional sentence (e.g. 'Cecilia would phone me if . . .'). Hence our choice of 'used to'.

In the next example, 'would' is just about possible, because the subjunctive after 'temevo che' implies doubt as to whether she will go out or not:

temevo che [. . .] uscisse	I was afraid [. . .] she would/might go out

However, 'would' perhaps suggests that he is pretty sure she will go out; in any case, in this context, it could still help to clutter the TT with unwanted conditional forms: 'might' is surely the better choice here.

The narrator pursues his hypothesis, with its inbuilt element of doubt, with more subjunctives:

non ci fosse, e io avessi a rimanere tutto il giorno nell'incertezza	she might not be there, and I would have to spend all day wondering about it

There are three points that need attention in the use of 'avere' here. First, it is a case of future in the past. Second, the context makes it clear that the obligation expressed does not involve any kind of *duty* (contrast 'dovevo' in ll. 1–2), but is a purely physical constraint; it corresponds to 'I'll be compelled to', not 'I ought'. Third, it is impossible this time to escape using an English conditional form, the future in the past having to be expressed as 'I would have to'. Fortunately, as this is clearly indirect speech ('I was afraid *that*'), there is little chance of confusing the reader here.

There is yet another subjunctive in ll. 8–9:

io volevo che Cecilia mi telefonasse	I wanted Cecilia to phone me

In this instance of future in the past, there is no translation problem. It is certainly true that any expression of will or wish logically entails uncertainty – 'I want her to, but will she?' But the Italian subjunctive is absolutely standard after 'volere che', so the element of uncertainty is not highlighted in any way; hence our choice of 'I wanted Cecilia to . . .' rather than 'I wished Cecilia would . . .', which would over-mark the subjectivity and doubt.

In l. 9, a particularizing translation of 'per poter' is doubly inevitable. First, the subject of 'poter' is different from the subject of 'telefonasse', so the alternative rendering, 'to be able to', cannot be used. Second, in a different context, 'I can' would be the right translation; here, the future in the past demands 'I could':

| per poter continuare a considerarla | so that I could still think of her/ continue to think of her |

In l. 10, there is an excellent example of the potential dangers in considering grammatical features in isolation from features on other levels, such as the prosodic, sentential or discourse levels. The 'se' clause presents no *grammatical* translation problem in respect of condition or future in the past:

| se invece fossi stato io a telefonarle | if, on the other hand, I phoned her |

However, this TT puts less emphasis than the ST on him phoning her rather than her phoning him; a hurried reader might even read it with the stress on 'phoned' (as distinct from 'e-mailed', 'called on', etc.). Grammatically, of course, this question of emphasis is different from those of condition and future in the past. But that is not all there is to it: if the translator gets the emphasis wrong, much of the emotional and thematic impact of the narrator's egocentric conjecture will be lost. How can the translator convey the full contextual force of this ST conditional? One standard English way of marking the required emphasis is to use voice stress and intonation, suggested here with italics: 'if, on the other hand, *I* were to phone *her*'. More emphatic still, if the translator thought it appropriate in context, would be: 'if, on the other hand, I were the one to phone'. And in each of these TTs, of course, the tone could be varied still further by using 'but' as the cohesion marker, instead of 'on the other hand'; the decision depends on how the translator reads the tone of the ST.

In the same line, the main clause, responding to the 'se' clause, is typical of a regular divergence between Italian and English in the expression of future in the past in conditional sentences:

| avrei dovuto pensare a lei | I would have to consider her |

The past conditional (e.g. English 'I would have done') is standard in Italian when, as here, what is envisaged as possibly going to happen has not yet actually happened. In English, this is generally conveyed by the present conditional (e.g. 'I would do'), especially in a text like this one, where the outcome of the protagonist's thoughts, decisions or plans is not immediately revealed. Here is another example:

| I thought he would kill her! | Pensavo che l'avrebbe uccisa! |

The correct use of conditional verb forms often causes difficulties for Italian and English-speaking student translators. Here are some examples for discussion in class. The first three are relatively straightforward, but the fourth may need more attention:

If you want to catch that train, you'll have to leave now.	Se vuoi prendere quel treno, devi partire adesso.
If only he could, I'm sure he would help us.	Se solo potesse, sono sicuro che ci aiuterebbe.
If he'd been the eldest brother, he'd have inherited the whole estate.	Se fosse stato il fratello maggiore, avrebbe ereditato l'intero patrimonio.
Se non ci vedremo alla riunione domani, ci sentiremo per telefono.	If we miss/don't see each other at the meeting tomorrow, we'll talk on the phone.

It is clear from the discussion so far that, where a past-tense narrative contains the projection of thoughts or actions into the future, the appropriate verb form to use can be a complex issue in both English and Italian; and in Italian there is the added complexity of the subjunctive, when it is required by grammar. Instances of this future in the past are especially common in literary texts, in indirect speech. A good example is the thriller, where there is much conjecture about who committed the murder and why. Conjecture and hypothesis are naturally also often present in reflective, analytical and scientific texts.

Conjecture and doubt are not only expressed in conditional sentences, of course. For discussion in the practical, translate the following sentences into Italian and make notes on the various possibilities:

1. That may be the book you're looking for.
2. That may have been the book you're looking for.
3. That might be the book you're looking for.
4. That might have been the book you're looking for.
5. That could be the book you're looking for.
6. That could have been the book you're looking for.
7. That must be the book you're looking for.
8. That must have been the book you're looking for.

Italian texts which propose a series of hypotheses tend to treat the verbal framework differently from English, because many verbs of thought, feeling and conjecture introduce a second verb, which often needs to be in the subjunctive. Thus there is often a preference for past narrative, direct speech or free indirect speech rather than orthodox indirect speech. In the following passage, allusion, conjecture, hypothesis and assumption are expressed in a variety of ways, which will repay discussion in class. (*Contextual information*. A murder has been committed in a church, and a Cardinal is being questioned by the Turin police.)

Nessun arresto ancora? Nessun serio indizio? Ah, e dunque non si escludeva nessuna ipotesi: né il terrorismo politico, allargato a colpire la stessa Chiesa... né una vendetta personale o il gesto di un folle... né forse una disgrazia, un malaugurato incidente di tipo, per esempio, pirotecnico?... In tanta
5   sciagura, comunque, il Signore era stato misericordioso a non permettere che ci fossero altre vittime: quell'ordigno – di cui il reparto scientifico ignorava la natura? o quanto meno il meccanismo? – quell'ordigno avrebbe potuto fare una strage... Erano tempi terribili, ma la Chiesa nella sua storia millennaria, aveva vissuto momenti ben più gravi, era stata minacciata da
10 ben più mortali pericoli...
    Il commissario ammirava. Silenzi, digressioni, incisi, frasi fatte, rapide aperture e pronte ritirate, tutto fluiva con una naturalezza quasi automatica e senza un intoppo.
    Finché [. . .] Sua Eminenza tornò al malinteso che aveva portato lui stesso
15 qui, questa notte, davanti a due funzionari della questura di Torino.
(Fruttero and Lucentini 1979: 223–4)

With respect to future in the past, English has greater flexibility in expressing future actions via indirect speech. Compare the four translations of the following Italian sentence, and say whether there are any differences in nuance between them:

Mario disse che sarebbe arrivato col prossimo treno.

(a)   Mario said he would be on the next train.

(b)   Mario said he would be arriving on the next train.

(c)   Mario said he was going to be on the next train.

(d)   Mario said he would have been on the next train.

One other form, used for the future in the past in a more restricted context, can be seen in the following example:

La Nona sarebbe stata/diventata la sinfonia più famosa di Beethoven.	The Ninth was to be/become Beethoven's best-known symphony.

To finish this practical, here is a text based on assumption, perceived obligation and conjecture. Translate it, and explain your decisions of detail in respect of the sections printed in bold type. (*Contextual information.* The text is the beginning of a piece entitled 'Preparando le vacanze', which was written immediately after the author's return from holiday.)

Questa doveva essere l'estate perfetta. Mi ero preparato con cura, a cominciare dal febbraio scorso. Due volte alla settimana – in palestra! Nessuno può immaginare che cosa accada ad un corpo umano quando sia torturato dalla ginnastica. E poi c'è la dieta. Ma da sole non bastano queste cose a
5 fare il miracolo. Avevo addirittura consultato gli oroscopi dei più noti veggenti.

Per il Leone **ci sarebbero state novità di rilievo**. Però, **dovevo pensare anche ad altre cose**; ad esempio, che fare di un corpo forte ma pallido? **Le esposizioni al sole artificiale mi avrebbero dato il giusto colorito** per
10 apparire vestito, semivestito, in costume da bagno e anche nudo, qualora la spiaggia prescelta fosse adatta. Però, la scelta della vacanza giusta comportava persino l'uso della calcolatrice: non è facile capire quanto possa costare un soggiorno, per quanto modesto e limitato.

20

Summary and conclusion

The only conclusion necessary to *Thinking Italian Translation* is a summing up of what it is the translator is supposed to be thinking about. The first thing to remember is that, whatever revision or editing the TT has undergone, it is the translator who is ultimately responsible for it. 'Thinking' translation implies a clear-sighted acceptance of this responsibility, but it also implies reducing the element of chance in how the TT will be received. If responsibility entails making decisions, applying the method presented in this book will enable the translator to make them intelligently and imaginatively enough to be confident of what the overall impact of the TT will be. This is why we have stressed throughout the course the need for a clearly formulated initial strategy, and for clearly formulated decisions of detail rationally linked to the strategy.

One thing we hope to have shown is that no strategy can be assumed a priori. Formulating an appropriate strategy means assessing the salient features of a particular ST and of the particular circumstances in which it is to be translated. The crucial question then is: 'How do I decide which features are salient?' What we have tried to do is equip the student translator with a way of answering this question, whatever the nature of the ST. For our purposes, the salient features of a text can be said to be its most *relevant* ones, those that have significant expressive function. Devising a strategy means prioritizing the cultural, formal, semantic, stylistic and genre-related properties of the ST according to two things: their relative textual relevance, and the amount of attention they should receive in translation. The aim is to deal with translation loss in as rational and systematic a way as possible. This implies being prepared, *if necessary*, to lose features that have relatively little textual relevance in a given ST (e.g. alliteration in a technical text on mining), sacrificing less relevant textual details to more relevant ones. And, of course, it implies using compensation to restore features of high textual relevance that cannot be more directly rendered (e.g. a play on words in a literary text).

'Textual relevance' is thus a qualitative measure of how far particular properties of a text are responsible for its overall impact. Textually relevant features are those that stand out as making the text what it is. Since it is the translator who decides what is textually relevant, the decision is inescapably subjective. But not necessarily damagingly so. A relatively objective test of textual relevance is to imagine that a particular textual property is omitted from the text and to assess what difference this would make to the overall impact of the text. If the answer is 'little or none', the property in question has little textual relevance. But if omitting it would imply a loss in either the genre-representative or the individual character of the text, then it has high textual relevance.

Developing a translation strategy by assessing textual relevance in an ST entails scanning the text for every *kind* of feature that might be relevant to producing an appropriate TT. For this scanning to be effective, it is vital to have in mind a systematic set of questions to ask of the ST. These questions correspond to the check-list of kinds of textual feature introduced in the schema of textual matrices on p. 5. The successive chapters of *Thinking Italian Translation* tackle the sorts of translation issue lying behind the questions that need to be asked of texts. The idea is that the translator learns to ask the questions systematically, one after the other. As students working through the book will have found, it only takes a bit of practice to be able to do this very quickly and efficiently.

Some comments are called for on aspects of the relation between the schema of textual matrices and the book you have read. First, the 'cultural' matrix is different in focus from the others. Unlike the others, it does not list types of feature that may *in themselves* be salient in the ST before the translator starts forming a strategy. Corresponding to Chapter 3, it lists types of feature whose relevance can only be decided when the translator starts to form a strategy. That is, it draws attention to features that force the translator to choose between source-culture and target-culture elements. As such, it does invite the translator to assess how far the culture-specificity of ST features is textually relevant – this is why we have included it in the schema of textual matrices.

The other matrices are more straightforward reminders of what sorts of thing to look for when asking what the relevant features of a text are. Chapters 5–7 correspond to the 'formal' matrix, introducing translation issues raised by the formal properties of texts. Chapters 8 and 9 correspond to the 'semantic' matrix; the translation issues addressed here are the ones most typically raised by literal and connotative meaning. Chapter 10 corresponds to the 'varietal' matrix; the questions to ask here concern language variety and its translation implications. Chapter 11, corresponding to the 'genre' matrix, gives a set of parameters to apply in identifying textual genre preparatory to translation. (As is explained in the Introduction and stressed throughout the course, genre is a primary factor in deciding a strategy, but can itself only be determined after the other salient features of the ST have been identified. Hence its position halfway through the course rather than at the beginning.) Chapters 12–14 then give a brief sample of the many sub-genres from which professional translators will normally choose their speciality.

Some vital topics in the book do not figure as such in the schema of matrices. This is because they either apply universally from top to bottom of the schema, or concern a translation operation, not a textual feature. Grammatical transposition, for example, is introduced in Chapter 2 but is of central relevance in every chapter and every practical. There is a case to be made for including it in the cultural matrix, but it is so all-pervasive that it is not useful to identify it as a discrete element in the matrix. It is in fact so important that Chapters 16–19 are given entirely to it – and there could have been many more than these four. The topic of grammatical transposition would have been altogether too big for Chapter 3.

Another absolutely crucial topic, introduced as such in Chapter 4 but everywhere relevant, is compensation. More than anything else, successful compensation exemplifies the combination of imagination and rigour that is the mark of a good translator. However, even though compensation very often involves cultural and/or grammatical transposition, it is a translation operation, not a textual feature. So too is revising, which is introduced as such in Chapter 15, but is a vital stage in the translation process and figures in a number of chapters and practicals.

One pre-eminent translation issue is neither a textual feature nor a translation operation. This is the translation brief – why the text is being translated, on whose behalf, and for what audience. As we suggest in Chapter 11, it is useful, for practical translation needs, to see the communicative purpose of a text as very closely linked with its genre. Genre, of course, *is* a textual feature, and as such figures at the head of the schema on p. 5. The reason why it is placed at the top is precisely that it shares a prime importance with communicative purpose: the translation *process* will result in a translation *product*, a text having specific textual features, and produced in order to meet a communicative demand. This demand, formulated by the work-provider, is the translation brief. As the brief is neither a process nor a textual feature, it does not have a chapter to itself. But it has decisive importance, and that is why we have everywhere stressed its role as a parameter in assessing the relevance of ST and TT textual features, and why, in practicals, you have been asked to produce your TTs as if in response to a specific commission.

It should be remembered that the schema of matrices can be used to analyse any text, not just an ST. It can be applied to draft TTs, their features being systematically compared with those of the ST so as to see which details will be acceptable in the final version. Published TTs can also be evaluated in the same way. But whatever the text that is analysed by this method, never forget that the watchword is ... *thinking* translation. This course encourages a methodical approach based on reasoned analysis of textual features and the translation problems they pose. But 'methodical' is not synonymous with 'mechanical' or 'automatic'. As we said in the Introduction, good translators know what they are doing: for thinking translation, there has to be a thinker, an individual person using flair and rigour to take creative, responsible decisions.

To sum up, then, we have tried to do two things in this course. First, to help you ask and answer the strategic questions we listed on p. 6: 'What is the message content of this particular ST? What are its salient linguistic features? What are its principal effects? What genre does it belong to and what audience is it aimed at? What are the functions and intended audience of my translation? What are the implications of these factors? If a choice has to be made among them, which ones should be given priority?' And second, to help you use intelligent, creative techniques for the translation operation, the battle with the problems of syntax, lexis, etc. that has to be fought in translating particular expressions in their particular context.

Postscript: A career in translation?

Having completed the course, you may feel you wish to know more about becoming a translator. This concluding section aims to provide some preliminary information and advice for aspiring entrants to the profession.

Translators are usually either 'in-house' or 'freelance'. The in-house translator is employed by a business, or a translation company or agency, to provide translations in the workplace, on either a permanent or a fixed-term basis. The advantage of being in-house for a newcomer to the profession is the opportunity to gain experience quickly, in an environment where mentoring and feedback are usually supplied. Though it may take time to find a placement or post, this kind of experience is extremely valuable. A good place to find companies who offer placements or posts in-house is the Institute of Translation and Interpreting (ITI) Bulletin. Newspapers, such as *The Guardian* on Mondays in the Media supplement, publish job vacancies, and your local 'Yellow Pages' directory will provide you with a list of translation companies or agencies operating in your area.

Setting up as a freelance is a more complex issue. Generally speaking, offers of work are only made to translators with a 'track record' and a specific qualification in translation, such as the Diploma in Translation of the Institute of Linguists (IoL), which can be considered the first step on the professional ladder, or membership of the ITI, which is gained by examination and experience. The IoL Diploma in Translation exam is held every November, and a number of institutions offer courses, whether on site or by distance learning. For details of these exams, do not write to us or to Routledge: contact the IoL and the ITI at the addresses given below.

The optimal freelance translator will need to be able to offer two or possibly more foreign languages at a very high level of competence. Moreover, experience and knowledge of a number of subject specialities is required; most translators concentrate on either technical translation (e.g.

IT, engineering, construction) or what is called 'general translation' and usually includes legal, financial and business texts. No translator worth his or her salt will attempt to cover a very wide range of subjects. In addition to these skills, the translator must possess suitable equipment, comprising a computer equipped with modem and e-mail (virtually all translation is sent back to the work-provider by e-mail these days), a printer (preferably laser), a scanner and a fax machine. Two phone lines are useful, so that one can communicate with work-providers while using e-mail or the Internet.

Working as a freelance means being self-employed, and it is important to find out before taking this step what self-employment entails. All translators have to grapple with taxation, pensions contributions, accounts, grants and subsidies, training, marketing and legal issues at some point. Help is at hand though, from bodies like Business Link, which exist throughout the United Kingdom and can provide information and advice (usually free of charge) about these matters. The Inland Revenue has offices in most towns and all cities, as does the DSS. Your local Chamber of Commerce may also be able to provide you with useful information, and sometimes they have their own lists of translators available for work, which you may be able to join.

One disadvantage of working from home is isolation. A body like the ITI offers a valuable lifeline to associates and members by providing a range of services. These include: links with the world of employment (e.g. DTI and other important bodies), guidance for new entrants to the profession (e.g. a forum for new translators at the annual conference), training and professional development (also in conjunction with universities and professional institutions), information on IT and reference materials, and the promotion of professional standards of competence through the Codes of Conduct and Terms of Business. Language graduates aiming at a career in translation may become associates, as may other language specialists such as abstractors and lexicographers. Membership is gained by assessment and examination only. Associates may attend ITI events, including courses, lectures and the annual conference.

The Bulletin published by ITI every two months contains useful articles and tips, job offers and a calendar of events and is a good way of keeping abreast of developments in the field of translation. Networking is also important, and ITI has a number of networks for subjects, languages and regions, which enable translators to share their experiences, meet and pass on work. Some new entrants, in fact, are offered their first job through networking.

If you do decide that you want to make a career in translation, bear in mind that you need to be enthusiastic, motivated and determined. Free-lancing, in particular, is not for the faint-hearted! Work flows are usually erratic, at least until you become established and have several work-providers. Therefore, if you are considering changing jobs and abandoning the nine-to-five office job for translation, make sure you have enough funds to see you through at least the first two years, when cash-flow and income will be irregular. However, once you have become successfully established, you will be unlikely to want to return to a routine job, as the independence of freelancing makes for an interesting and stimulating occupation.

An excellent book giving detailed advice for aspiring and practising translators is Samuelsson-Brown (1993).

Useful contacts:

The Institute of Translation and Interpreting
377 City Road
London
EC1V 1NA

Tel: 020 7713 7600

Web site: http://www.ITI.org.uk

The Institute of Linguists
Diploma in Translation Department
48 Southwark Street
London
SE1 1UN

Tel: 020 7940 3100

E-mail: info@iol.org.uk

Web site: http://www.iol.org.uk

Local Business Link networks.

Local Chambers of Commerce.

Glossary

---

affective meaning   a type of **connotative meaning**, affective meaning is the emotive effect worked on the addressee by using one particular **linguistic expression** rather than others that might have been used to express the same literal message.

alliteration   the recurrence of the same sound or sound-cluster at the beginning of two or more words occurring near or next to one another; not to be confused with **onomatopoeia**.

allusive meaning   a type of **connotative meaning**; in a given **linguistic expression**, allusive meaning consists in evoking the meaning of an entire saying or quotation in which that expression figures. NB If a saying or quotation appears in full, that is a case of *citation*: e.g. 'The darling buds of May are just beautiful this year'; *allusion* occurs where only part of the saying or quotation is used, but that part evokes the meaning of the entire saying or quotation: e.g. 'Brrr . . . No darling buds yet awhile, I'm afraid'.

anaphora   see **grammatical anaphora** and **rhetorical anaphora**.

associative meaning   the **connotative meaning** of a **linguistic expression** which takes the form of attributing to the referent certain stereotypically expected properties culturally associated with that referent.

assonance   the recurrence of a sound or sound-cluster within words occurring near or next to one another; not to be confused with **onomatopoeia**.

attitudinal meaning   the **connotative meaning** of a **linguistic expression** which takes the form of implicitly conveying a commonly held attitude or value-judgement in respect of the referent of the expression.

back-translation　translation of a **TT** back into the **SL**; the resulting text will almost certainly not be identical to the original **ST**.

calque　a form of **cultural transposition** whereby a **TT** expression is closely modelled on the grammatical structure of the corresponding **ST** expression; a calque is like a moment of **exoticism**, although exoticism proper is a feature of whole texts or sections of texts. NB Calque is different from **cultural borrowing**, which imports the ST expression verbatim into the TT.

code-switching　the alternating use of two or more recognizably different language variants (varieties of the same language, or different languages) within the same **text**.

coherence (adj. **coherent**)　the tacit, yet intellectually discernible, thematic or affective development that characterizes a **text**, as distinct from a random sequence of unrelated sentences.

cohesion (adj. **cohesive**)　the explicit and transparent linking of sentences and larger sections of **text** by the use of overt linguistic devices, such as conjunctions or **grammatical anaphora**, that act as 'signposts' for the **coherence** of the text.

collocative meaning　the **connotative meaning** lent to a **linguistic expression** by the meaning of some other expression with which it frequently collocates; e.g. 'social intercourse' almost inevitably acquires a connotation of 'sex' from the common collocation of 'sexual intercourse'. Collocative meaning is thus the 'echo' of expressions that partner a given expression in commonly used phrases.

communicative translation　a mode of **free translation** whereby **ST** expressions are replaced with their contextually/situationally appropriate cultural equivalents in the **TL**; i.e. the **TT** uses situationally apt target culture equivalents in preference to **literal translation**.

compensation　a technique of reducing **translation loss**: where any conventional translation (however literal or free) would entail an unacceptable translation loss, this loss is mitigated by deliberately introducing a less unacceptable one, important **ST** effects being approximated in the **TT** through means other than those used in the ST. N.B. unlike e.g. an unavoidable, conventional **grammatical transposition** or **communicative translation**, compensation is not forced on the translator by the constraints of **TL** structures – it is a conscious, free, one-off choice.

compensation by splitting **compensation** that involves dividing up a feature carried in a relatively shorter stretch of the **ST** and spreading it over a relatively longer stretch of the **TT**; an ad hoc choice, not a grammatical constraint.

compensation in mode **compensation** that involves using a different mode of textual effect in the **TT** from the one used in the corresponding part of the **ST**; most compensation is compensation in mode, whatever other features it has.

compensation in place **compensation** that involves a **TT** textual effect occurring at a different place, relative to the other features in the TT context, from the corresponding textual effect in the **ST** context; an ad hoc choice, not a grammatical constraint.

connotation see **connotative meaning**.

connotative meaning (or **connotation**) the implicit overtones that a **linguistic expression** carries over and above its **literal meaning**. NB The *overall meaning* of an expression is compounded of its literal meaning plus these overtones and its contextual nuances.

cultural borrowing taking over an **SL** expression verbatim from the **ST** into the **TT**; the borrowed term may remain unaltered in form, or it may undergo some degree of **transliteration**. NB Cultural borrowing differs from **calque** and **exoticism**, which do not use the ST expression verbatim, but adapt it into the **TL**, however minimally.

cultural transplantation the highest degree of **cultural transposition**, involving the wholesale deletion of source-culture details mentioned in the **ST** and their replacement with target-culture details in the **TT**.

cultural transposition any departure from **literal translation** that involves replacing **SL**-specific features with **TL**-specific features, thereby to some extent reducing the foreignness of the **TT**.

decisions of detail translation decisions taken in respect of specific problems of **lexis**, **syntax**, etc.; decisions of detail are taken in the light of previously taken **strategic decisions**, although they may well in their turn lead the translator to refine the original **strategy**.

determiner a word which specifies the range of reference of a noun (*a* car, *the* car, *that* car, *my* car, *which(ever)* car, *both* cars, *such* cars, *any* driver *whose* car fails, etc.).

dialect a language variety with non-standard features of accent, vocabulary, **syntax** and sentence formation characteristic of the regional provenance of its users.

discourse level the level of textual variables on which whole **texts** or sections of texts are considered as **coherent** or **cohesive** entities.

editing the final 'polishing' of a **TT**, following revision, and focusing on matching TT style and presentation to the expectations of the target readership.

exegetic translation a style of translation in which the **TT** expresses and comments on additional details that are not explicitly conveyed in the **ST**; i.e. the TT is an explication, and usually an expansion, of the contents of the ST.

exoticism the lowest degree of **cultural transposition**, importing linguistic and cultural features wholesale from the **ST** into the **TT** with minimal adaptation; exoticism generally involves multiple **calques**. NB Exoticism is different from **cultural borrowing**, which does not adapt ST material into the **TL**, but quotes it verbatim.

free translation a style of translation in which there is only a global correspondence between units of the **ST** and units of the **TT** – e.g. a rough sentence-to-sentence correspondence, or an even looser correspondence in terms of even larger sections of **text**.

generalization see **generalizing translation**.

generalizing translation (or **generalization**) rendering an **ST** expression by a **TL** **hyperonym**, e.g. translating 'sonaglio' as 'bell'. The **literal meaning** of the **TT** expression is wider and less specific than that of the corresponding ST expression; i.e. a generalizing translation omits detail that is explicitly present in the literal meaning of the ST expression.

genre (or **text-type**) a category to which, in a given culture, a given **text** is seen to belong and within which it is seen to share a type of communicative purpose with other texts; that is, the text is seen to be more or less typical of the genre.

gist translation a style of translation in which the **TT** expresses only the gist of the **ST**; i.e. the TT is at the same time a synopsis of the ST.

grammatical anaphora the replacement of previously used **linguistic expressions** by simpler and less specific expressions (such as pronouns) having the same contextual referent; e.g. 'I dropped the bottle and *it* broke'.

grammatical level the level of **textual variables** on which are considered words, the decomposition of inflected, derived and compound words into their meaningful constituent parts, and the **syntactic** arrangement of words into phrases and **sentences**.

grammatical transposition translating an **ST** expression having a given grammatical structure by a **TT** expression having a different grammatical structure containing different parts of speech in a different arrangement.

hyperonym a **linguistic expression** whose **literal meaning** includes, but is wider and less specific than, the range of literal meaning of another expression; e.g. 'vehicle' is a hyperonym of 'car'.

hyperonymy-hyponymy the semantic relationship between a **hyperonym** and a **hyponym**; a lesser degree of semantic equivalence than **synonymy**.

hyponym a **linguistic expression** whose **literal meaning** is included in, but is narrower and more specific than, the range of literal meaning of another expression; e.g. 'car' is a hyponym of 'vehicle'.

illocutionary particle a discrete element which, when added to the **syntactic** material of an utterance, tells the listener/reader what affective force the utterance is intended to have; e.g. 'alas', 'ma di un po'!'

inter-semiotic translation translating from one semiotic system (i.e. system for communication) into another.

interlinear translation a style of translation in which the **TT** provides a literal rendering for each successive meaningful unit of the **ST** (including affixes) and arranges these units in the order of their occurrence in the ST, regardless of the conventional grammatical order of units in the **TL**.

intertextual level the level of textual variables on which **texts** are considered as bearing significant external relationships to other texts, e.g. by allusion or imitation, or by virtue of **genre** membership.

intralingual translation the re-expression of a message conveyed in a particular form of words in a given language by means of another form of words in the same language.

lexis (adj. **lexical**) the totality of the words in a given language.

linguistic expression a self-contained and meaningful item in a given language, such as a word, a phrase, a sentence.

literal meaning the conventional range of referential meaning attributed to a **linguistic expression**. NB The *overall meaning* of an expression in context is compounded of this literal meaning plus any **connotative meanings** and contextual nuances that the expression has.

literal translation an **SL**-oriented, word-for-word, style of translation in which the **literal meaning** of all the words in the **ST** is taken as if straight from the dictionary, but the conventions of **TL** grammar are respected.

nominal expression a **linguistic expression** which either consists of a noun or has a noun as its nucleus.

nominalization the use of a **nominal expression** which could be replaced by a **linguistic expression** not containing a noun.

onomatopoeia a word whose phonic form imitates a sound; not to be confused with **alliteration** or **assonance**.

partial overlap see **partially overlapping translation**.

partially overlapping translation (or **partial overlap**) rendering an **ST** expression by a **TL** expression whose range of **literal meaning** overlaps only partially with that of the ST expression, e.g translating 'professoressa' as 'lecturer'; i.e. the literal meaning of the **TT** expression both *adds* some detail *not* explicit in the literal meaning of the ST expression (she works in a university, not a school) and *omits* some other detail that *is* explicit in the literal meaning of the ST expression (she is female); partially overlapping translation thus simultaneously combines elements of **generalizing** and of **particularizing** translation.

particularization see **particularizing translation**.

particularizing translation (or **particularization**) rendering an **ST** expression by a **TL hyponym**, e.g. translating 'bell' as 'sonaglio'. The **literal meaning** of the **TT** expression is narrower and more specific than that of the corresponding ST expression; i.e. a particularizing translation adds detail to the TT that is not explicitly expressed in the ST.

phonic/graphic level the level of **textual variables** on which is considered the patterned organization of sound-segments (phonemes) in speech, or of letters (graphemes) in writing.

prosodic level the level of **textual variables** on which are considered 'metrically' patterned stretches of speech within which syllables have varying degrees of *prominence* (e.g. through stress and vowel-differentiation), varying degrees of *pace* (e.g. through length and tempo) and varying qualities of *pitch*.

reflected meaning   the **connotative meaning** given to a **linguistic expression** by the fact that its form (phonic, graphic or both) is reminiscent of a homonymic or near-homonymic expression with a different **literal meaning**; i.e. reflected meaning is the 'echo' of the literal meaning of some other expression that sounds, or is spelled, the same, or nearly the same, as a given expression.

register   see **social register** and **tonal register**.

rephrasing   the exact rendering of the message content of a given **ST** in a **TT** that is radically different in form, but *neither* adds details which are not explicitly conveyed by the ST *nor* omits details that *are* explicitly conveyed in it; perfect rephrasing is rarely achieved.

revision   checking a **TT** against the **ST** to eliminate errors and inconsistencies; compare **editing**.

rhetorical anaphora   the repetition of a word or words at the beginning of successive or closely associated clauses or phrases.

rhyme   rhyme occurs when, in two or more words, the last stressed vowel and all the sounds that follow it are identical and in the same order.

sentence   a complete, self-contained linguistic unit capable of acting as a vehicle for communication; over and above the basic grammatical units that it contains, a sentence must have sense-conferring properties of intonation or punctuation, and may in addition contain features of word order, and/or **illocutionary particles**, which contribute to the overall meaning, or 'force', of the sentence. NB In this definition, a sentence does not necessarily contain a verb.

sentential level   the level of **textual variables** on which **sentences** are considered.

SL   see **source language**.

social register   a style of speaking/writing from which relatively detailed stereotypical information about the social identity of the speaker/writer can be inferred.

sociolect   a language variety with features of accent, vocabulary, **syntax** and sentence-formation characteristic of the class affiliations of its users.

source language (or **SL**)   the language in which the **ST** is expressed.

source text (or **ST**)   the **text** requiring translation.

ST   see **source text**.

strategic decisions   the initial decisions that constitute the translator's **strategy**; strategic decisions are taken, in the light of the nature of the **ST** and the requirements of the **TT**, as to which ST properties should have priority in translation; **decisions of detail** are taken in the light of these strategic decisions.

strategy   the translator's overall 'game-plan', consisting of decisions taken before starting to translate in detail – e.g. whether and when to give **literal meaning** a higher priority than style, to address a lay readership or a specialist one, to maximize or minimize foreignness in the **TT**, to use formal language or slang, prose or verse, etc.

synonym   a **linguistic expression** that has exactly the same range of **literal meaning** as one or more others. NB Synonymous expressions usually differ in **connotative meaning**, and are therefore unlikely to have identical impact in textual contexts.

synonymy   the semantic relationship between **synonyms**; synonymy is the highest degree of semantic equivalence.

syntax (adj. **syntactic**)   the branch of grammar that concerns the arrangement of words into phrases and sentences.

target language (or **TL**)   the language into which the **ST** is to be translated.

target text (or **TT**)   the **text** which is a translation of the **ST**.

text   any stretch of speech or writing produced in a given language (or mixture of languages – cf. **code-switching**) and assumed to make a **coherent** whole on the **discourse level**.

text-type   see **genre**.

textual variables   all the demonstrable features contained in a **text**, and which could (in another text) have been different; i.e. each textual variable constitutes a genuine *option* in the text.

TL   see **target language**.

tonal register   a style of speaking/writing adopted as a means of conveying an affective attitude of the speaker/writer to the addressee. The **connotative meaning** of a feature of tonal register is an **affective meaning**, conveyed by the choice of one out of a range of expressions capable of conveying a particular literal message; e.g. 'Excuse me, please' versus 'Shift your butt'.

translation loss   any feature of incomplete replication of the **ST** in the **TT**; translation loss is therefore not limited to the omission of ST features in the TT: where the TT has features not present in the ST, the addition of these also counts as translation loss. In any given TT, translation loss is inevitable on most levels of **textual variables**, and likely on all. NB The translation losses in the TT are only significant in so far as they prevent the successful implementation of the translator's **strategy** for the TT.

transliteration   the use of **TL** spelling conventions for the written representation of **SL** expressions.

TT   see **target text**.

Bibliography

Anderson, A. and Avery, C. 1995. 'Checking Comes in from the Cold', *ITI Bulletin*, February 1995.

Ballestra, S. 1991a. 'Compleanno dell'iguana', in *Compleanno dell'iguana*. Milan: Mondadori.
Ballestra, S. 1991b. 'La via per Berlino', in *Compleanno dell'iguana*. Milan: Mondadori.
Bassani, G. 1989. *The Garden of the Finzi-Continis*, Quigly, I. (trans.). London and New York: Quartet.
Bassani, G. 1991. *Il giardino dei Finzi-Contini*. Milan: Mondadori.
Bausi, F. and Martelli, M. 1993. *La metrica italiana*. Florence: Casa Editrice Le Lettere.
Boccaccio, G. 1995. *Cinque novelle dal Decamerone* (a cura di M. Spagnesi). Classici italiani per stranieri, 2. Rome: Bonacci editore.

Calvino, I. 1976. *The Path to the Nest of Spiders*, Colquhoun, A. (trans.). Hopewell, NJ: The Ecco Press.
Calvino, I. 1993. *Il sentiero dei nidi di ragno*. Milan: Mondadori.
Carbosulcis. 1997a. 'Logistica del trasporto di materiale tramite mezzi gommati in miniere di carbone', *Euroabstracts*, 35/533-35/803.
Carbosulcis. 1997b. 'Material Transport by Tyred Vehicles in Coal Mines', *Euroabstracts*, 35/533-35/803.
Carducci, G. 1994. *Selected Verse*, Higgins, D.H. (ed. and trans.). Warminster: Aris & Phillips.
Catalano, E. 1987. 'Una proposta urbana per Montecalvario', in Alisio, G. et al. (eds) *Progetti per Napoli*. Naples: Alfredo Guida.
Chaucer, G. 1974. *The Complete Works of Geoffrey Chaucer*, Robinson, F.N. (ed.). 2nd edn. Oxford: OUP.
Chiriotti, M. et al. 1997. 'VignaleDanza', in *Piemonte dal vivo*. Turin: Regione Piemonte.
Colucci, R. 1990a. 'Cilento da scoprire', *Stagioni d'Italia*, 2/90.
Colucci, R. 1990b. 'The Cilento: An Area to Explore', *Stagioni d'Italia*, 2/90.

Dalisi, R. 1987. 'Calata S. Francesco (una strada degli occhi)', in Alisio, G. et al. (eds) *Progetti per Napoli*. Naples: Alfredo Guida.
De Carlo, A. 1981. *Treno di panna*. Turin: Einaudi.
Djalma Vitale, E. 1996. 'Roast canguro', *L'Espresso*, 14 November 1996.

Eco, U. 1963. *Diario minimo*. Milan: Mondadori.
Eco, U. 1994. 'A Rose by Any Other Name', Weaver, W. (trans.), *Guardian Weekly*, 16 January 1994.
Eliot, T.S. 1963. *Collected Poems 1909–1962*. London: Faber.

Fiat. 1993a. *Cinquecento. Uso e manutenzione*. Turin: Fiat Auto SpA.
Fiat. 1993b. *Cinquecento. Owner Handbook*. Turin: Fiat Auto SpA.
Flick, G.M. 1999. 'Un mondo imbottito di mazzette', *La Stampa*, 1 May 1999.
Fruttero, C. and Lucentini, F. 1971. *La donna della domenica*. Milan: Adelphi.
Fruttero, C. and Lucentini, F. 1979. *A che punto è la notte?* Milan: Mondadori.

Garioch, R. 1983. *Complete Poetical Works*. Loanhead: Macdonald.
Graham, J.D. 1983. 'Checking, Revision and Editing', in C. Picken (ed.) *The Translator's Handbook*. London: Aslib.

Halliday, M.A.K. and Hasan, R. 1976. *Cohesion in English*. London: Longman.
Hervey, S. 1992. 'Registering Registers', *Lingua*, 86.
Hollander, J. 1981. *Rhyme's Reason: A Guide to English Verse*. New Haven and London: Yale University Press.
Holmes, J.S. 1988. *Translated!* Amsterdam: Rodopi.

IBM Italia. 1996. Advertisement in *L'Espresso*, 21 November 1996.
Irwin, M. 1996. 'Translating Opera', in Taylor, J. et al. (eds) *Translation Here and There, Now and Then*. Exeter: Elm Bank Publications.

Jakobson, R. 1971. *Selected Writings*, vol. II. The Hague: Mouton.

Keats, J. 1958. *The Poetical Works of John Keats*, Garrod, H.W. (ed.). 2nd edn. Oxford: Clarendon Press.
Koller, W. 1995. 'The Concept of Equivalence and the Object of Translation Studies', *Target*, 7.

Leech, G. 1974. *Semantics*. Harmondsworth: Pelican Books.
Levi, P. 1976. *Se questo è un uomo*. Turin: Einaudi.
Levi, P. 1996. *If This is a Man. The Truce*, Woolf, S. (trans.). London: Vintage.
Loris Rossi, A. 1987. 'Napoli 2000', in Alisio, G. et al. (eds) *Progetti per Napoli*. Naples: Alfredo Guida.

Machiavelli, N. 1995. *Il principe. Sette capitoli scelti* (a cura di S. Maffei). Classici italiani per stranieri, 3. Rome: Bonacci editore.
Menichetti, A. 1993. *Metrica italiana: Fondamenti metrici, prosodia, rima*. Padua: Antenore.
Moravia, A. 1952. *The Conformist*, Davidson, A. (trans.). London: Secker and Warburg.
Moravia, A. 1981. *Il conformista*. Milan: Bompiani.
Moravia, A. 1989. *La noia*, in *Opere 1948–1968*. Milan: Fabbri, Bompiani, Sonzogno.
Morgan, E. 1968. *The Second Life*. Edinburgh: Edinburgh University Press.
Morgan, E. 1997. 'Aprire la gabbia a John Cage', Fazzini, M. (trans.), *FMLS*, 33,1.

Newmark, P. 1981. *Approaches to Translation*. Oxford: Pergamon.
Nicolai, G.M. 1994. *Viaggio lessicale nel paese dei soviet*. Rome: Bulzoni.

Nida, E. 1964. *Toward a Science of Translating*. Leiden: Brill.

Paoli, G. 1981. 'Sapore di sale', in Pinzauti, F. (ed.) *'Sono solo canzonette'*. Florence: CI.ELLE.I.
Pascoli, G. 1905. *Myricae*. 7th edn. Leghorn: Giusti.
Petrignani, S. 1997. 'Lingua e linguacce. Perché il romanesco è diventato sinonimo di volgarità', *Panorama*, 4 September 1997.
Pinchuk, I. 1977. *Scientific and Technical Translation*. London: Andre Deutsch.
Pirro, U. 1991. *Il luogo dei delitti*. Milan: Frassinelli.
Pittàno, G. 1993. *Così si dice (e si scrive)*. Bologna: Zanichelli.
Pradella, R. 1982. 'Intervista con Riccardo Pradella: il Teatro dei Filodrammatici', in Messora, N. and Quartermaine, L. (eds) *Italia, anni '80. Corso di lingua e cultura (Unità N. 1, Parte terza)*. Exeter Tapes. Exeter: Exeter University.

Russo, V. 1996a. *Santità!* Milan: Joppolo.
Russo, V. 1996b. *Holiness!*, Cragie, S. (trans.). London: Minerva Press.

Samuelsson-Brown, G. 1993. *A Practical Guide for Translators*. Clevedon, Bristol PA, Adelaide SA: Multilingual Matters.
Saponaro, M. 1992. 'Il cavallo morello', in Mollica, A. and Convertini, A. (eds) *L'Italia racconta*. Lincolnwood, Ill.: National Textbook Company.
Scialoja, T. 1984. *La mela di Amleto*. Milan: Garzanti.
Shakespeare, W. 1967. *Macbeth,* Hunter G.K. (ed.). The New Penguin Shakespeare. Harmondsworth: Penguin.
Snell-Hornby, M. 1988. *Translation Studies: An Integrated Approach*. Amsterdam: John Benjamins.
Spinosa, N. 1990. 'La pittura di veduta a Napoli dal ritratto urbano al paesaggio d'emozione', in *All'ombra del Vesuvio: Napoli nella veduta europea dal Quattrocento all'Ottocento*. Naples: Electa Napoli.

Tabucchi, A. 1988. *Piccoli equivoci senza importanza*. Milan: Feltrinelli.
Tabucchi, A. 1995. 'Dio ci salvi dai nipotini di Craxi', in *L'Espresso*, 9 June 1995.
Tomasi di Lampedusa, G. 1963a. *Il Gattopardo*. Milan: Feltrinelli.
Tomasi di Lampedusa, G. 1963b. *The Leopard*, Colquhoun, A. (trans). London and Glasgow: Collins.

Vaccari, L. 1997. 'Capello, ma tu che fai per un povero diavolo?', *La Gazzetta dello Sport*, 20 October 1997.

Welsh, I. 1996a. *Trainspotting*. London: Minerva.
Welsh, I. 1996b. *Trainspotting*, Zeuli, G. (trans.). Parma: Ugo Guanda.

Index

Bold type denotes a term that figures in the glossary, and the page where it is first defined.